D1253293

BATTLE FLAGS SOUTH

The Story of the Civil War Navies on Western Waters

BATTLE FLAGS SOUTH

The Story of the Civil War Navies on Western Waters

JAMES M. MERRILL

Fairleigh Dickinson

Rutherford • Madison • Teaneck
FAIRLEIGH DICKINSON UNIVERSITY PRESS

© 1970 by Associated University Presses, Inc.

Library of Congress Catalogue Card Number: 71-86652

Associated University Presses, Inc.
Cranbury, New Jersey 08512

SBN: 8386 7448 8

Printed in the United States of America

Contents

Preface

This book is the story of the struggle between the navies of the Confederacy and the Union for the control of the Mississippi River. Early in the conflict Generals Grant, Sherman, Halleck, and Pope earned reputations by victories achieved with the support of the Western Flotilla. These combined actions together with naval engagements on the Atlantic and Gulf coasts gave the Union its first victories of the war, shored up a tottering Lincoln Administration, and sustained Northerners with the belief that despite the reverses and inactions of the Army in the East, ultimate victory would be theirs.

On the Mississippi River, in contrast to the situation on the Atlantic and in the Gulf, both North and South started with nothing. Both sides were forced to build river navies; both sides had the men and the shipyards with which to build them. Yet, by the spring of 1862, only a year from the start of hostilities, the Confederate Navy on western waters was all but obliterated.

This book tells of the race to build these gunboats—the "stinkpots" and tinclads, the Pook turtles and the cottonclads—the construction of the engines and ordnance, and the recruitment of the landlubbers to man the flotillas. It is the story of the Union Navy Department's neglect of its bastard squadron, of intense jealousies between the Army and Navy, and of changing strategies, strategies that forced the Rebel armies away from the river—away from their strongholds at Columbus, Memphis, and New Orleans—to fight the Union armies. It is a study of command that demonstrates the ineptness of Southern naval commanders, the complete mental and physical breakdown of Admiral Andrew Hull Foote, the heroics of Farragut at New Orleans and his lapses before Vicksburg, and the meteoric rise of the boisterous, the hard-to-handle David Dixon Porter. It underscores the difficulties saltwater sailors had in adjusting to a new type of warfare in the muddy, turbulent waters of the Mississippi River.

This book could not have been written without a most generous fellowship from the John Simon Guggenheim Foundation and help from Whittier College and the University of Delaware. It could not have been attempted without the continued encouragement of Dr. John Haskell Kemble of Pomona College; Dr. Brainerd Dyer of the University of California, Los Angeles; Dr. Robert E. Johnson of the University of Alabama, and Dr. David B. Tyler of Wagner College. I also appreciate the assistance of Dr. Albert W. Upton, Dr. Benjamin Whitten, and Mrs. Ann Dahlstrom Farmer, all of Whittier College, Carol Morris of the University of Delaware and the patience of my wife, Ann, who, in addition to performing her homely tasks, blue-penciled and proofread the manuscript.

Acknowledgments

My thanks go to the librarians and archivists who helped make my bibliography possible. Special thanks go to Elmer Parker and the staff, Naval Branch, National Archives; Captain Victor Gondos and staff, Civil War Branch, National Archives; David C. Mearns and the staff, Manuscript Division, Library of Congress; Admiral E. M. Eller, Naval History Division, Navy Department; Mary Isabel Fry, Henry E. Huntington Library; V. L. Bedsole and staff, Louisiana State University; Wilmer Leech, New-York Historical Society; Mattie Russell, Duke University; Charlotte Capers and Carl Ray, Mississippi Department of Archives; Carolyn Wallace, Southern Historical Commission, University of North Carolina; Jacqueline Bull, University of Kentucky; William T. Alderson and Mrs. Frank Owsley, Tennessee State Library; Clyde Watson and Margaret Flint, Illinois State Historical Library; James A. Fleming, Virginia Historical Society; John Dudley, Virginia State Library; Gladys Webster, New Hampshire Historical Society; Caroline Dunn, Indiana Historical Society; Elizabeth Martin, Ohio Historical Society; Mrs. Ernest Stadler, Missouri Historical Society; and John M. Dawson and staff, especially Charles Mason, Mrs. Rachel J. Elliott, and Mrs. Elizabeth Russell, University of Delaware Library.

J. M. M.

BATTLE FLAGS SOUTH

The Story of the Civil War Navies on Western Waters

"We all knew the Navy's value and necessity for exterior purposes, but were not aware of its internal strength in sustaining the government. Our armies in the west would have been comparatively powerless without the gun-boats. . . ."

Gideon Welles to Andrew H. Foote
June 24, 1862

1
"Give the Pirates a Roaring Rout!"

It was Saturday afternoon, May 1861, in wartime Cincinnati. Down at the foot of Lawrence Street, Captain Air, as was his custom, pocketed fifteen cents from each passenger who boarded the steamboat *Cincinnati Belle* for the day's excursion to Camp Clay. On the same wharf in a recruiting tent, Army officers signed up boisterous youths but rejected teenage Laurie Donovan, who wanted to join her lover in the 3rd Ohio Regiment. Up in Washington Park, Strobel's Silver Cornet Band tuned up for the evening concert honoring the hero of Fort Sumter, Major Robert J. Anderson. Other Cincinnatians waited impatiently in double lines for tickets to Dan Rice's Circus under the big top on Court Street, while in the bookshops readers casually leafed through copies of *How to Save a Life in War* and the illustrated songbook *The Star-Spangled Banner*.[1]

The Little Miami Railroad train belched cinders as it ground to a stop at the Cincinnati Depot. From the rear car a naval officer, dressed in a faded uniform with the stripes of a commander, climbed down into the dust and grime, collected his bags, and waded through the crowd out into the street. Here Commander John Rodgers, U. S. N., hailed a cab and drove to the Burnett House, a mammoth, domed hotel where, after signing the register, he walked up the marble stairway and entered Room 22 on the second floor. Rodgers, a balding, heavy-jowled man with an aristocratic thirst for champagne, unpacked his bags and pulled out a set of confidential orders dated May 16, 1861. He had been sent west to create a fresh-water navy to blockade the Mississippi River and thus halt steamboat traffic to and from the Confederate states.[2]

A month before, a confused and rudderless nation, torn asunder by the issue of Negro slavery, had drifted into tragic internal conflict. On April 12, 1861, Southerners had cannonaded Fort Sumter, in Charleston Harbor, South Carolina. Union troops, after mustering on the parade ground inside the fort, had marched to the wharf with drum and fife playing "Yankee Doodle" and had boarded a transport. The Federal garrison had surrendered. It was civil war.

The firing on Fort Sumter electrified the North. Thousands of New Yorkers, yelling, shouting, pushing, and holding placards aloft, swarmed through their city's streets. "Northernmen, come out! Give the pirates a roaring rout!" some placards said. In Union Square, a crowd listened to a senator rave, "All Southerners should be blown to the Devil without mercy." Another orator exhorted a cheering throng with, "Who will fight? I will. Will you?" Five thousand citizens surged after him to a recruiting station on Canal Street chanting, "We'll go! We'll go!"[3] From New York to Chicago, Northerners from hamlet and city sprang to the colors.

Washington was chaotic. Troops poured into the city. Congressmen fended off lobbyists in hotel corridors, commission-hungry contractors buttonholed guests, and volunteer officers jammed into the bars and saloons along Pennsylvania Avenue.

Unperturbed by the confusion in Willard's Hotel, President Lincoln's Secretary of the Navy, Gideon Welles, hung his black Quaker hat on a rack in the ornate dining room and sat down to order from a menu that offered fresh shad, wild pigeon, pig's feet, and oysters. A curious-looking man wearing a flowing white beard and a wig with gray ringlets that fell to his shoulders, he peered at the selection through iron-rimmed spectacles.[4]

Gideon Welles was a former Democrat and newspaper editor from Hartford, Connecticut, whose sole claim to naval knowledge derived from a stint as Chief of the Bureau of Provisions and Clothing in the 1840s. Lincoln had appointed him to the Cabinet as a sop to New England politicians. Back in Connecticut, political enemies spread ugly stories that "Old Gid," while in the Bureau of Provisions and Clothing, had profited from the purchase of worthless merchandise. They pointed to the disastrous business failure of Welles and his brother, Thad, which had rocked Glastonbury to its very foundations.[5]

Finishing his dinner with a flourish, this odd-appearing man retired to his second-floor room at Willard's. Outside his open window he heard the tramping of troops in the street below. Far off, near the Long Bridge, soldiers chanted, "We are going to win the war. We are going to win the war."

Mrs. Welles and son Tom, after visiting the camps of Connecticut troops, had departed that very afternoon for New England. Houses were scarce in wartime Washington, but Welles, through influential friends, had purchased a home on H Street near 16th that would be ready for occupancy in two weeks. As the Secretary stood at the window, though, listening to the drums outside, moving his family was the least of his worries.

Over at the Navy Department, working late into the night, Gustavus Vasa Fox, Assistant Secretary, finished writing a report and then put on his black coat and hat and stepped out of the office, closing the door behind him. "Captain Fox," as Welles called him, had been a professional seaman, serving eighteen years as an officer in the Navy, cruising on board ships in the Mediterranean, East Indian, and Pacific waters. He had surveyed the southern coasts from New York to Panama, participated in the blockade of the Mexican coast during the previous war, and witnessed the British naval operations off the Syrian coast in the 1840s.

Resigning his commission in 1856, Fox had operated a cotton mill in Massachusetts. He came to Washington in early 1861 with a plan for the relief of Fort Sumter. Lincoln was impressed with this little man's aptitude for organization and with his energy and had first appointed him Chief Clerk and later Assistant Secretary of the Navy. Fox had high political connections as the son-in-law of Lincoln's Postmaster General, Montgomery Blair. Unlike the quiet, plodding, and sometimes slow-appearing Welles, Fox was imaginative and aggressive, albeit a "conceited ass." Despite his conceit and his erudite vocabulary, naval officers respected Fox as the best executive in the Department for, said one, "What little brains there were . . . he found them."[6]

Unlike the stodgy Secretary, Fox fancied himself the perfect host; his home was always open to Congressmen, military and naval brass, visiting dignitaries, and even to crackpots like the Prussian with a scheme to blow Richmond to kingdom come. The President called often to discuss naval operations.

The two secretaries had enormous capacity for work. Night after night, they toiled together on the second floor of the Navy building, Fox pontificating, Welles carefully weighing the significance of things.

The Administration had handed the Navy a Herculean assignment. On April 19, 1861, a week after the fall of Fort Sumter, President Lincoln issued his Blockade Proclamation, which sent Federal ships down the southern coast, over 3,500 miles of it, to cut off enemy ports from European trade and to hunt down Confederate privateers at sea. To accomplish this job, Welles and Fox started with almost nothing—a few dilapidated ships commanded by "rum sucking, good for nothing old fogies."[7] Officers with secessionist sympathies had long since packed sea bags and fled southward. Everything relating to the naval campaign had to be solved after the shooting war commenced, and the Navy Department, with no established doctrine, lacked machinery for strengthening the fleet or for securing intelligence on Southern installations.[8]

To complicate these problems, Welles and Fox discovered that the navies of the world were in an age of transition. A revolution was dramatically changing the whole concept of naval warfare. Iron was superseding wood. Steam was replacing sail. The old sailing ships, splendid, awe-inspiring in their day, ships that had fought the British in the American Revolution and in the War of 1812, were passé, except, perhaps, as floating batteries towed to the target. The shell was displacing the solid shot. The construction of marine engines and guns was improved. This new technology outdated former theories and intro-

duced the sailor to new ships, new cannon, and a new
type of warfare.

For almost fifty years, moored in the backwash of
America's march westward, the Navy had had no chance
to attract attention. The Navy Department building itself, a two-story brick structure to the west of the White
House, had a "gone-to-seed appearance." This orderly,
quiet oasis misled newspaper reporters, who, used to the
bustle and confusion of Capitol Hill, concluded that all
the officials, the naval officers, and the clerks were either
lazy or extremely dull fellows.[9] Here the "Old Man of
the Sea," Gideon Welles, labored quietly and patiently,
but his mildness and gentleness contributed to the low
esteem in which the Navy was held by the uninformed.

The Department and the entire North received a
severe blow when, in late April, the Navy yard at Norfolk
—the largest and most important of the Government's
yards in the South—fell to Rebel hands and, with it, the
frigate *Merrimack*. Northerners stormed at the Administration. They pointed to Norfolk, to Confederate blockade
runners, to privateers that were scouring the seas, and to
the enemy coastline still uncaptured. They demanded the
scalp of Gideon Welles. "If only we had that old fossil
Welles out of the Navy, we might do something," argued
a Westerner.[10] But amid these abuses, the President held
firm and Welles sailed steadily on.

President Lincoln, who knew little about ships,[11] called
upon his secretary to run the naval establishment almost
independently. Steering the Department with a free hand,
Welles was pleased with Lincoln's confidence in him and
could not be pressured into hasty decisions regarding
strategy.

In the Cabinet, the wizened, white-haired Secretary

of War, Simon Cameron, predicted that if the North re-
covered Fort Sumter and captured Charleston, the South
would "fret" itself into submission.[12] William Seward,
Secretary of State, complained that the Administration
could not use the Navy to its best advantage because no-
body knew anything about a Navy.[13] Philosophically,
Gideon Welles, twisting his war wig and adjusting his
ringlets, asserted that only time would determine the
best strategy.[14] Postmaster General Montgomery Blair
wanted the Eastern Army to capture Richmond, the
Western Army to invade Texas.[15] Edward Bates, St.
Louis lawyer and Lincoln's Attorney General, suggested
that the Army and the Navy take and hold New Orleans
and other Southern ports and that a giant force be created
to control the Mississippi River. This would strangle
the South by severing its supply line from Europe and the
trans-Mississippi West and thus starve it back into the
Union. The high spirited, militaristic Southerners, explained Bates, could not stomach the steady pressure applied by the Union. "They *must sell* [cotton] or sink into
poverty and ruin."[16]

On April 17, just two days after Bates had submitted
his ideas to the Cabinet, he wired his friend James B.
Eads, a St. Louis businessman, to hurry to Washington
and aid the Government with his knowledge of western
rivers.[17] Climbing out of a sickbed, Eads hurried eastward. In Washington, Bates quickly explained his views
on fortifying Cairo, Illinois, and operating steam gunboats on the Mississippi. He introduced Eads to the Cabinet and, together, they considered the whole gamut of
river operations. Secretary Cameron vetoed the idea as
useless, but Welles, seeing the importance of the Mississippi River to ultimate victory,[18] asked Eads to pre-

pare a written statement. Eads suggested blockading all commerce moving southward on the river by establishing at Cairo a strong force with batteries afloat and ashore. He urged the Government to purchase one strongly built boat—he knew just the one, as he owned her[19]—and arm her with guns and protect her with cotton bales. This could overhaul enemy steamers and prevent the Rebels from erecting river batteries. Even a one-boat blockade could devastate the economy of the South by damming up the main artery through which Confederates received goods from the Northwest. With a shutting off of this flow at Cairo, the only outlets remaining for shippers from the Southwest would be the Tennessee and Cumberland Rivers and the railroads from Louisville to Nashville and Chattanooga. If the Union closed the approaches to the Mississippi River, reasoned Bates, the South inevitably would die of malnutrition.[20]

In his gold-embroidered coat with epaulets, the aged General of the Army, Winfield Scott, sat in his office. Under his overall plan to destroy the Confederacy, Scott wanted to rely heavily upon the Navy to shut down the Southern ports and cut off European aid. Together with these operations, the general hoped to send a powerful force down the Mississippi River from St. Louis to New Orleans, cleaning out the Rebels and keeping open this line of communication. With such strategy, Scott emphasized, the North would crush the South like an anaconda and force it to terms with little bloodshed. Unlike the Eads plan, Scott's underscored offense. To be successful, he believed, such a force on the Mississippi would have to muster twenty gunboats, forty transports, and

80,000 men; progressing down the river to the Gulf, this amphibious contingent would capture and hold Rebel fortifications, including New Orleans. Meanwhile, as military brass recruited this unit, a few shotproof gunboats, operating alone from Cairo, could seriously annoy the Rebel camps on the river.[21]

Scott's basic strategy was to destroy the South's economy by closing the river and the port of New Orleans to the commerce of the Northwest. The wants of the section were not considered. At first, Northwesterners believed that it would be a short war and that, despite the loss of their southern outlets, their produce would get to market in the East by railroad, the Erie Canal, and the Great Lakes. Out west in Cincinnati, St. Louis, and other river towns, business was hit hard when the river trade collapsed. In St. Louis, markets shut down; businesses went bankrupt; steamboats idled at the wharf. The farmers of Illinois, Wisconsin, Minnesota, and Iowa no longer shipped crops by river, but sent them East on the railroads. The West clamored for the Army to crush Richmond and paid scant heed to Scott's anaconda policy.[22]

In Cincinnati, General George B. McClellan, commanding the Department of the Ohio, galloped around the countryside on a powerful charger and wanted no truck with gunboats. "Little Mac" was ready immediately to march his 80,000 troops across the mountains into Virginia toward Richmond, simultaneously with a Union advance on the eastern front.[23] Scott turned thumbs down. The anaconda policy was paramount.[24]

At his Washington headquarters, General Scott, hampered by scant funds and the confusion in the War Department, forwarded instructions to McClellan on the importance of gunboats to any offensive or defensive operation. By June 1861, he had requested the War Department to build sixteen gunboats by September 20, gunboats that were to protect Army transports, destroy Rebel steamers, and cooperate in the landing of troops for assaults upon enemy forts.

Quartermaster of the Army Montgomery C. Meigs paced the floor of his rented office at the corner of F and 17th Streets in the national capital. As an Army officer he was loath to undertake the responsibility of fitting out river gunboats, but he had the foresight to advocate the building of at least two ironplated, light draft gunboats, slow in speed, strong in fire power. Writing to General McClellan, Meigs underscored Scott's plan for the western flotilla. Its sole function was to meet Rebel steamers that tried to interrupt the descent of the Army transports down river. He told the General that Confederate river batteries were too strong for the gunboats to attack and that to capture them, Army units would have to assault or besiege them.[25]

The idea of a river navy was so novel, so strange, that official Washington was uncertain whether this auxiliary belonged to the Army or to the Navy. Secretary Welles, whose officers and men were to operate the flotilla, found the situation anomalous and embarrassing. Meigs, whose department was to build the gunboats, complained that his officers understood little about shipbuilding. Officers of both branches were unwilling to shoulder the responsibility of directing this bastard force.[26] Problems were multiple. Who actually directed the flotilla? Who paid for it? If the Army built the boats and the Navy manned them, who supplied the guns and ammunition? Could Army officers earn sea pay and prize money? Who planned joint Army and Navy assaults? Commanders out west lacked funds, men, boats, guns, and confidence. Naval officers knew little about fighting gunboats on rivers; the Army knew less.

At the Navy Department, Welles, on the strength of the Eads report, readied an officer to accompany the St. Louis businessman west to purchase and fit out gunboats. Up to this point the Navy had acted independently. Cameron was indifferent. But suddenly, at a Cabinet meeting, the Secretary of War claimed jurisdiction.[27] After tedious delays arising from the War Department's lack of interest, Welles finally issued orders that sent Commander John Rodgers to Ohio. John Rodgers—brother-in-law of the Quartermaster General of the Army, Montgomery Meigs, and son and namesake of the naval hero of the War in 1812—was a veteran officer who had seen duty in the Seminole War, sailed in Mediterranean and Atlantic waters, and served with the North Pacific Exploring Expedition in the 1850s. Now placed under the command of General McClellan, Rodgers buckled down. No sailors, no vessels, and no guns belonged to the United States Government on the Ohio and Mississippi Rivers. He would have to buy the boats and arm and man them; in short, create a fresh-water navy.

2

Stinkpots 'Round the Bend

At Army headquarters John Rodgers met a boyish-looking man with a "Napoleon figure," a general who might have passed for a private. McClellan, although he had been advised of the anaconda plan, told Rodgers that he had no notion of the Administration's views regarding gunboats and offensive operations. "Little Mac" was sure that Washington wanted Cairo defended and the river blockaded. The Army had already erected batteries at that Illinois river town and sent troops there. To shield Cairo further from Rebel invasion, McClellan suggested that Rodgers purchase three gunboats and arm them with two guns apiece.[1]

Rodgers searched the Ohio River for vessels. After discussions with Naval Constructor Samuel Pook, who had come out from Washington, Rodgers, with McClellan's blessing, invested $62,000 in three side-wheelers, the *Tyler, Conestoga,* and *Lexington.* With high pressure boilers on deck, their steam connections exposed, and with "three story houses" planted on their hulls, such boats differed radically from Union warships and could hardly be expected to withstand the incessant hammering of enemy cannon fire. Rodgers decided that heavy bulwarks would have to be built. Armed with plans and specifications, he contracted with mechanics and carpenters to alter the three boats from the bottom up and dispatched the bills to Gideon Welles.[2]

Four hundred laborers swarmed over the *Tyler, Conestoga,* and *Lexington* at the Marine Railway and Drydock Company. They chopped down the vessels' superstructures, lined the interiors of the hulls with two-and-a-half-inch oak plank, and lowered the boilers and placed them between the engines, leaving the decks clear for action. Carpenters made compartments watertight and erected solid bulwarks around the ships for protection. Discarding the suggestions for ironplating, they cased the pilot houses with five-inch oak plank, added heavy wrought iron shutters, and pierced the bulwarks for three guns on each side.[3]

When the *Conestoga* was completed, one newspaper reporter asked, "What is it?" and then answered himself, "A slaughter pen!" Citizens dubbed the *Conestoga, Lexington,* and *Tyler* "tubs," "tea kettles," "ready-made coffins," and "stinkpots" and joshed that a man with a pair of heavy-soled cowhide boots could kick in the sides.

News of Commander Rodgers' purchases drifted up and down the river. Shipping bosses in Pittsburgh complained that the Navy had no jurisdiction on the river and that salt-water sailors had no business commanding river boats. The *St. Louis Republican* snickered that the Administration's plan, if it existed, of sending a squadron down river was impracticable, dangerous, and humbug.[4]

Amid mounting criticism, Rodgers berated the contractors. Upon close examination of the *Tyler, Conestoga,* and *Lexington,* he and his recently arrived assistant, Lieutenant S. Ledyard Phelps, discovered that on each vessel there were no boat davits, no iron ties and bars over the boilers, and no hatchways for ascending to the upper decks, and that there was no entrance to the pilot house and no way for boarding the vessels from small boats.[5]

To complicate Rodgers' task in Cincinnati, the Navy had no "understanding" with the Army quartermasters to supply the vessels. Without authority the commander purchased quantities of dried beef, ice, vegetables, spoons, dishes, rope, pillow slips, chairs, frying pans, mattresses, canvas, lamp wicks, scissors, and monkey wrenches.[6] An angry Gideon Welles, beset by worries over the Atlantic and Gulf Blockading Squadrons, upbraided Rodgers for sending requisitions to the Navy Department. This was Army business.[7] General McClellan saved Rodgers further embarrassment by signing the necessary requisitions, but he was too busy with military affairs to worry about the gunboats.[8]

Rebuked by Washington, hampered by contractors, strangling in red tape, Rodgers plunged into his next assignment—manpower. He chartered the steamer *Ohio No. 2* for a receiving ship, anchored her opposite the levee, opened a recruiting office,[9] and hired two agents to hunt down likely prospects. But along the river banks recruiting was slow. In one week twelve men stepped forward in St. Louis, seventeen in Cincinnati.[10]

Grudgingly, Gideon Welles sent out two naval officers to command the gunboats but, again, ordered Rodgers to recruit all further personnel. Naval officers hated the river service,[11] as they resented stepping down from gallant men-of-war with their pitching decks and salt spray to tubs operating in the muddy waters of the Mississippi River. No officer, no experienced salt-water sailor was prepared to command a river gunboat in the treacherous waters of the Mississippi. "What I would have regarded as madness on the coast," reported Lieutenant Phelps, "here, on the river, under other circumstances, becomes a different act."[12]

In late June the Ohio River started falling rapidly. Alarmed that the low water would prevent his gunboats from reaching the Mississippi, Rodgers ordered the dock superintendent to spare no expense to ready the gunboats.[13] He handed out small arms to crew members, bought groceries on credit, and, with such hands as he could muster under the command of Lieutenant Phelps, turned over the engines of the unfinished *Tyler, Conestoga,* and *Lexington* and sent them off to Cairo, Illinois, home base of the squadron. Chances of grounding were great, but this was war.

Three miles below Louisville, the flotilla slowed down and stopped. Water over the Portland Bar was too shallow. Phelps hired dredges to deepen the channel, but the drift of the river filled up the artificial channels as rapidly as the machines cut them.[14] "Now," chuckled the pro-Southern Louisville *Daily Courier,* "if it takes twenty-four hours to travel two and a half miles, how long will it be before the flotilla reaches New Orleans?"[15]

Inexperienced in river navigation, Lieutenant Phelps was upset when rivermen reported that farther downstream the river was too shallow to float the gunboats and that it might be months before he ever made Cairo. Days slipped by. Finally the boats, tugging and snorting, pushed into deep water, steered down-river, but stopped again at New Albany, Indiana, where the *Tyler* ran into a mudbank. After three tugs hauled her off, the side-wheelers got under way again.[16]

On their approach to Cairo, Phelps and the crews

passed a low, sandy point that jutted out from the main shore between the Ohio and Mississippi Rivers. They watched blue-clad pickets on the levee as they cruised by the army camps, and the earthworks stretching out in all directions. The sailors heard the boom of the cannon at Cairo and exchanged recognition signals with the Army on shore. The *Tyler, Lexington,* and *Conestoga* slid into the wharfs and tied up.

Cairo, the "city of stinks," filth, and disorder, was "hotter than hell" the day Phelps arrived. Peddlers, merchants, and ruffians lined the river front. Refugees from the South were streaming into the city. "When the world was made," reported one Ohioan, "the refuse materials were washed up at the junction of the Ohio and Mississippi and the composite is Cairo. It is, in fact, nature's excrementitious deposit."

The town of Cairo—the main base for the river squadron, the terminus of the Illinois Central Railroad, the Army's strategic area for the defense of St. Louis—sat on a low, marshy, and boot-shaped site, protected from the overflow by stone levees. For years Cairo had lagged in growth; it was a ragged, straggling town sunk in a basin. The war had transformed it into an armed camp, a brawling, rioting, drunken town, a vast depot of supplies for the Army and Navy.[17]

Southward ran the Mississippi River—strong, twisting, unpredictable—past the swamps, plantations, Negro huts, hamlets, and sugar fields and past the bustling river towns of Memphis, Vicksburg, Natchez, Baton Rouge, and New Orleans, 1,700 miles away. The Mississippi was the Red and the White Rivers, the Yazoo and the Arkansas, the Black and the Tallahatchie, the Ohio and the Tennessee. Death came swiftly among the Mississippi's snags, from explosions of the overtaxed boilers of the steamboats and from yellow fever, malaria, and typhoid.

There in Cairo, John Rodgers, relieved that his gun-boats had weathered the shallow waters, began readying them for war. Almost single-handedly, he recruited, appointed river men as officers, contracted his gun carriages, and hired old steamers to serve as receiving ships. Mustering his crews, Rodgers realized that he lacked one half the force needed to man the side-wheelers. On a routine inspection Rodgers discovered that the magazines on board the *Tyler* and *Lexington* were incomplete. The *Conestoga* leaked. This makeshift force, described as a cross between a fleet of Chinese junks and Noah's Ark, was powerless to attack and would have been hard-pressed to defend Cairo from an enemy attack.

When the cannon, the leftovers from the Erie, Pennsylvania, arsenal, arrived months late, gunners hauled them on board and secured them: six 64-pounder broadside guns and one 32-pounder on the *Tyler;* four 64-pounder broadsides and two 32-pounders on the *Lexington;* and three 32-pounders on the *Conestoga.*[18]

Washington was hot and sultry on the 4th day of July when Congress met in special session. That evening, down Pennsylvania Avenue, twenty-three regiments of New Yorkers, bands playing, snaked their way behind President Lincoln and Cabinet officers Seward, Welles, and Bates, who sat high on floatlike platforms. In the torchlight before the White House, Lincoln ascended the steps and spoke to the excited multitude.[19]

In his office, oblivious to the fanfare, General Winfield Scott worked late. With the approval of the Secretary of

War and convinced of the feasibility of his anaconda plan, Scott was ready to begin offensive operations down the Mississippi River. He had ordered the Quartermaster's Department to construct a fleet of ironclad gunboats for western service and urged Congress to appropriate $1,100,000 for their construction.[20]

Promptly, the Administration transferred the responsibility of supervising the building of these ironclads to Commander John Rodgers. Naval Constructor Samuel Pook drew up plans and specifications with the advice of river boatmen and designed flat-bottomed, light draft, and low freeboard centerwheelers, each measuring 175 feet in length, fifty feet in width, and six feet in depth.[21] The gunboats, 512 tons each, had sloping, rectangular, armored casemates covering their entire decks and enclosing almost everything but their stacks. The casemates were of heavy timber, faced with iron plates on the forward end and on the sides abreast of the machinery. Placed as low as possible in each boat, two horizontal high-pressured engines operated a twenty-two foot paddle wheel. The estimated cost of each vessel was $55,000.[22]

Quartermaster General Montgomery Meigs advertised for bids from western builders for constructing seven Pook gunboats and dispatched plans and specifications to all inquirers. But James B. Eads, the St. Louis businessman who had first recommended the use of gunboats on the Mississippi, was first in line. Unlike the other bidders, Eads had never built a boat, but he had the backing of Edward Bates, the Attorney General.[23] Prominent Missourians, including Postmaster General Montgomery Blair, clamored for the gunboats to be built in St. Louis. Government contracts for Missouri would insure high employment, pulling St. Louis from the brink of financial ruin and squelching once and for all disaffection and traitorous talk.[24]

The Eads bid of $89,000 for each boat was the lowest and he promised the earliest delivery date. He agreed to build and equip seven ironclads in sixty-three days. If he failed to deliver the vessels on time, he promised, he would forfeit $250 a day until each boat was completed.[25]

When word leaked out that James B. Eads had won the coveted contract, western boat builders charged corruption and chicanery. One bidder labeled Eads an "unscrupulous speculator." He had no timber, no machinery, no boatyard, no anything, and would be lucky to complete the boats in two years, let alone two months.

Although Eads was not a boatbuilder, he proved to be an administrative genius. This Missouri speculator had spent his youth on river boats, and, in the 1840s, had formed a partnership to recover steamboats (and their cargoes) that had sunk in the Mississippi. He sold out and entered the glassware business, but later returned to the river, organizing a new company into a $500,000-a-year business.

When, in mid-August, Eads arrived back in St. Louis with his lucrative contract, business all over the city was at a standstill. Factories and rolling mills, foundries and forges were silent. Overnight, Eads marshalled all the machine shops in St. Louis into service. Telegraph lines hummed between St. Louis, Pittsburgh, and Cincinnati with instructions to factories and foundries for the construction of steam engines and boilers. Within days the whole city of St. Louis reverberated.

Mechanics laid down the keels for four of the gunboats

at the drydocks in Carondelet, seven miles to the south, and for three more in Mound City, near Cairo. Promising whopping bonuses for speed, Eads hired 800 men, signed up thirteen sawmills to cut and saw oak lumber, and parceled out the work of manufacturing iron plates to three different rolling mills.[26]

Still struggling to fit out the *Tyler, Conestoga,* and *Lexington* at Cairo, John Rodgers now was burdened with the responsibility of supervising the construction of the Eads ironclads. Reading the plans and specifications, inspecting the keels and decks, Rodgers ordered each gunboat to be armed with five rifled 42-pounders and ten 9-inch Dahlgren broadside guns. He planned to mount the rifled cannon in the bow of each vessel, pointed through the forward end of the casemate and positioned to sweep the river ahead. Two smoothbores would be planted aft, one on each quarter, the other light smoothbores in broadside. The commander rechecked the armament, the steam plant, and the iron plating and concluded that the ironclads bore most of their weight abaft the beam, trimming each gunboat astern. To remedy this, Naval Constructor Samuel Pook changed the plans at Rodgers' insistence, moving the boilers forward twenty feet.[27]

Mechanics plated the forward end of the casemates with the prescribed two and a half-inch iron and employed three-quarter inch iron on the deck forward of the casemate. The sides abreast of the engines and boilers were covered with two and a half-inch plates. The steam plant was located below the water line; the remainder of each gunboat was left unprotected.[28]

Since Eads and Rodgers wanted to test the strength of the iron plates against artillery, they conducted tests across the river from the Carondelet docks. On a sandy beach, officers bolted iron plates to oak blocks positioned at an angle of forty-five degrees, the same slant as the gunboats' sides, and began firing from various distances. To the satisfaction of naval officers, builders, and ordnance experts, the experiment proved the resisting power of the two and a half-inch plates, but underscored that the method of securing the plates to the sides of the gunboats—with bolts with heads—was hazardous. The decision was made to countersink the bolts. Impressed with the overall results, the Gaylord Foundry, in St. Louis, proudly displayed the targets and ball fragments in front of their establishment.[29]

At the dockyards, James Eads's gunboats began to take shape. To river men, the ironclads resembled "snapping turtles," "mud turtles," "Pook turtles," but, to a newsman, they were unlike "anything on the earth, or under the earth, or above the earth."[30] Rodgers believed that these unorthodox, "suffocating stinkpots" would outfight and outmaneuver any frigate in smooth water,[31] but Eads was not so optimistic.

The War Department in Washington used one pretext after another to withhold money, and Eads was forced to pour his own funds into the venture after first exhausting his credit. He had contracted with other firms and was heavily in debt. The builder, requisitioning the War Department for $100,000, suggested that unless the Government paid promptly, all work would stop. Unanswered telegrams to Eads for money forced engine builders in Pittsburgh to complain that they were in the hole $25,000.[32]

Washington seemed deaf to all requests, including those of Rodgers. To arm the Eads gunboats, the commander dispatched a five-page request to the naval Bureau of Ordnance for cannon, shells, grape, cartridge balls, revolvers, carbines, primers, bayonets, and cartridge bags. When the Bureau chief read this request, he thought Rodgers crazy: this was strictly an Army undertaking, and the Navy was not responsible. Across town, Army Ordnance dilly-dallied, complaining that gunboat ordnance was unknown to the military service.[33] Cameron snapped that the Army could furnish only two rifled 42-pounders for each gunboat.[34]

After a month's delay and under extreme pressure from the Navy Department, Army Ordnance sent a trickle of small arms westward, but no heavy cannon. From the Philadelphia Navy Yard, Rodgers finally received 2,000 rifle cartridges, three gun chain slings, and three gallons of lacquer.[35]

While Rodgers pleaded for help, the Army shook up its western command. In late July 1861, Rodgers reported for duty to General John C. Fremont, the famed western explorer, who had succeeded McClellan in command. The Administration set up Fremont as military commander of the Western Department—a department embracing Illinois and the states and territories from west of the Mississippi River to the Rocky Mountains, with headquarters in St. Louis.[36]

The sun was merciless the day Fremont took command. At the corner of St. Ange and 14th streets, on a point overlooking the whole city, General Fremont set up headquarters at the camp of the distinguished Hungarian officer Captain Zagonyi. Three hundred picked men—lawyers, physicians, and school teachers—composed Fremont's bodyguard.[37]

At noon he called a staff meeting. By afternoon, after

searching through records and asking questions, he concluded that he had inherited a mess. His troops had not been paid; several units threatened mutiny; veterans left the service; the new levies were too raw, too young. To march this unmanageable mob before the enemy would be suicide.[38] But Westerners were encouraged, positive that Washington had sent Fremont to St. Louis to move an expedition southward to New Orleans.[39]

In mid-August intelligence reached Rodgers at Cairo that enemy troops were camped en masse near New Madrid, Missouri, and that 1,000 had already captured Commerce. The *Lexington, Conestoga,* and *Tyler* got underway and moved down-river. At Commerce, bluejackets discovered that the Rebels had retreated westward with a train of fifty wagons loaded with corn, after wantonly destroying homes, barns, and other property. Up on the hill Confederate cavalry showered the gunboats with small-arms fire. Union gunners quick retaliated, their shells scattering the enemy in all directions. Rodgers and his gunboats, taking women and children on board, steamed northward for Cairo.[40]

Rumors spread up river that enemy units were massing at Benton and at Big Island—below Commerce; that Confederate cargo steamers were lying unmolested at Paducah; that Rebel ironclads had reached Memphis on their way to Cairo. Rodgers wired Fremont that his wooden gunboats, his inexperienced sailors, and his puny weapons were no match for ironclads.[41]

Operating near Hickman, Kentucky, Rodgers, with the *Tyler* and *Lexington,* spotted a gunboat with the Stars and Bars twoblocked at the mast. The Confederates fired. Masked batteries ashore fired. The *Tyler* and *Lexington's* guns peppered the enemy but, caught in the river current, which sent them swirling toward the shore batteries, the *Tyler* and *Lexington* turned and headed away. At that moment, Rodgers realized that his wooden gunboats, equipped only with small arms and antiquated ordnance, were no match for shore batteries.[42]

In St. Louis, General Fremont, worried about the rumors of enemy ironclads, demanded the removal of Commander John Rodgers. "I don't like Rodgers," he told Montgomery Blair, the Postmaster General, "will you ask to have him removed." He insisted that Rodgers be replaced by a captain, an officer with experience.[43]

In far-off Brooklyn, New York, the career-conscious naval captain Andrew Hull Foote worked unnoticed, momentarily forgotten at the Navy Yard. This thirty-nine-year veteran of the naval service yearned for promotion and fame;[44] he had written his old schoolmate, Gideon Welles, congratulating him upon his appointment as naval secretary, and, later, he went off to Washington to see him. In friendly confidence, Foote told the secretary his opinions of various naval officers and asked for a command, any command. Gideon Welles was impressed with Foote's qualifications.[45]

On August 30, 1861, the Navy Department ordered Foote to St. Louis to command naval operations on western rivers and to cooperate with General Fremont.[46] Without fanfare or publicity, this quiet, silvery-haired veteran slipped into St. Louis, where he listened to Fremont bewailing conditions on the river. The enemy had ironclad steamers; the Union, three wooden gunboats that could be sunk within a matter of minutes. From the outset, Foote was fearful. "I expect, of course, to be shot by a rifle soon," he confided to a friend, "but I mean to die game."[47] He saw that the western command lacked money, credit, ordnance, men, supplies, a navy yard, and prestige.[48]

Down at Cairo there was little left for John Rodgers. His brother-in-law, Montgomery Meigs, Quartermaster General, had been shocked and surprised at the Foote appointment, but there was nothing he could do.[49] Welles lamely told Rodgers that as the western command grew, officers with more experience were indispensable and pushed the blame for his removal on the War Department.[50] In early September Rodgers packed his bags, left Cairo, and headed eastward. This outstanding naval officer was to win fame in the monitors on the Atlantic Coast.

At his Cairo office on the wharf, Captain Foote expressed dissatisfaction with James Eads's gunboats—they lay too low in the water; their engines had limited capacities; they could not make headway up-stream. He reiterated that the gunboats were purely experiments and that all experiments were defective. Foote heaped invective upon the ordnance bureaus, Army and Navy, for failing to supply guns. "This fitting out of the vessels when no one knows anything about it," he said, "is truly discouraging . . . it is darkness ahead."[51]

The military commander at Cairo in charge of southeast Missouri was an obscure man named Ulysses S. Grant, a West Pointer who, at the start of the war, was in the leather business at Galena, Illinois. Appointed by President Lincoln as Brigadier General, he had established headquarters at Stafford's Bank, up the street from the waterfront.[52]

No sooner had Foote arrived in Cairo than Grant

started offensive operations. Gunboats and transports
loaded with the 9th and 12th Illinois regiments steamed
off for Paducah, Kentucky, at the mouth of the Tennessee
River. Foote stepped on board a fast steamer, overhauled
the squadron, and, at 8:30 a.m. on September 6, saw the
troops under Grant disembark. Marching into town, the
Yankees learned that a company of Rebel troops had just
left by railroad, hauling off all the rolling stock. With
Federal forces in Paducah and others at Smithland, at
the mouth of the Cumberland River, Union gunboats
now blockaded both rivers that led from the Ohio into
the heart of Tennessee.[53]

Four days later, the *Conestoga* and *Tyler* covered a
military advance southward from Cairo. Passing the
Union soldiers on shore, *Conestoga* steamed down-river
to examine Island No. 2, where she discovered enemy
forces on the Missouri side at Lucas Bend. *Conestoga*
opened fire. From shore, sixteen rifled guns roared in
unison. Rushing down-river at full speed, the *Lexington*
joined the fight and, after a brisk engagement, she and
the *Conestoga* retired out of range to lure the Rebels into
an ambush of advancing Union soldiers. Off in the distance, below the land batteries, the Confederate gunboat
Jackson opened fire. The *Lexington* and *Conestoga* responded, but the shot from their outmoded guns failed
to reach the enemy.

During the afternoon, the *Conestoga* and *Lexington*
dropped down to engage the *Jackson* at close quarters.
A lucky shot demolished the latter's wheelhouse. Injured
and leaking badly, she limped off toward Columbus, Kentucky. The *Conestoga* and *Lexington* returned up-river,
their guns sputtering at the enemy's shore installations
on the Missouri side. In forty minutes, they silenced

the Rebels and drove them inland. Hiding in an out-building, other Confederates bushwhacked the *Conestoga*, killing Nelson Castle, quartermaster, the first sailor to fall in the river war.[54]

A month after this engagement, the *Conestoga* and *Tyler* began patrolling the river to Iron Bluff's Bank, where, near Columbus, they spotted the Rebel steamer *Jeff Davis*. Steaming gingerly toward her, the Union gunboats came within view of the gun emplacements two miles above Columbus and opened fire. From the banks, five enemy rifled cannon belched shells that went whizzing over the gunboats, one shot splashing within a few feet of their bows. Impotent against heavy cannon, the side-wheelers rounded to and returned to Cairo.[55]

Although these preliminary skirmishes on the river were of minor importance, Foote had learned that the Confederates had difficulty hitting a moving target at long range and that gunboat fire power was superior to troops operating on shore without shelter of fortifications.

3

"The Poor Damn Bastards Ought'a Have a Plan"

At 2:00 a.m. on November 7, 1861, a messenger roused General Grant from a sound sleep. The enemy was transporting troops across the Mississippi from Columbus, Kentucky, to seek out and destroy the Union forces then operating in Missouri. Grant determined to attack.[1] Hurriedly, the 22nd, 27th, 30th, and 31st Illinois regiments, the 7th Iowa, and a company of artillery, 3,500 men in all, boarded transports and moved down-river, escorted by the *Lexington* and *Tyler*.[2]

Southward at Columbus, twenty-one miles below Cairo, General Leonidas Polk, an Episcopalian bishop who had forsaken the cloth for the uniform, commanded the Confederate forces. At the first streaks of dawn an officer awakened the general. The Yankees were moving transports down-stream. Word flashed across the river to Belmont, Missouri, where Gideon Pillow, a compact little general, readied his division.[3]

Two miles north of Belmont, the Federal expedition nosed into the bank on the Missouri shore, out of range of the Columbus cannon. Hardly had the Yankees mustered in battle formation, when the Rebel infantry fired.

Union soldiers advanced. From tree to tree, through the woods and out into an open field, the undermanned Confederate force fought each step of the way, strengthening their positions by chopping down trees and sharpening the limbs to throw up an abatis.

Out in the river the *Lexington* and *Tyler* steamed, firing toward the batteries on Iron Banks, a short distance above Columbus, and zigzagging to elude the shots zooming overhead. The superiority of the enemy position and their field cannon, planted high on a bluff overlooking the river, proved too formidable. The gunboats withdrew but, at 2:30 p.m., the sound of the battle inland persuaded naval commanders to renew the attack. Their paddlewheels churning, the *Lexington* and *Tyler* maneuvered toward the Columbus battlements. Running inside the shell fire, out of range of the guns, the sidewheelers discharged broadside after broadside. Gradually the Rebels corrected their range. A shot slammed into the starboard bulwarks of the *Tyler* and smashed through the spar deck, decapitating seaman Michael Adams.[4]

The battle raged ashore. Rebels and Yankees fought stubbornly and viciously in hand-to-hand combat. Grant's horse was shot out from under him. A 100-pounder shell screamed over the general and his staff, burying itself in the ground less than fifty feet away, but failed to explode. The Yankees pressed back the Rebels, who suddenly broke and ran to the river banks.

Grant had gained his objective, the capture of the Confederate camp with all its stores and artillery, but Belmont was nothing as a military position and could not be held without the capture of Columbus. To attack this stronghold was foolhardy.

Flushed with victory, the overconfident and boisterous Blue scattered to loot the neighborhood, giving the Confederates precious time to regroup. General Leonidas Polk dispatched three regiments from Columbus to reinforce the faltering lines. They poured out of the transports on a bank near the Federal position and heard their embattled comrades scream: "Don't land! Don't land! We are whipped! Go back!"[5]

Grant's men, reforming, their pockets loaded with boodle, fired at the boats arriving from Columbus. From the heights across river, General Polk ordered the heavy guns into action. As shells zipped into Union lines, Grant gave the order to retreat.

Fresh Rebel troops advanced, giving time for their battleworn friends to move up-river, turn the Union's position, and attack in the rear. Caught in a murderous cross fire, the Yankees fell back, struggling toward their transports. More Confederate reinforcements arrived, while General Gideon Pillow's command gained on the fleeing Yankees.[6] Suddenly, the Southerners ran into fire from the guns of the *Lexington* and *Tyler,* which lay on the river bank protecting the transports. The gunboats drove shot and shell into the Rebels with deadly effect. Exploding shells hurled horses, guns, and men into the air and mowed down Confederate ranks. It was madness for troops armed only with muskets and field artillery to attack. Under the covering fire of the *Lexington* and *Tyler,* Yankees swarmed on board the transports.[7]

Sneaking through the brush, the Rebels hastened up-river to wait the passing of the transports and gunboats. When the flotilla appeared, Confederates fired. The Yankees rushed to the opposite side of the transports, where sergeants forced them back with bayonets to pre-

vent capsizing. The expedition steamed on to safety up-
river. Back on the field of battle, Rebels buried 295
soldiers. One Confederate wrote home, "We've had an
awful battle and victory."[8]

Triumphantly, General Polk wired Richmond, "The
enemy fled . . . It was a complete rout." Confederate
losses numbered 641 killed, wounded, or missing;[9] the
Union's, 500, plus twenty-five baggage wagons, 100 horses,
1,000 overcoats, and 1,000 blankets.

The results of the Belmont battle were clear and un-
mistakable. Union forces supported by the gunboats had
foiled Rebel attempts to send reinforcements into Missouri and established the fact that Columbus was so
strongly fortified that a large field force must cooperate
with the gunboats to move successfully beyond that
point. The battle brought home to Southerners the power
of enemy gunboats. "The most terrifying [part] of the
day's work was when we were exposed for half an hour
to the shell and grape from the gunboats," testified a
young officer.[10] General Pillow agreed. He confided to
authorities in Richmond that if the Confederacy possessed
gunboats, it could meet and destroy the enemy.[11]

The river reverberated with talk of gunboats and Federal naval might. Memphis trembled. Old men and young
in broadcloth and jeans drilled in the streets. New organi-
zations—the Confederate Guards, the Liberty Guards,
and the Independent Guards—sprang to the colors. At
Vicksburg citizens searched the city for guns.[12] The
governor of Tennessee dispatched letters to Alabama,
Mississippi, and Louisiana, asking for troops.[13]

Westerners were shocked at Grant's losses and his
management of the entire operation. His blunders, grumbled an officer to his senator, proved that he was wholly

incapable of command.[14] When the news was flashed
from Belmont, Captain Foote was supervising the construction of gunboats in St. Louis. The captain assaulted
Washington with protests. Grant had failed to telegraph;
he had failed to consult; he had failed to inform the
gunboat captains until, at the last minute, he directed
them to convoy the transports. The captain complained
bitterly of the Army's lack of consideration toward the
Navy and demanded promotion to flag officer rank.[15]

The irritated Foote shuttled back and forth between
Cairo and St. Louis, inspecting, ordering, planning. He
learned that Fremont, haunted by the thought of Southern ironclads, had unilaterally and without authority,
purchased from James Eads the steamer *Submarine No.
7*, invested in the ferryboat *New Era*, and contracted for
the construction of a fleet of mortar boats. The Congressional appropriation of $1,100,000 for the seven ironclads
and for the *Tyler*, *Lexington*, and *Conestoga* had long
since been spent. Money earmarked for the Quartermaster Department in St. Louis had been handed over
for these additional river steamers and thirty-eight mortar boats.

The *Submarine No. 7*, rechristened the *Benton*, had
been a Mississippi wrecking boat; Eads had tried to
peddle her to Rodgers by offering a Government agent
$100 to use his influence.[16] Rodgers had rejected this
boat for being on "her last legs." Fremont paid Eads
$26,000 and moved her to the St. Louis drydocks, where
carpenters tore down her superstructure, pulled up decks,
and left only the bottom and sides. Amid piles of lumber,
rivets, and iron plates, mechanics hoisted the pennant
"Benton—For Memphis and New Orleans" and began
replacing the decayed timbers, cutting off the forward

part of the *Benton*, attaching a new bow, and rebuilding the entire boat.[17]

At his headquarters in St. Louis, General John C. Fremont sent his friend, Theodore Adams, to Louis V. Bogy, president of Wiggin's Ferryboat Company, to persuade him to sell the largest ferryboat then operating on the upper Mississippi River, the *New Era*. At first Bogy refused Adams's overtures, but after repeated threats of government seizure, he relented and sold the vessel for $22,000, a figure well below his asking price. Once this transaction was completed, General Fremont handed Theodore Adams the job of converting the *New Era* (rechristened *Essex*) into an ironclad.[18]

A stranger to St. Louis and to the ways of the river, Adams was both inexperienced and lacking in capital, but this did not deter him from dickering for another Government contract to construct mortar boats. In the summer of 1861, Gustavus Fox, in Washington, had thought of placing mortar guns on rafts and floating them down-river.[19] Now Adams was proposing solid pine-timbered rafts, sheathed with boiler iron and equipped with a steering oar and "doors" for the free swing of the guns.[20]

General Fremont had complete faith in Theodore Adams and, without testing their merits, ordered thirty-eight of these "peculiar craft." Adams demanded and received $8,250 for each boat. Fremont had not advertised for bids, and contractors protested that a total stranger, and a Californian to boot, was lining his pockets with staggering profits. These rafts, reported a river man, were "little more than piles of logs securely pinned together."[21] In Washington, Montgomery Meigs, pleased with the mortar idea but believing that only one would be constructed for experimental purposes, was dumbfounded to learn that the general had ordered thirty-eight. The Quartermaster Department's depleted funds were not sufficient to pay for them.[22]

Fremont's giveaway program lined other pockets. In St. Louis, Fremont's quartermaster, without legal sanction, appointed favorites to the posts of director, superintendent, and agent for steamboat transportation. The purchase of steam tugs afforded remunerative employment for Government pets. The tug *Wonder*, bought by a firm for $1,500, was passed on to the Government for $4,000. Another boat, regularly chartered at $200, was hired by the Government for $1,800 a month. The condemned steamer *Lake Erie No. 2* was chartered by the Government at $1,350 per month. Owners whose steamers had remained idle for months suddenly saw their rates skyrocketing, and deck hands who, before the war, worked contentedly for $15 a month, had their wages hiked to $30 while in the transport service.[23]

From the time Fremont arrived in St. Louis, fraud, corruption, extravagance, and inefficiency rocked the western command. In one transaction, a total of $191,000 went to build five forts, $110,000 of it being profit to the contractor.[24] Lincoln hastened a Congressional committee westward to examine conditions and to probe all unsettled claims against the Western Department.[25] With this investigation wrapped around his neck, Fremont's quartermaster revamped the system for chartering transports, fired the superintendents and directors, and placed a competent Army captain in charge of all Mississippi River transportation in a frantic effort to clean up the frauds.[26]

Senator Lyman Trumbull of Illinois stepped into town and found deplorable conditions. The Army was demoralized. Thousands had no guns; others were ragged and half-clad. The command lacked money. "If the Government has not confidence in Fremont's financial capacity," stormed Trumbull, "in Heaven's name send somebody here with funds to purchase necessary supplies in which it has confidence." The Senator complained about Washington's refusal to supply Foote. "What earthly use can there be for gunboats without arms and ammunition?" he snorted.[27]

Down in Cairo in his grubby waterfront office, Foote sought comfort in his Bible.[28] He needed credit and money, guns and ammunition, men and support from Washington. His rank of captain was subordinate to that of an Army colonel, and this lack of status rankled.[29] Foote complained that he was expected to be a business office—a one-man bureau of ordnance, provision, yards and docks, construction, and personnel.[30] "We want money and men," he cried. If delays were to continue, if offensive operations were to bog down, his professional reputation would vanish. The captain was tired of coming in second to the Army.[31] Finally on November 13, Washington promoted Andrew Hull Foote to flag officer, commanding the United States naval forces on western rivers.[32]

Foote's biggest headache was ordnance. Washington ordered the Fort Pitt Foundry to furnish Fremont with sixteen 9-inch Navy shell guns and thirty 8-inch Army mortar pieces. The shell guns, stored in the foundry since the 1850s, were rejects, too defective to serve on board the Atlantic frigates. In the emergency, inspectors had pronounced them fit, but Captain John Dahlgren, the gunnery expert at the Washington Navy Yard, warned that they should not be fired beyond 300 rounds per gun.

The foundry promised to forward them at once and to manufacture mortar pieces at the rate of four per week.[33]

The War Department wrote Foote that thirty-five 42-pounder rifled cannon would be sent to him, but suggested he hound the warehouses at Sackett's Harbor, Erie, and Buffalo for any additional ordnance.[34] Eventually, after repeated pleas, the Erie Arsenal dispatched their left-overs: twenty-five 32-pounders, ten 68-pounders, ammunition, one sponge, and one rammer.[35]

The sixteen Navy shell guns from Pittsburgh arrived in Cairo. but the Army's thirty-five 42-pounders did not. Foote petitioned his old shipmate, John Dahlgren, to send out twelve howitzers, along with ammunition and thirty good gun captains. Finding no gunpowder in St. Louis, Foote continued to bombard Washington with requests, but the worries, the setbacks, the responsibilities, began to wear him down. "May God grant that I never again in this world . . . be placed in the painful state I am now in . . . I have worked myself, body and mind, almost to death."[36]

Foote—"Old Flags" to his men—dispatched his ordnance officer to Cincinnati and to Pittsburgh to look after the flotilla's interests.[37] Refusing to go through channels, Foote prodded the Allegheny Arsenal to hurry.[38] If the promised cannon failed to arrive, the gunboats would be powerless. He urged Washington to send out $75,000 for current expenses to fit out the flotilla, to pay for Navy clothing, to reimburse officers and crew for back wages.[39]

Recruiting continued to plague Foote. Upon his arrival in Cairo, he had reopened stations along the Great Lakes and in major western cities. For every Navy recruiting station, the Army had thirty, which dangled bounties and advances before the eyes of youths. The Navy could not match it. Lack of funds forced Foote to reduce the advance of $36, paid in Eastern ports, to only $10 in the Great Lakes area.[40] Sailors hesitated to leave home ports to serve in the muddy waters of western rivers.

Concerned over the situation in the West, Welles picked fifty men ticketed for the blockading squadrons and shipped them to the flotilla.[41] Foote himself appointed river men as officers. Undisciplined, ignorant of naval regulations, they proved, in the opinion of Lieutenant Phelps, to be poor and unreliable. "They understood the business of steamboating and questions of freight," complained Phelps, "but seemed capable of nothing else."[42]

In the East, recruiting for the blockading squadrons had gone slowly. To step it up, the Navy Department ordered the steamer *Michigan* to cruise in the Great Lakes, to dock at various ports, and to sign up men for Atlantic duty, which took priority over duty in Foote's command.[43] Welles verbally paddled Old Flags for recruiting on the Great Lakes and for competing with the Navy's efforts for the blockading squadrons. Foote closed down all stations except Chicago and Pittsburgh, but countered by demanding 500 men.[44] Seeing that the Army and Foote had milked the Great Lakes region dry, Welles reversed his policy and sent word to the steamer *Michigan* to recruit for the Western Flotilla.[45] Although a draft of 542 was sent to Cairo late in 1861, fifty-eight of these deserted at various station stops along the way.[46]

At the dockyards, Eads's ironclads began sliding down the ways. General Grant and an excursion party of men and women journeyed northward from Cairo to see the *Mound City* launched. Out in the Ohio River, at Mound City, the *Lexington* lay anchored, her hull newly painted black, bluejackets lining the hurricane deck. Colonel Morgan's regiment was drawn up in line and presented arms as the band played "Hail to the Chief." A lady smashed a whiskey bottle filled with river water, rather than effete champagne, across the *Mound City's* bow, and the gunboat plunged into the Ohio. When she struck the water, guns salvoed from the *Lexington* and its band blared out "Hail Columbia."[47]

After the launching, James Eads worried over the ironclad's defects. The chief error was the lack of depth in the hold. Steam drums could not be placed beneath the decks, and engineers refused to sheath them with iron plates since the boats, already trimmed at the stern, could not stand the additional weight. With the fantail only thirteen inches above the water line, Foote was concerned because the mechanics still had to fit rudders, water buckets, and heavy cannon. He suggested chopping off the deck and beams covering the stern wheels. Eads urged caution, pointing out that the heavy armament and the additional plates, which went forward, would trim the boat fore and aft. At Cairo, when the *Mound City* was fitted with cannon in the bow, Foote's fears were proven groundless.[48]

That same November Winfield Scott retired as General-in-Chief. General George B. McClellan's appointment to the post was heralded by a parade that went down Pennsylvania Avenue, through the grounds of the White House, and on past the home of the Secretary of War, to McClellan's residence at the corner of 16th and H streets. Fireworks soared, and bands played the "John Brown Tune," while thousands, waving red, white, and blue torches, sang:

We have seen our last defeat
We have seen our last defeat
We have seen our last defeat
McClellan's marching on,
Glory, glory, Hallelujah!

The hullabaloo brought Little Mac to the porch, where, silhouetted against the torchlights, he proclaimed: "The war cannot be long."[49]

Over at the Navy Department, his desk piled high with books and charts, Assistant Secretary Gustavus Vasa Fox pondered the blockading squadrons' next moves in the Atlantic and Gulf. Already Union land-sea expeditions had struck and captured Hatteras Inlet, off the North Carolina sounds, and Port Royal, South Carolina. Once these areas were secured and bases for the squadrons established, Fox turned his attention to the seizure of New Orleans, gateway to the Mississippi River, and, in the word of Gideon Welles, "the most important place in the insurrectionary region and the most difficult to blockade."

During his maritime days Fox had ascended the river in an ocean steamer at night without a pilot and he was now reasonably certain that the forts guarding New Orleans from the Gulf, built in the days of sailing vessels, would prove ineffective against steamers operating under cover of darkness. Checking charts and survey reports, he saw that once the gunboats passed New Orleans, they could steam up-river and cooperate with the Western Flotilla, which was moving southward. Fox wanted New Orleans for the Navy. Both he and Welles knew that the War Department was committed to the strategy of descending the Mississippi to capture the Crescent City from the north.

On November 14, 1861, Fox went to the White House and saw Lincoln about New Orleans.[50] The President was interested in the project, but doubted its feasibility. Fox argued that steam had revolutionized naval warfare. The Confederates would be expecting an attack from above, not past strong forts and against raging currents. An assault up to New Orleans from the Gulf would be less difficult, less exhausting, less costly, and far more fatal to Rebel commerce and morale than a mere blockade.

The evening of the next day, November 15, Lincoln, Welles, Fox, Secretary of State William H. Seward, and Commander David Dixon Porter, who had just arrived in Washington from Gulf blockading duties, consulted with McClellan at his headquarters. When the delegation headed by the President marched in, officers lounging on sofas snapped to attention. Upstairs, Lincoln and the others found McClellan in his shirt sleeves, sitting on the edge of a camp bed. Lincoln, Welles, Fox, Seward, and Porter sat down around the general's table, which was littered with papers, journals, and torn envelopes.

Engrossed in the problems of the Army of the Potomac, Little Mac hoped to establish a base for his Army on the Peninsula, the shortest route to Richmond. Simultaneously, the Western Army could march into Memphis. Once this happened, the Army at Port Royal could move into Charleston, and General Don Carlos Buell's units, then in Kentucky, could push into Tennessee and Alabama.[51]

Patiently, McClellan listened to Fox's detailed plan for New Orleans. When the secretary stopped talking, the general stood up, put down his cigar, and walked over to a wall map, which he studied. Such a plan, he snapped, might possibly divert the Rebels from the Virginia front, but such an operation would take at least 50,000 of his own men. Fox emphasized that this was to be a naval expedition and that the gunboats would need only 10,000 soldiers to hold the city once it was captured. The debate continued. Finally McClellan agreed, but he had little faith in the venture.

By December 1861 two plans for the river campaign had been blocked out. The Navy was expected to capture New Orleans from the Gulf, while the Western Army and Foote's gunboats, sticking with General Scott's anaconda plan, were to move down the river and strike Columbus, Kentucky, or maneuver up the Cumberland and Tennessee rivers toward Nashville. Memphis would be their next step, then Vicksburg and New Orleans.[52]

Winter came early to St. Louis. General Henry W. Halleck arrived in the city and took command of the Western Department. Fremont's bungling policies and financial incompetence, coupled with his defiance of Lincoln's stand on the slavery question, had forced the President to dismiss him. In his place the War Department assigned the cigar-chewing Halleck, who, though never having enjoyed an opportunity to demonstrate what he could do in field command, was a distinguished military theorist, lawyer, and administrator. There was no pomp or ceremony about Henry W. Halleck. He resembled a country parson, not a general, dressing as he did in simple blue flannel and stiff-rimmed black hat.

Down at Cairo the dreary military routine was broken only when generals from Washington reviewed the troops or when firing squads executed horse thieves and Army deserters. On the waterfront, Flag Officer Andrew Foote was painfully frank with newspaper reporters. Prominent in his encyclopedia of complaints was the Navy Department's lack of sympathy with the Western Command, which resulted in undermanned gunboats and second-rate ordnance. James Eads's ironclads had been improperly designed and lay too low in the water, and their engines were deficient in power.[53]

Reporters swarmed on board the *Louisville*, tied up to the Cairo wharf. From the weight of the machinery, the iron plates, and the crew, her hull lay so deep in the water that the deck was almost awash. Newsmen inspected the lower deck and the casemate, with its sloping sides, climbed the ladder to another deck, entered the iron-sheathed pilot house, and squinted through the eight peep holes. They remarked on the massive plates covering the bow and sides as far back as the boilers and machinery.[54]

Astern of the *Louisville* lay the thirty-eight mortar boats, ready for their guns and beds. Foote hated these contraptions and awoke mornings with "a mortar boat on his heart." But Gustavus Fox, sure that the rafts were the flotilla's most efficient weapon, had insisted on their construction and use.

The Navy needed mortar guns and 800 volunteers to man them. Foote appealed to Meigs, but the Quartermaster General passed the buck to Halleck, who refused to help and vetoed all suggestions.

When Lincoln heard of the mortar-boat imbroglio, he was furious and badgered the Naval Ordnance Bureau, demanding to know what was being done and ordering daily telegrams sent to him from the Western Flotilla. After investigating the matter, he became "much put out" at the War Department over the delays and became so exasperated that he telegraphed the foundry in Pittsburgh

himself, simultaneously threatening to fire the Army ordnance chief. At the White House, Fox and Meigs met
with the President for two hours. Lincoln instructed
Meigs to fill Foote's needs.[55]

On the 15th of January, 1862, it was cold in Cairo, but
Foote, as usual, was up early. He breakfasted in his room
at the St. Charles Hotel and then picked his way toward
the wharf, careful to keep on the plank walks to avoid
the slop, the manure, and the mud which was everywhere. Foote's stroll to the river took him past the horse
stable and pig yard adjoining the hotel, past Stafford's
Bank, where Grant's headquarters were, past the express
office with the rough board coffins waiting for the train,
and past the gamblers, the speculators, the ruffians, the
truckmen, and the fighting hogs and chickens. Toward
the Mississippi levee lay the soldiers' barracks, miserable
sheds stretching far up-river. Surveying the Mississippi,
Foote saw the hulking receiving ship, the ironclads
moored astern, and the cluster of mortar boats along the
banks. His ears were assaulted by the clang of hammers
and the buzz of saws and the snorting and puffing of tugs
and steamers out in the stream.[56]

Foote had labored six months to put this squadron into
fighting trim. Although he still needed 1,700 men to bring
the flotilla up to full strength, he was cheered when he
learned that the nation's arsenals and foundries were
sending out more cannon and ammunition to Cairo for
Eads's ironclads, the *Cairo, Pittsburg, Louisville, Mound
City, St. Louis, Carondelet,* and *Cincinnati.*

The year 1862 opened with the Union armies, East and
West, idle in their camps. Across the nation, prolonged

inaction increased discontent, and indignant Northerners, Illinois farmers and Boston bankers, berated the Lincoln Administration. "The poor damn bastards ought'a have a plan," stormed a Michigan senator.[57] Northwesterners dubbed Lincoln an imbecile, and, claiming that Eastern-owned railroads were robbing them blind, demanded the speedy opening of the Mississippi.[58]

Southward, down the swirling waters of the river past Columbus, Memphis, and Vicksburg to New Orleans, the Confederates, like the Yankees, were hastening to float a Navy. They, too, lacked men, guns, tools, and support from the central government. The problem that faced the North also faced the South.

4

"This Is No Time to Mince Words"

One autumn day in 1861 New Orleans toasted the Confederate ram *Manassas,* "The Invincible Sea-King," which had just rammed into a Yankee blockader and sent her scurrying out into the Gulf. The ram had moved southward in the early mists of October 14 toward the Head of the Passes in the Mississippi. The forward hatch opened a few inches, and the pilot peered out and distinguished the dim outline of the blockader *Preble* dead ahead. Instantly, he sang out to the engineer: "Let her out, Hardy, let her out *now!*" Coal heavers threw tar, tallow, and sulphur into the furnaces. The *Manassas* shot forward, crunching and clawing her way into the wooden sides of the *Preble.* The ram shuddered until her engines were reversed. She backed away, wrenching loose huge chunks of coppering and solid oak.

Most of the *Preble's* crew, fast asleep below, fell from their hammocks at the moment of impact. Recovering their senses, they rushed topside and gaped at the *Manassas.* Some leaped overboard. "We're sinking!" screamed a bluejacket, "We're all lost! Oh, my God!"

The Rebels saw a Union cruiser nearby, her broadside exposed. Again the pilot shot an order to the engineer: "Now let her out, Hardy, and give it to her." But a condenser broke, and the *Manassas* failed to attack. Working one engine, the skipper turned the ram around and headed her up-stream.

By this time the Union gunboats realized what had happened. Guns flashed from the *Richmond* and *Vincennes,* but most of their shells sailed harmlessly over the enemy. A lucky shot from the *Richmond* ricocheted into the *Manassas,* knocking down her second stack and choking off the outlet. Sulphur and tallow fumes spread and threatened to suffocate the crew. Grabbing an axe, engineer Hardy sprang up the companionway, chopped away the fallen stack and its guys, and opened the vent. Smoke rushed skyward.

Blazing Rebel fire rafts charged the Yankee cruisers. But the wind blew them ashore, where they burned without inflicting damage. The blockaders steamed off hastily, the *Preble* in tow, and scrambled across the bar headed for sea. The first skirmish for the control of New Orleans had ended.[1]

Six months earlier, at the start of the war, the Confederate Secretary of the Navy, Stephen R. Mallory, had taken charge of a department that owned not even a rowboat. This charming Floridian not only had to organize and administer the affairs of the Navy, but had to build the ships, scrape up the ordnance, and recruit the men—all in a nation that was soon shut off from outside help by a blockade, a nation that controlled pitifully limited resources, a nation that had no maritime tradition.

The Confederacy thought of its Navy primarily as a defensive weapon. The ability of the South to wage war on the high seas, to win a war rather than merely avoid being conquered, and to win it at a minimum of cost in blood and treasure, depended upon its ability to carry the fight to the blockaders. No war can be won simply by standing on the defensive; any "victory" so won would be hollow. Regardless of how impregnable the Confederacy's coastal defenses were, they could never be perfect, and the security of the South would be jeopardized if it could not inflict vital injury to the enemy that menaced its coast and its rivers.[2]

During the summer of 1861, lacking the foresight to demand that the Government create a Navy, Richmond newspapers begged for the construction of forts along the seacoasts to repel Yankee armadas and prepared the public mind for the disasters that would ensue when "Massa Lincum's" gunboats began "swimming in Southern waters."[3] At the capital, President Jefferson Davis—a former United States Secretary of War, a Mexican War veteran, and a West Pointer—disparaged the Navy and turned his energies and those of the nation to propagating a military colossus.

The sums appropriated for building and strengthening a fleet were indicative of the Government's myopic policy. While the North poured millions into the blockade and that July spent $1,000,000 for Eads's ironclads, the Confederate Congress alloted the Navy a mere $278,500. A second bill earmarked a sop of $50,000 to buy or build gunboats for coastal defense and $160,000 for the construction of two ironclad gunboats for the defense of the Mississippi River. If $160,000 would build and equip two gunboats, the Government miscalculated if it believed that an additional $50,000 would purchase many steamers. The Confederate Congress voted to spend $800,000 for "floating defenses" at New Orleans and another $197,000 for fitting out the *Merrimack* at Norfolk. Naval officers objected to the monies given New Orleans since they implied that the Government planned to build "float-ing defenses" and not "honest-to-God" gunboats and cruisers.[4]

At his office in Richmond, Secretary Mallory concen-trated upon the problems of naval strength. Stumpy and fat, he made up for lack of brilliance and dash with pa-tience and capacity for hard work. In the Davis Adminis-tration, Mallory enjoyed fame as the best-informed man in the South on naval warfare, although his only sea experience had been gained on board his own yacht. Before the war, his career as United States Senator from Florida had been chiefly associated with the Navy, for he served for many years as chairman of the United States Senate Committee on Naval Affairs.

The secretary realized from the outset that the enemy already commanded a "built Navy" and could turn out 100 wooden ships to the Rebels' one. Just two Confederate naval yards, Norfolk and Pensacola, were operating, and at that, Norfolk had been badly damaged by the retreat-ing Federals, and Pensacola's yard was geared to ship repair. Small private yards in the East were incapable of turning out warships. Although the South had a supply of raw naval stores for the old-style wooden vessels, it lacked sufficient workmen with the know-how to convert them into fighting craft.

Focusing upon ironclads, Mallory's objective was to make Southern ships so powerful as to compensate for the Rebels' numerical inferiority. Ironclad vessels were vital, and Mallory wanted to revolutionize naval warfare by showing the world what could be done despite limited resources.[5] He estimated that an iron-plated fleet carrying 300 rifled cannon could subdue any squadron, any fort, any defensive work. Mallory dreamed of an ironclad navy patrolling the entire Atlantic seaboard, preventing the blockade and whipping the enemy fleet. The need for economy dictated the decision to fight with iron against wood.[6]

The Navy Department begged Congress for money to build iron-plated craft, sent agents to Europe, and stimulated the construction of rolling mills to manufacture iron plates. To meet the crisis of securing marine engines, the Department canvassed factories and purchased steamers to gain their machinery. The Navy hastily signed up at double wages all applicants, mechanics, carpenters, and common laborers willing and able to work on vessels and called upon the Army for more.

At Norfolk, workmen raised the *Merrimack*, which had been scuttled by the Federals, docked her, and began repairing the machinery and the hull, bolting on three-inch iron sheathing. The Department contracted with private enterprise to manufacture naval guns, established a laboratory to turn out powder, shells, shrapnel, and fuses, and sent 531 heavy cannon, captured at Norfolk, to the various naval commands.[7]

While John Rodgers was tramping the Cincinnati wharves and converting the wooden-hulled *Tyler, Lexington,* and *Conestoga* into gunboats, Confederates in New Orleans were busy purchasing steamers and arming them for active operations. Unlike the battle for control of the high seas, where the terms were unequal, the odds were nearly even, the Confederates discovered, in the campaign for the Mississippi River. Here, both North and South had started the war without fleets, naval guns, or a clear-cut strategy, and, on the other hand, both possessed river boats, officers to man them, and, at least on paper, the drydocks, facilities, and materials to build ships.[8]

When the initial shock of Fort Sumter had died away, New Orleans—proud city, Queen City of the South, the Confederacy's major seaport—continued to bask in the sun, remote from hostile guns. "A couple of millions of dollars, a few batteries of artillery, ten or twenty thousand extra rifles and hands to use them, will determine upon the Potomac rather than upon the Mississippi whether this experiment is to succeed or Lincoln is to triumph," reported the *Daily True Delta*. The Confederacy—especially Virginia with her empty treasury—needed men, arms, and money. If New Orleans were to escape the turmoil and damage of war, Louisianans strongly believed, no time should be lost in throwing into Virginia every man, gun, and cent not required for home protection.[9]

When rumors of General Scott's anaconda plan circulated along the river, minor precautionary steps were adopted, but Southerners were positive that a Yankee descent of the river was impossible. The Confederate stronghold at Columbus, Kentucky, the gateway to the Mississippi River, would stop any Federals who hankered to go farther.[10] But even early in the war, there were dissenters. On an inspection tour of the Mississippi's fortifications, one Confederate congressman complained that the river's defense system lacked organization and leadership and that 30,000 Yankee soldiers, supported by gunboats, could move down river without opposition. Batteries along the banks could not halt an invading army. "The possession of the river," he warned the War Department, "will decide the fate of the Confederate

States." One Louisianan wrote President Davis that Federals were planning to draw attention to Virginia, then send an Army and fleet down the Mississippi to the Gulf.[11] The Common Council of New Orleans traveled to Richmond and pointed to the defenseless condition of the city.[12]

As days dragged into months and the war settled down to a planned strategy and as Union shipyards sent cruisers to the blockade, more and more Louisianans wondered about the defenses of the Gulf and of the Mississippi River. "What should they be? What have we to resist the new gunboats?" asked a news editor.[13] It behooved New Orleans to investigate. The lower South gradually began asking for and then demanding gunboats to protect New Orleans and the river cities. The *Planters' Banner* hounded citizens of St. Mary's Parish to construct gunboats to meet the attacks. "This is not time to mince words . . . Light draft steam gunboats are a positive security."[14]

Citizens of New Orleans, proud of their tradition of building river steamboats, trusted in their ability to turn out gunboats at a cost far below the price asked for Mississippi river boats. Across the river, Algiers boasted eight drydocks, experienced builders, and skilled mechanics. New Orleans bragged about Leeds and Company—the largest and oldest foundry in the South for manufacturing marine engines—and pointed to the steamboats lining the river banks, boats that could be transformed into warships. Live oak, yellow pine, and cypress abounded in the forests of Louisiana, Florida, and Texas. Tennessee could furnish copper, iron, and hemp cotton. At the start of the war the facilities for hauling materials into New Orleans were adequate. If the Confederacy acted with dispatch, thirty Mississippi steamboats could be altered into gunboats and other gunboats built within ninety days.[15] In Richmond, Congress voted resolution after resolution for the defense of the Mississippi River and, in August, appropriated $1,000,000 for floating defenses of western rivers.[16]

Amid rumors, threats of actual warfare, and gunboat talk, the elegant carriages of New Orleans' wealthy still drove out Shell and Gentily roads Sunday afternoons, crowds still thronged City Park in the evenings, and sightseers continued to overload the Carrollton Railroad trains for the trip to Camp Lewis.

The rains came in the summer, but, as usual, they failed to clean the gutters. After a day's excessive heat, the stagnant water and the garbage slopped in the streets spread fetid odors throughout the city. Yet for all her squalor, New Orleans was indeed the Queen City of the South. Canal Street, reported one visitor, was the prettiest in America. The shade trees and the iron fences formed a series of parks for its entire length.

In the cafes, billiard rooms, oyster bars, and saloons, visitors noticed the "French air." Driving through the city, sightseers spotted the steamboats at the levee, the multitude of well-dressed citizens radiating wealth and comfort. Rebel flags flew from every public building and from many private homes. Military companies paraded in the parks and along the streets. Walls were covered with placards of volunteer companies—the Pickwick Rifles, the Lafayette Guards.

By late summer and early fall, the din of preparation, the tramp of marching soldiers, and the sound of martial music were everywhere. In certain private homes behind closed doors, Louisianans staunchly held that an invasion of New Orleans was impossible. Federals would never reach the city except as prisoners.[17]

After the first six months of the war, nothing from above Cairo moved southward along the river and few merchantmen from the Gulf passed the blockade. From the Mississippi and its tributaries below the Ohio River, the Rebels drew unlimited supplies, while the war excluded the Northwest from the lower river markets and from the Gulf. The vast, fertile regions west of the Mississippi River, especially Texas, were remote and untouched by the war. Products of the soil and of the range flowed into the South as if there were no conflict. Texas supplied the Rebel Army with immense loads of beef and sent cotton, destined for Europe, through the inept blockade off Galveston. To the Confederate Government, the control of the Mississippi River was vital.

The Navy Department in Richmond strove to float a naval force on the Mississippi hefty enough to battle the Cairo gunboats. Congress passed an act that dangled rewards before the eyes of owners who would arm their vessels and put them to sea as privateers to search out enemy merchantmen.[18] Under this act, a syndicate of Louisiana businessmen converted the Boston-built tug *Enoch Train* into the ram *Manassas* and dreamed of lucrative bounties.[19] At New Orleans, carpenters reconditioned her with massive beams, made a solid bow, and equipped her with an iron turtleback, sheathed with one-inch iron, extending below the water line. Her oval deck, resembling half an eggshell, was composed of five-inch timber covered lengthwise with a layer of railroad iron. She carried only one gun and depended for offensive power upon her bow sheathed with iron, which would stave in the wooden sides of blockaders. To prevent boarding by enemy sailors, workmen provided the engine with pumps for ejecting steam and scalding water from the boiler. On the negative side, although engineers drove her with a powerful propeller, she was unwieldy, unmaneuverable, unable to stem the strong current of the Mississippi River.[20]

The Confederate Navy in New Orleans purchased and armed three steamers. The 520-ton steam sloop *Sumter* already had slipped through the Federal blockade, reached the Gulf, and started to prey upon Union commerce. The steam sloop *McRae*, armed with one 9-inch pivot gun and six 32-pounders and manned by a crew of 152, lay at the wharf in New Orleans watching for an opportunity to escape to sea. Rechristening a Mississippi tugboat the *Jackson*, the Navy fitted her out for river patrol and sent her steaming off to Memphis.[21]

The commander of the naval establishment at New Orleans, Captain Lawrence Rousseau—charged with the defense of the Louisiana coast and the Mississippi River— was authorized to construct five river gunboats and to purchase, arm, and equip four others for duty in Lake Pontchartrain. Rousseau walked the streets of New Orleans searching for wrought iron plates, pricing Mississippi steamboats, and consulting with builders.

During the fall of 1861, Captain Rousseau was recalled, and a veteran of the War of 1812, George Hollins, hobbled into New Orleans and took the helm.[22] With an unsparing hand, he squandered $30,000 for the steamboat *Red Rover*, $65,000 for the *Pontchartrain*, $8,000 for the *Edward Howard*, $40,000 for the *Maurepas*, $40,000 for the *Ivy*, $35,000 for the *Pamlico*, $37,000 for the *Mobile*.[23] Most of these light-drafted side-wheel river boats, built for commerce, were too frail to withstand the recoil of heavy ordnance. Most of these river steamers—large, high, and deep—differed from those of the Union in that they bore partial decks above the main deck. Such vessels came with wheels located well aft and were propelled by a vertical one-cylinder low-pressure engine on each wheel. Mechanics encased their bows with iron, secured cotton bales to the decks for protection, and manhandled on board aging smoothbore cannon.[24]

In October the Navy Department bought the ram *Manassas* from the New Orleans syndicate. When they inspected their new purchase, officers were surprised to find no prow and no armament. She bore only an old-fashioned 68-pounder, which was lashed down and could not be fired, and four double-barreled shotguns. One engine ran high pressure; the other ran low.[25] The Government had laid out $100,000 for this monstrosity and spent $30,000 for the tumble-down tugboat *Yankee*, appraised at $5,000. Swindlers and speculators had a carnival, ensnarling the Confederate naval command. Unlike the North, the South could ill afford to expend its treasure upon chaff and husks.[26]

Citizens, finding nothing with which to resist a heavy enemy attack, asked, "Where is our fleet?" They grumbled over incompetents handling the river defense, over speculators placing gain before country, over the shilly-shally policies of the Navy Department. "It is clear to everyone," reported the *Daily True Delta*, "that there is much dangerously wrong."[27]

At the Confederate capitol in Richmond, Stephen R. Mallory was shocked at Commodore Hollins' spending orgy. Without official authority, the naval command had purchased vessels at prices that far exceeded estimates. After a recheck of the reports from the ordnance laboratory in New Orleans had revealed that $146,000, instead of the allotted $4,000, had been spent, Mallory reprimanded Hollins and warned him to observe caution in the future.[28]

When money from Richmond failed to arrive in New Orleans, ship construction slowed down. Money finally became so scarce that Governor Thomas Moore, fearing for the defense of the city, wired the Confederate Treasury that he was placing $2,000,000 earmarked for the war tax into local banks for the Navy. Quickly, Richmond responded that all naval requisitions had passed and that the naval command would be amply supplied with funds.

The Navy Department began contracting with various builders in New Orleans to construct warships—the floating batteries *New Orleans* and *Memphis*, the wooden gunboats *Carondelet, Livingston,* and *Bienville*, and the ironclads *Louisiana* and *Mississippi*.[29] At Bayou St. John, the boat builder, John Hughes, launched the 800-ton *Bienville* in four months from the day her keel was laid.[30] Already Hughes had on his stocks the frame of a vessel that could easily be converted into a fighting craft. The Navy Department signed contracts with Hughes for a gunboat to be made from this hull, which would be christened the *Livingston*. This side-wheel, light-drafted gunboat, like the *Carondelet*, which was being constructed by Sidney Porter, had no breastworks and was armed with military leftovers.[31]

A twenty-year veteran of the river, E. C. Murray, proud of having built 120 steamboats, started construction of the 1,400 ton ironclad *Louisiana*.[32] Clambering over the boat under construction, peering at the unwieldy superstructure and at the single stack, the Confederate Navy's engineer mistrusted the design of this warship. In theory the *Louisiana's* four engines—transplanted from the river steamer *Ingomar*—were to work two paddle wheels located amidships, one forward of the other, and two propellers, one on each quarter.[33] After looking at the machinery, the engineer predicted it would "poop out" in the strong current of the Mississippi. Gunner's mates called attention to the faulty portholes, at which the guns could neither be elevated nor depressed and which, therefore, gave no angle of fire.[34]

Unconcerned over the torrent of criticism, Murray went forward with construction. He happened upon 1,700,000 feet of timber in the Lake Pontchartrain area and in the forests along the tracks of the New Orleans and Jackson Railroad. Early in November, he prodded factories to roll iron plates, but found no one in New Orleans willing to do so except Clark and Company. The owner assured Murray that his plant was ready to roll, but by midwinter of 1861, upon closer inspection, the building boss discovered that Clark was reneging on the project. To urge Clark forward, Murray paid out $5,000 from his own pocket.

Construction on the *Louisiana* commenced to lag. Mechanics struck for higher wages; iron was slow in coming; the propeller shafts did not fit.[35]

Across a wooden fence, in an adjoining area, the Tift brothers, Asa and Nelson—former merchants, railroad presidents, and owners of considerable property in Mallory's home state, Florida—superintended the construction of another ironclad, the *Mississippi*. To overcome the handicaps of insufficient timber and trained workmen, the Tifts recruited ordinary house carpenters to build the vessel from green pine timber, plentiful in Southern forests.

New at this game of shipbuilding, the Tifts had perfected the model of the *Mississippi* early in the war, traveled to Richmond, and optimistically submitted its plan to their intimate friend, Secretary Mallory. Blinded by friendship and the Tifts' patriotism, the Navy Department ignored the bids of experienced shipbuilders with superior facilities at Algiers and awarded the contract to the two tycoons.

The Tifts' plan was revolutionary, if unsound. Discarding the old but standard practice of curved frames, they designed the *Mississippi* with straight lines. Carpenters were to start from the bottom and work up. The *Mississippi* had no frames, but was solid, with three-foot thick timber covered by three-inch iron plates.

At the Jefferson City shipyard the Tifts built a sawmill, a blacksmith's shack, and sheds for the workmen. They explored New Orleans for marine engines. The famous Leeds and Company was too busy, but the Patterson Iron Works, with the same capacity as Leeds, promised to devote full time to the engines of the *Mississippi*.

Confident that the first hurdle was past, the brothers rechecked their engine specifications and discovered that they had grossly miscalculated. Calling in experienced engineers for advice, Asa and Nelson Tift came to see that the boiler capacity was insufficient and drew up new plans and specifications, which called for sixteen double-flued boilers in two different sets, three propellers, and three engines. The Patterson Iron Works promptly hiked the price of the redesigned machinery—to include an additional $20,000 for the engines, $8,000 for the boilers.

The Tifts' theory of using ordinary house carpenters to build ships failed in practice. Even the simple lines of the *Mississippi* stumped the unskilled. The work was arduous and difficult. Some men, more experienced than others, ran off the job for greener fields or were pressed into

military service. Others gravitated to the more established shipbuilding firms. Desperately, the Tifts smuggled
foremen into the Algiers yards to bribe workmen away.
A labor strike stopped work on the *Mississippi* for a
week.[36]

The Southern states' lack of iron seriously handicapped
ship construction in the state of Louisiana. Mallory requested the Secretary of the Treasury to turn over the
iron, copper, steel, and lead stored at the New Orleans
mint.[37] A War Department agent explored each plantation in the state for scrap iron.[38] One shipbuilder asked
permission to start his own mill and prodded the Secretary
of War to purchase the Mexican Gulf Railroad iron, then
up for sale.[39]

While western shipbuilders scoured the hinterlands,
the Tredegar Iron Works, of Richmond, with heavy eastern commitments and under contract to furnish iron for
the *Virginia* (ex-*Merrimack*), had dispatched an agent to
the Mississippi River. Seventeen thousand feet of one-
quarter-inch gas pipe, 11,000 pounds of zinc, 900 tons of
pig iron, fifty-eight boxes of ingot copper moved eastward
from New Orleans.[40] At Nashville other Tredegar agents
loaded 1,000 tons of iron upon freight cars for Richmond.[41]

Familiar only with peacetime pursuits, citizens of New
Orleans were ignorant in the ways of turning out weapons
for war. There were no preparations to produce cannon
and no foundries willing to cast them. Bujack and Company, satisfied to manufacture only shot and shell, hoarded
iron and complained they could not make cannon, for
Navy tests and inspections for new guns were too severe.

Lieutenant Beverly Kennon, C. S. N., ordnance expert,
was constantly on the move contracting for the manufacture of guns of assorted sizes and, with John Armstrong

and Company, for the production of ammunition.[42] Kennon badgered merchants who stored powder, and, if they refused to sell, he had it seized. The lieutenant ordered many guns, but only a few were cast. By November 1861 he had accepted only one 32-pounder rifled gun and one 12-pounder brass cannon.

Other naval officers ransacked the city for all types of ordnance. When the windfall of the Navy yard at Norfolk accrued to the Confederacy, New Orleans received eight 8-inch guns, one 9-inch smoothbore, and twelve 32-pounders. But this was a paltry amount compared to New Orleans' needs. Agents for Governor Moore traveled throughout the South in quest of more cannon, while the merchants of New Orleans banded together and promised to donate sixteen.[43] Guns manufactured in the East finally began rolling westward in the fall and winter, including one hundred and one 32-pounders—smoothbore and rifled, three 7-inch Brooke rifles, eight 9-inch Dahlgrens, and two 8-inch Army Columbiads.[44]

The recruiting station at New Orleans stayed open twenty-four hours a day and sent agents into the bayous.[45] To spur recruiting, the Navy promised $50 in bounty money to each new enlistee and tried devious means to lure skilled sailors from the Army, as seamen in the military ranks were numerous. Daily, the Navy Department received applications from privates for service afloat, but Army officers, short on their quotas, were unwilling to part with their men.[46]

The Confederate military worked on an extensive system of fortifications in and around the city, but, expecting a land attack, they neglected the two forts—Jackson and St. Philip—guarding the approaches from the Gulf. Tucked

into an elbow in the Mississippi River at Plaquemine
Bend, twenty miles above the Head of the Passes and
seventy miles south of New Orleans, Fort St. Philip was
an outdated, ramshackle affair originally built by the
Spaniards. On the point across the river, Fort Jackson
was formidable, modern, and well-built. It was a heavy
pentagon with massive walls of solid masonry.[47]

When informants spread rumors of a gargantuan gunboat flotilla readying at Cairo,[48] apprehension about a
Gulf attack gradually diminished. The real source of danger, officials believed, was the ironclad fleet of the enemy
up-stream. But certain quarters, including the Governor's
Mansion, still feared that Northerners could easily ascend
the river from the Gulf, pass the forts, and level New
Orleans.[49]

To General Mansfield Lovell, who commanded the
military forces at New Orleans, the main objective of the
enemy was the lower Mississippi River. He argued both
with President Jefferson Davis and the Secretary of War
that Federal steamboats could run the forts guarding the
city. President Davis could not believe that New Orleans
would be attacked, but, if it were, its fine defenses and
its energetic commander would deter the assault.[50]

Lovell went to work. Army work gangs built earthworks in, around, above, and below the city. They accu-
mulated flour and meat supplies for a sixty-day siege and
replaced the 24-pounders *en barbette* at Forts Jackson
and St. Philip with 42- and 32-pounders that arrived from
Norfolk. Lovell, lacking heavy caliber guns, appealed to
Richmond, Pensacola, and other points for 10-inch Columbiads and seacoast mortars. But none could be spared.
The general arranged with New Orleans' foundries to

cast shot and shell and converted one half of the Marine Hospital into an arsenal, in which he installed machinery to turn out ammunition.[51]

To prepare New Orleans further, Lovell tried to integrate Commodore Hollins' naval forces into his military defense system.[52] President Davis, however, warned him that the fleet took its orders from Richmond, not from the military commander at New Orleans, and requested that he not tamper with the gunboats.[53]

After this rebuke, General Lovell, on orders from the War Department, was given his own flotilla. Urged upon Congress by the Mississippi delegation and by speculators, this fleet numbered fourteen converted river steamers and cost the Government $563,000. Lovell chose river men to command and ordered each of them to arm his own boat, search out his own crew, and ready his own ship for action. Captain James Montgomery was placed in overall command. Theoretically, this force received its orders from Lovell, but the general realized that his fourteen Mississippi riverboat captains were individualists and that with each captain fitting out his own gunboat the lack of unity was multiplied.[54]

To compound the confusion, the State of Louisiana, under the leadership of Governor Moore, equipped and commissioned two additional vessels, the *Governor Moore* and the *General Quitman*.[55] Lovell and Hollins were appalled by this action. There were already two independent commands on the river and a third was unnecessary.[56]

A group from the House Naval Affairs Committee, which inspected the defenses in midwinter, declared that New Orleans was impregnable.[57] Despite General Lovell's forebodings,[58] other Army and Navy officers convinced the committee that the Crescent City was safe.

By February 1862, New Orleans, the river, and the Gulf coasts of Louisiana and Mississippi were defended by the *General Polk* (ex-*Edward Howard*), *Jackson, Ivy, Maurepas, Livingston, Pamlico,* and *Red Rover*; the floating battery *New Orleans*; eight steamers of the River Defense Squadron stationed at Memphis under the command of Army officers; the gunboats *Segar* and *Mobile* in Berwick's Bay; and the cruiser *Florida,* in Mobile Bay, ready to flee through the blockade. At New Orleans the *Louisiana,* launched and almost ready for action, mustered 250 crew members and sixteen 6- and 7-inch rifled guns; the wooden steamer *McRae* had 120 men who worked one 8-inch cannon and six 32-pounders; and the ram *Manassas* had one 9-incher. The state-owned gunboats *Governor Moore* and *General Quitman,* both converted Galveston mail steamers, carried two 32-pounder rifles each. Operating in the same area, the River Defense Fleet, under orders from General Lovell and commanded by Captain Montgomery, included the *Defiance, Warrior, Resolute, Reliance,* and *Stonewall Jackson,* each equipped with one or two 32-pounders. The ironclad *Mississippi* and the wooden gunboats *Carondelet* and *Bienville* were still under construction.[59]

Rejecting wooden ships as ineffective, New Orleans and the Confederacy pinned their hopes on the two ironclads, the *Louisiana* and the *Mississippi*. The executive officer of the New Orleans command, after a minute inspection of the *Louisiana,* concluded that she and the *Mississippi* were the two most powerful ships that had ever floated and could, despite the Union's superior resources, defeat and obliterate the Yankee fleets.[60] Commodore Hollins believed that the *Mississippi* was the greatest ship in the world.[61] Mallory himself boasted that the *Louisiana*, the *Mississippi*, and the *Virginia*, then fitting out on the East coast, were already revolutionizing naval warfare.[62]

Commander William Whittle, who came west in February 1862 to take over the naval command at New Orleans, was not clear about his responsibilities. He was outranked by Commodore Hollins, and he knew nothing about navigating the Mississippi River. Confused and troubled, Whittle assumed that the command of the naval station did not involve the command of gunboats, believing that Hollins was responsible for the operation of the flotilla.[63] Neither Whittle nor Hollins—nor General Lovell for that matter—was sure who was accountable for supervising the construction of the ironclads.

The Rebel Navy at New Orleans, like the Yankee Navy at Cairo, floundered in a sea of difficulties. In the history of sea power, all navies traditionally have tried to squeeze from their money and materials the maximum in fighting strength. To do so has always involved a balanced fleet, balanced in accordance with the soundest and most advanced strategic theories of the time. Such theories cannot be fully tested until war comes, which means that errors are inevitable. The nation with the largest resources holds an initial advantage, but a less generously endowed power that makes fewer mistakes and husbands its resources wisely can achieve superiority.

New Orleans, with its tradition of river steamboating,[64] well-established foundries, and experienced shipbuilders, was the only river port in the South equipped to turn out fighting craft, whereas St. Louis, Cincinnati, Pittsburgh,

and other towns along the Ohio River teemed with ship-
yards, foundries, sawmills, and mechanics. The Confederacy had no overall plan to marshall the forces of industry
for war. It contracted with various builders, some trained
in, others ignorant of, naval architecture and, early in the
war, wasted its substance on worthless hulks. The Navy,
the Army, and the State of Louisiana all engaged in building and converting ships. Interchange of ideas between
river men and the Navy was infrequent. Rousseau,
Whittle, and Hollins understood little of command organization. Business and industry failed to cooperate.

Confederates on the upper Mississippi, at Memphis, at
Columbus, and on the rivers and creeks of Tennessee,
watched the activities of those Yankee "cutthroats" at
Cairo. The War Department, in Richmond, direly predicted that Union forces would harass the Mississippi
River and burn, pillage, and level ports.[65] Tennesseans
demanded that the Volunteer State be defended. If the
Rebels could not stop the Federals in Tennessee, they
argued, the enemy could control "the whole damn river"
and slice the Confederacy in two. "Such an amputation,"
diagnosed General Gideon Pillow, "will require all the
surgical skill of President Davis to restore the patient."[66]
To prevent this calamity, the Confederate Secretary of
War ordered four batteries erected along the Mississippi;
to arrest the southward movement of Yankee gunboats,
citizens of Memphis blockaded the river with chains and
buoys.[67]

Richmond reshuffled the military command, assigning
General Albert Sidney Johnston to Department No. 2,
which embraced the states of Tennessee and Arkansas
and part of the state of Mississippi, and clothing him with

the authority to call up troops from these states for the defense of the Mississippi Valley and to call upon the Navy in New Orleans for support. General Leonidas Polk was assigned the first division of the department, charged with the actual defense of the Mississippi River.[68]

Working feverishly to throw up defenses, Johnston told Richmond that his forces had collected all the gunpowder in the state of Tennessee, requested more guns, and stood firm in the belief that the defense of the upper Mississippi was as important as that of New Orleans at its mouth. Johnston's command commandeered supplies before they could be shipped east.[69] Sensing imminent danger, the governor of Tennessee demanded that his troops be sent home from the Virginia front and hinted that the security of Tennessee was essential to continuance of the steady eastward stream of ordnance equipment produced in the state.[70] General Lovell sent up-river to Columbus the 13th Louisiana and the 3rd Mississippi regiments. The general reported to Johnston that he had reinforced him only because the danger was more apparent in Tennessee.[71]

Johnston was alarmed. He was sure that a Yankee Army supported by gunboats would assault Columbus and move up the Cumberland River while General Carlos Buell's Army of 20,000, operating in Kentucky, would advance simultaneously upon Nashville, the principal depot and manufacturing center in the West.[72] At Columbus, Polk hastened to completion the river fortifications;[73] on the Cumberland River, Army work gangs strengthened Fort Donelson with four 32-pounders; on the Tennessee River, twelve miles overland from Fort Donelson, Confederates hurried construction on Fort Henry.

As the pressure mounted against Tennessee, Commodore Hollins in New Orleans ordered the *Ivy, Tuscarora,* and *General Polk* to get under way and steam northward to protect the rivers in Tennessee. Not far from Memphis the *Tuscarora* caught fire, exploded, and sank.[74]

In December 1861, the mayor of Nashville traveled to Richmond and urged conversion of river boats into gunboats and the construction of gunboats for the protection of the Cumberland and Tennessee rivers. Nashville was, he said, in peril—a Union Army under General Buell was nearing Bowling Green. Promptly Congress appropriated $500,000 for the defense of the Tennessee rivers and the Navy Department sent Lieutenant Isaac N. Brown west to purchase vessels and convert them into gunboats.[75] Upon his arrival in early January 1862, Brown bought the *James Wood, James Johnson,* and *Dunbar* and started the job of conversion.[76] At Columbus, General Polk seized the steamer *Eastport* for river operations and asked Richmond for an additional $60,000.

Time was running short. With a six months' head start the Federals at Cairo were massing their flotilla for offensive operations. But the Confederate military on the upper river had not demanded an adequate force of gunboats and for this they were to pay dearly at Forts Henry and Donelson.

5

In the Wake of Old Flags

A hard rain drenched Washington on February 6, 1862.
It had stormed for a week. The ungainly Army of the
Potomac, axle-deep in mud, rested outside the city. At
the White House that night, as the Marine Band played
lively airs, President and Mrs. Lincoln welcomed 800
guests in the East Room. At midnight the visitors
swarmed about the tables helping themselves to sand-
wiches and to punch from a huge bowl. In the dining
room, a select few sat down to a meal prepared by the
famous Malliard, of New York, and enjoyed steamed
oysters, boned turkey, aspic of tongue, chicken salad,
roast beef, turkey with truffles, quail, canvasback ducks,
fruit glaze, and bonbons. At the head of the table, the
caterer had placed a spun sugar helmet, signifying war,
and, beside it, a fancy basket fashioned into the pagoda
temple of liberty.[1]

It also rained in Tennessee. Union bluejackets inside
fallen Fort Henry inspected the damage. Guns were shattered, and the ground was red with blood. Under a gray
blanket lay six corpses, one with its head blown off, its
body blackened with powder. On his flagship out in the
Tennessee River, Flag Officer Andrew Foote, silhouetted
in the lamp light, finished his official report. Down-stream

lay the smouldering *Essex*. On her decks, scalded seamen were screaming in pain as surgeons removed their clothing, applied linseed oil and flour to their blackened bodies, and wrapped them in blankets.[2]

The Union assault upon Fort Henry had been difficult to plan but easy to execute. On February 1, 1862, General Halleck, in St. Louis, pinpointed on a map the Union armies in the Mississippi Valley. The Army of Ohio, led by General Don Carlos Buell, operated in Kentucky; the Army of Tennessee, under Ulysses S. Grant, waited in Cairo; the Army of the Mississippi, under General John Pope, was massing at St. Louis; the Army commanded by General Samuel R. Curtis was marching and countermarching in southwest Missouri. To Halleck, the Rebels' line of defense for the valley rotated around three points. They held Bowling Green, Kentucky, to prevent a Union advance by railroad from Cincinnati to Chattanooga; Forts Henry and Donelson, on the Tennessee and Cumberland rivers, to guard these arteries from enemy gunboats and transports; and Columbus, Kentucky, to halt an armada from descending the Mississippi River to Memphis, Vicksburg, and New Orleans. How to smash through this line of defense troubled the military in St. Louis and Washington. Upon the solution hinged the Union's initial success in the West.

In St. Louis, Halleck was laid up with measles. Smoking cigars as he lay in bed reading reports, Halleck knew that as long as the enemy dominated the river below Columbus, he could not chance sending General John Pope's Army of the Mississippi into New Madrid, on the opposite shore. Before he executed this move, he would have to send Grant up the Cumberland or the Tennessee and threaten Columbus from the rear; otherwise, a Rebel force might, at any time, be thrown from Columbus, march southward, retake New Madrid, and drive Pope back into St. Louis. Halleck hesitated. For three weeks no word came from Washington.

Emaciated from his illness, Halleck sipped hock wine to put on weight. In his room on the second floor of the Planter's House one night, as he chatted with his chief of staff, General George W. Cullum, talk ran to the advance southward. Slumped in his chair, Halleck pointed out that Lincoln was insisting upon a descent of the Mississippi to Columbus. Confederate Generals Pillow and Polk, Halleck reported, commanded a minimum of 20,000, equipped with cannon planted high on the bluffs. Suddenly, Halleck heaved himself out of his chair, paced the floor with his hands behind his back, and strode to the large map on the table. He asked Cullum, "Where is the Rebel line?"

Cullum drew the pencil through Bowling Green, Forts Henry and Donelson, and Columbus.

"Now," retorted Halleck, "where is the proper place to break it?"

Cullum replied, "Naturally, in the center."

Halleck traced a line perpendicular to Cullum's, near its middle. It coincided with the course of the Tennessee River. Turning to his aide, he said calmly: "That's the true line of operation."[3]

In Cairo, Foote wired Halleck that Grant and he were sure Fort Henry could be stormed easily.[4] Grant followed the telegram with a letter informing Halleck that after the capture of Henry, Federal units could race up the Cumberland River to Fort Donelson or down to Columbus.[5] Halleck ordered Grant to gather up all available troops at Smithland, Paducah, and Cairo and move upon Henry.[6]

The *Lexington* and *Conestoga* lay at Paducah, blockading the mouth of the Tennessee River; the *Essex* was moored at Cairo; the *Tyler* and the ironclad *St. Louis* operated in the Mississippi a few miles to the south. Trial runs of the other six Eads ironclads down-river from St. Louis had revealed that the boilers worked water instead of steam. These gunboats were laid up temporarily while engineers changed the position of the steam drums to the top of the boilers. Black gangs revamped the machinery on board the *Benton*, whose engines were incapable of stemming the current up-stream. Mortar boats languished on the river banks, waiting for guns and beds.

Under orders to attack Fort Henry, Foote lacked men enough to get under way. For want of crews, he angrily reassigned all men stationed on the five gunboats left to guard Cairo and distributed them throughout the attack force.[7] Instead of steaming up the Tennessee River toward the enemy with gunboats in battle trim, Foote got under way with untested guns and ships, manned only partially and by crews of untrained landlubbers and undisciplined river men.

Cairo stirred with excitement. Regiments were under marching orders. On Saturday, it rained. The movement of troops into the Army transports were tedious. Hour by hour on Saturday and Sunday, soldiers filed wearily on board. There was no sign of departure. Rain turned to sleet and snow. Crammed into overloaded transports, the troops grew impatient. They cursed their detention, the muddy decks, the cold rations. Wrapping themselves in blankets, troops stowed away as best they could on open decks. Monday morning they were still in Cairo.[8]

The gunboats *Tyler, Essex, Carondelet, Cincinnati,* and *St. Louis* pulled away from the wharves on February 2, followed by the Army transports, bulging with 10,000 restive soldiers. Whistles screeched and bands played. A bewildered Army colonel fell overboard and drowned. It alternately rained and snowed. Arriving at Paducah the same afternoon, the expedition made contact with the gunboats *Lexington* and *Conestoga*.[9]

Up the Tennessee River the expedition steamed. The snow stopped and the sun shone. Men, women, and children, black and white, lined the riverbanks, cheering and waving, catcalling and cursing.

A decrepit farmer, clad in butternut, shouted, "Glory to God, it has come!"

"Hurrah for Jeff Davis!" cried an urchin. "Hurrah for Jeff Davis! Hurrah for Jeff Davis!"

"Oh, you little villain!" roared a Union major. "You're a secession, are you? Hell is your portion, thank God! Hail Columbia!"[10]

Soldiers spotted four women at a cabin door. "There's a gal up there that's got hoops on," shouted one private. "Three cheers for the gal with hoops in this country!"

Located at Pine Bluff Landing, ninety-nine miles from the mouth of the Tennessee, and built on the river bottom of clay, brick, and layers of thatched hickory poles, Fort Henry was surrounded, or nearly so, by the river during high water. Soldiers could approach it only by a causeway. At one angle of the camp, a road led to the town of Dover, on the Cumberland River near Fort Donelson, twelve miles away. Above Henry, the railroad—vital to the defense of Tennessee—connected Memphis with Bowling Green, headquarters for the Western Army under General Albert Sidney Johnston.

Stout and pompous General Lloyd Tilghman ordered gunners to position the ten 32-pounders, two 42-pounders, one rifled 42-pounder, and one 10-inch Columbiad. He inspected the 10th Tennessee, 4th Mississippi, companies of the 3rd Alabama, and a company of artillery—1,185 undrilled, poorly disciplined, and indifferently armed men.[11]

Early on the morning of February 4 inside Fort Henry, a sentinel for No. 3 gun awakened Tilghman. He reported rockets, signaling the approach of enemy gunboats. The Confederate transport steamers were moved out of range up-river, and a courier was sped to Fort Donelson.[12]

Before dawn that morning, twelve miles below, Federal transports lay moored along the east bank. Four ironclads bobbed at anchor a mile above. At daylight, the expedition got under way and moved up-river to within four miles of the fort.

Union soldiers disembarked and spread out along the wooded bluffs. Campfires dotted the valleys and hillsides that night, and the melody of "Rock of Ages" rose from a cluster of men holding a prayer meeting.[13] Rumors were whispered about that Beauregard himself, the best general in the South, had taken personal command at Fort Henry. Out in the stream, transports moved down-river to pick up General Charles F. Smith's command, which was marching up the opposite side of the river from Federal-held Paducah. All day Wednesday the *Alex Scott, Uncle Sam, Minnehaha, Chancellor, Fanny Bullet, Illinois, January,* and *City of Memphis* hauled soldiers, guns, and horses to the opposite bank. The gunboats *Conestoga* and *Tyler* removed six mines from the channel.

At dusk on February 5, Grant and his generals boarded the ironclad *Cincinnati* for final conferences with Foote. The troops were to march for the fort, while the gunboats blasted it from the river. As they talked, men on board the *Conestoga* were unloading a huge mine onto the *Cincinnati's* fantail. The strategy meeting finished, Army officers, accompanied by Foote, stepped down the ladder to the stern to see the mine. Grant was curious and expressed a wish to see the firing mechanism. The ship's armorer, working with a monkey wrench, hammer, and chisel, began to dismantle it. He unscrewed the cap. Gas hissed. Two officers hit the deck, face down. Foote sprang up the ladder, stampeded by Grant. Realizing that the danger had passed, Foote turned to Grant, remarking, "General, why this haste?"

"That the Navy may not get ahead of us," Grant laughingly responded.[14]

Foote left the *Cincinnati* for the *Essex*. Climbing on board, he mustered the crew, inspected and drilled them, and roused them with a pep talk. Having an eye toward thrift, he concluded his remarks with a note of caution: "Every charge you fire costs the Government about eight dollars. If they reach home, you demoralize the enemy and get your money's worth."[15] The inspection over, Foote returned to the *Cincinnati*. He never slept better.[16]

Off at Fort Henry, General Tilghman recalled the troops from the west bank of the river, at Fort Heiman, and funneled his main force—2,600 men—into the rifle pits beyond range of gunboat fire. He cursed the wretched position of Fort Henry and the smallness of his command.

At 11:00 a.m. on February 6, the gunboats appeared from the chute at Panther's Island, two miles below. Mired in the mud, Grant slogged up the east bank of the river with 10,000 men. General Smith, with 6,000, plodded up the west bank toward Fort Heiman.

Alternatives raced through Tilghman's mind. Fort Donelson could be held, if properly reinforced, even if

Henry fell. The contrary was not true. The defense at Henry must either defeat the enemy or serve as a delaying action until Donelson was reinforced. If Henry capitulated, the fate of the Rebels' right wing, at Bowling Green, would depend upon a concentration of troops at Fort Donelson. If Henry could delay the enemy long enough, Tilghman's entire command could retreat to Fort Donelson while other regiments streamed there from other fronts.

Tilghman did not hesitate to sacrifice Fort Henry. His only chance was to delay the gunboats long enough to pull out his command, now stationed in the rifle pits, for Fort Donelson. Only the heavy artillery company, seventy-five men, remained inside to ward off the enemy.

At 11:45 the gunboats opened fire. Before the echo died away, guns of the fort thundered. The gallant seventy-five threw off their coats with a wild hurrah, stripped to the waist, and worked the spikes, ropes, and rammers with a vengeance.[17]

Yankees fired only their bow guns. Belching shot and shell, the gunboats pushed forward, straight for the target in an even line. The range closed to 600 yards. Repeatedly, Rebel shells thudded against the ironclads, but failed to penetrate the plating. The damage was done by shells entering the gun ports or bursting through the boats' unprotected parts.[18]

On board the *Essex*, Captain William Porter, "Dirty Billy," peered out of the port, checking the effect of his 9-inch Dahlgren smoothbores, swearing at Foote for failing to give him a rifled cannon. Suddenly, the *Essex* lurched and buckled. A shell had hit the only vulnerable point in her bow. Porter watched transfixed: the shell had decapitated a young man named Brittain and exploded in the starboard boiler. Instantly, the *Essex* filled with hot, blistering steam. Bluejackets leaped overboard. James Coffey, shot man at No. 2 gun, who was passing a shell from the box, died on his knees. In the pilot house, two pilots scrambled for the escape hatch, but it was shut tight. Struggling, screaming, they ran their arms through the ports as they scalded to death. The *Essex* drifted helplessly down-stream. Porter himself was badly burned. Marshall Ford, the helmsman, was found dead at his post, standing erect, his left hand holding the spoke, his right hand grasping the signal bell.[19]

The ironclads *Cincinnati, Carondelet,* and *St. Louis,* supported by the *Tyler* and *Conestoga* astern, hammered away, firing deliberately, slowly. Shells ripped up the embankment, tearing up the sandbags, and one burst directly over a cannon, blowing up its entire crew.

The Rebels stood to the guns, but the odds were fearful. Fifty-five guns against eleven; sixteen thousand men against seventy-five. The gunboats advanced, their accuracy improving. Fired too often, the Rebels' most reliable gun, the rifled 24-pounder, burst. The 10-inch Columbiad jammed. A premature explosion destroyed another cannon. A fourth gun broke down. The Confederates lacked proper ammunition for the 42-pounders.

Rebel hopes had soared when the *Essex* drifted downstream. Tilghman observed a weakness of the ironclads; their exposed "roofs" were vulnerable to the plunging fire.

When the ironclads closed to point-blank range, thoughts of escape occurred to Tilghman. He dismissed them. By 1:00 p.m., only five guns worked. When informed of the casualties and of the men's exhaustion, Tilghman jerked off his coat, sprang to the nearest gun, loaded it, and fired. Directly in front of the Rebel cannon, the ironclads blazed away. Further Confederate resistance was useless. Neither tactics nor bravery could stop the incessant pounding of the ironclads.[20]

Someone in the fort yelled, "Cease firing!" Colonel Milton A. Haynes instantly countermanded the order. A soldier ran up and shouted, "Look, look! Someone has raised a white flag!"

Haynes retorted, "God damn the man who would raise a white flag now! Go, quick, and pull it down and shoot the man who raised it!"

The private raced to the spot, returned, and reported that it was hoisted on General Tilghman's order. Stumbling through the debris, Haynes found the general and asked if he intended to surrender.

"Yes," Tilghman said tersely. "It is vain to fight longer; our gunners are disabled; our guns dismounted; we can't hold out five minutes longer."

Haynes shouted, "As I do not belong to this garrison, I shall leave the fort—I will not surrender." Shaking hands with the general, he climbed on a horse and sped away.[21]

As they hastened along the road to Fort Donelson, Tilghman's main command, whom he had dispatched before the battle, made contact with Grant's advanced cavalry units and repulsed them.

On board the ironclads, bluejackets saw the Rebel flag go down. They dropped lanyards, rammers, sponges, and tackle and, clapping hands and tossing caps in the air, hugged and kissed shipmates and cheered. Foote ran among the men, conking their heads with a belaying pin to restore order. Above the din, the surgeon hollered to Foote that it was like coming from death to life.

Far behind in the mud, the Union Army toiled toward the fort.[22]

A rowboat came alongside the *Cincinnati,* and General Tilghman stepped on board. Disheartened and worn out, the general decried the fall of Fort Henry as the most damaging blow of the war and stoutly maintained that if his 24-pounder had not burst, his men would have blown the flotilla to pieces. "You did perfectly right, sir, in surrendering," consoled Foote.[23]

The general said something about his reputation's having vanished with the defeat.

Foote replied: "General, there is no reason that you should feel this way . . . To continue the action would involve needless sacrifice of life and, under the circumstances, you have done right. Come, General, you have lost your dinner, and the steward has just told me that mine is ready." Taking the general by the arm, the two walked into the next cabin.[24]

Half an hour later, the Navy handed the fort and the prisoners over to Grant and his Army, which had just arrived.

That evening Foote sat writing dispatches.[25] In his hour of triumph, the old veteran was filled with tension. He had gone into action wretchedly unprepared. The *Cincinnati* had been hit thirty times. He had had the breath knocked out of him on two occasions when shot smashed into the ironclad's sides. He had been shaken by the sight of a dead sailor lying among nine wounded men, who were groaning horribly. Foote never forgot those moans, rising above the whine of shells and the thunder of cannon. That night he slept fitfully, thinking of the poor devils.[26]

Down-stream, the scene on the *Essex* was horrible. When the news flashed of victory, Captain Porter, burned severely, raised himself on his elbow, rallied his men, called for three cheers, and fell back, exhausted. Seaman Jasper Breeze, badly scalded and stark naked, climbed to his feet and waved his jacket, screaming, "Surrender! I must see that with my own eyes!" Before his shipmates could stop him, Breeze ran crazily up the ladder to the spar deck to see the Stars and Stripes floating over Fort Henry. He whimpered pitifully, "Glory to God!" and sank dead to the deck.[27]

Inside the Rebel barracks, Union soldiers found camp-fires still blazing, dinners boiling, and half-baked biscuits in their pans. Heaps of flintlock muskets of the 1828 pattern, double-barreled shotguns, homemade sabers, meat cleavers, fowling pieces, and bowie knives were strewn about. Grant's men ransacked the trunks, donned Rebel coats and hats, armed themselves with revolvers, and stuffed their pockets with books. A few staggered under loads of Rebel whiskey.[28] An aging Negress stumbled about in the rubble, repeating to officers, "De big balls, dey come whizzing and tearing about, and I thought de las' judgment was cum, sure."

"Where are all your soldiers?" questioned a lieutenant.

"Lord A'mighty knows. Dey just runned away like turkeys, nebber fired a gun."[29]

Foote pushed his victory. Before he descended the river for Cairo on board the *Cincinnati*, with Rebel flags flying beneath the Stars and Stripes, he sent Commander Phelps in the *Conestoga*, together with the *Tyler* and *Lexington*, up the Tennessee River. The three vessels arrived at the Memphis and Bowling Green Railroad bridge, twenty-five miles above the fort, from where Phelps could see Confederate steamers escaping in the distance. The *Tyler* landed a force to demolish the railroad track and to secure military stores, while the *Lexing-*

ton and *Conestoga* shadowed the Rebel steamboats. In five hours, the *Conestoga* closed the gap and forced the Southerners to abandon and set fire to three steamers loaded with ammunition. Afraid that gunpowder explosions would destroy its boats, the flotilla stopped engines 1,000 yards short. When the Rebel boats blew up, the concussion smashed the *Lexington's* skylights, raised the upper deck, and buckled the hatches. The whole river for a mile was showered with falling fragments, shot, and balls. The *Tyler* rejoined the *Conestoga* and *Lexington,* and the three boats chugged on up-river.

At dusk they arrived at Cerro Gordo, where bluejackets jumped ashore and discovered the half-finished gunboat *Eastport* abandoned. In the mists of early dawn, the Federals passed Eastport, Mississippi, and, at Chickasaw, farther up, near the state line, they seized the *Sallie Wood* and *Muscle.* They left these astern, entered Alabama, and maneuvered into Florence, 250 miles from Paducah. Within sight of the town, Yankees set afire three steamers, the *Kirkman, Julius,* and *Time,* and confiscated iron plates for the *Eastport* and supplies marked "Fort Henry." Once the citizens of Florence realized that the Yankees would not harm them, they sang the "The Star-Spangled Banner" and invited the invaders to a fancy dress ball that evening.[30]

Returning that night, the Federals took in tow the *Sallie Wood* and *Muscle,* hauled off the *Eastport* at Cerro Gordo, and lumbered down-river, destroying abandoned camps and sawmills and stealing stores and ammunition. All along the river, hundreds of Tennesseans—persecuted by the Rebels for their Unionists sympathies—lined the banks and greeted the Federals with hurrahs. The *Tyler* stopped and began recruiting. Two hundred and fifty signed on. Finally, after destroying the railroad bridge, the expedition returned to home base.[31]

On Sunday, Foote attended the Cairo Presbyterian Church. For half an hour, the worshipers waited in silence for their pastor. When he failed to appear Foote stepped in the aisle, marched forward to the pulpit, and opened the service with prayer. After the hymn, he took his text from Acts, chapter 14, verse 1, and "preached such a sermon as had not been heard in that Presbyterian church for years." The sermon finished, the congregation stormed toward the pulpit, striving to reach the commander and honor him. Foote stared and exclaimed, "This is the Sabbath day, and this is God's house, and no time or place to glory over the downfall of an enemy."[32]

The North reveled in its first Western victory. "Three times three cheers, and another, and yet another, and one cheer more!" exhorted the Cincinnati *Gazette*.[33] The North has a "Foote-hold in Tennessee," punned the Louisville *Daily Journal*.[34] In Washington, President Lincoln danced at the news, praised his Navy boys, and promised full cooperation in fitting out the mortar boats.[35]

Concurrently, news spread in the North that General Ambrose E. Burnside and Commodore Louis M. Goldsborough had assaulted and captured Roanoke Island, in Pamlico Sound, North Carolina, eliminating blockade running in that area. Roanoke Island, coming on the heels of Fort Henry, lifted the nation from its despondency and uncertainty and made clear to millions that the Union had taken a giant step toward ultimate victory.[36]

Sitting in the State House in Nashville, Governor Isham G. Harris of Tennessee clamored for help.[37] But Tennessee could not expect aid from Georgia, Alabama, Mississippi, or Louisiana when Yankee fleets had already captured Hatteras Inlet, Port Royal, and Roanoke Island and threatened the entire Atlantic seaboard. "Like the inmate of the fatal chamber which daily closed in gradually upon its victim," commented the Louisville *Journal*, "the Confederacy is involved in an inextricable peril."[38]

At Bowling Green, Kentucky, General Albert Sidney Johnston considered the situation serious. The slight resistance at Fort Henry indicated that the best earthworks were not capable of resisting the pounding of the ironclads. The gunboats alone, even without Grant's forces, were a threat to Fort Donelson.[39]

The day after the fall of Henry, crowds thronged the railroad depot at Nashville to cheer General P. G. T. Beauregard, who had come west to assist Johnston. "The name of Beauregard," cried a newsman, "is as good as thirty thousand men. He'll lead our armies to the banks of the Ohio!"[40] But General Beauregard, proclaiming that he was a man of action, not of words, was despondent when he saw Johnston's pitifully small force. It seemed essential to give up minor points and concentrate troops to protect important sectors.[41]

At headquarters, Generals Johnston and Beauregard evaluated their position. The Federals now controlled the Tennessee and had broken communications between the Confederate Army at Bowling Green and Polk's command at Columbus. They determined to evacuate Bowling Green and fall back across the Cumberland River to Nashville. In the event of further retreat, the generals chose Stevenson as a point to make a stand. Johnston elected to fight for Nashville at Fort Donelson and gave the best part of his Army to it, retaining only 14,000 to cover his front.[42]

Grant resolved to strike Fort Donelson with gunboats and his Army.[43] But in St. Louis, the Assistant Secretary of War, Thomas Scott, sent west by Washington to investigate the various commands, became alarmed and feared that Grant's force marching toward Donelson was imperiled by Confederate detachments in and around Bowling Green and Columbus. It took Halleck two days to calm him down. If Donelson fell, Halleck believed, any immediate further advance would be too dangerous, since the enemy had the facilities to concentrate troops at almost any point.[44]

He wired Foote to send the ironclads up the Cumberland River to support Grant.[45] The day before, the *Carondelet*, on duty at Paducah, had received orders from Grant to ascend the Cumberland and cooperate with the Army.[46]

At Fort Henry, Grant had decided to march part of his Army overland toward Donelson and move the other contingent up the Cumberland on transports. His ground force trudged out on the morning of February 12. The route lay along the Dover Road, through high ridges and dense forests. The weather turned mild and progress was rapid. In four hours, the advance columns entered the ravines to the rear of Fort Donelson and took position within two miles of the Johnnies. Rapidly, Grant extended his lines parallel with the river, enclosing the fort in a semicircle.[47]

The Confederates were primed for the Union assault. After Fort Henry had collapsed, every drop of sweat was expended to mobilize Donelson, embedded on a sloping bluff, 150 feet above the river. In command, General Gideon Pillow saw reinforcements stream in and fatigue parties extend the lines of infantry cover. Officers placed the first river battery twenty feet above the water and mounted five 32-pounders. Sixty feet higher, the second battery held a 10-inch Columbiad and four 32-pounders. On the summit, the third battery was equipped with a rifled gun, an 8-inch howitzer, and one 32-pounder.[48]

On the day Grant arrived at the rear of Donelson, General John B. Floyd galloped into the fort to replace Pillow in overall command. One look convinced him that neither the troops nor the fort could withstand the enemy. The situation would be hopeless, Floyd believed, even if General Johnston's entire force, which was headed for Nashville, were rerouted to Donelson.[49]

On the afternoon of February 12, the ironclad *Carondelet* steamed near Donelson and, after lobbing shells into the fort to announce her arrival to Grant, dropped downstream to anchor for the night. Early on the morning of the thirteenth, Grant notified Lieutenant Henry Walke, skipper of the *Carondelet*, to advance toward the fort at 10:00 a.m. The ironclad got under way, maneuvered toward the Rebel guns, and opened fire. The fort's cannon blazed. A lucky shot rammed through the *Carondelet's* port casemate forward, glancing over the boilers and steam drum, and fell into the engine room, though without injuring the crew. The *Carondelet* continued to fire, throwing forty-five shells into the bastion, while, inland, Grant's artillery boomed and sharpshooters harassed Rebels who exposed themselves above the trenches. The *Carondelet* withdrew down-river during the afternoon watch to await orders from Grant. Reinforcements from the transports joined the Army to the rear of the fort.[50]

The next day, the *Louisville, Pittsburg, St. Louis,* and two wooden gunboats arrived. Foote felt ill-prepared to silence the water batteries, pass the forts, and, from the river, bombard the upper batteries to support the Army's assault upon the rear of the works.[51]

At 2:00 p.m., February 14, four ironclads stood toward Donelson, holding their fire. At a range of one mile, they commenced their barrage and steamed to within 400 yards. The firing was rapid, destructive. Shot and shell ripped into the lower batteries at pointblank range, demolishing the guns, scattering their crews.

The Confederates fired in volleys. A shell exploded on the *Carondelet.* She faltered. Walke was knocked senseless for five minutes. Suddenly, a sailor yelled "Fire!" Flames spread throughout the boat while fire crews manned the pumps. Masters Mate Brennan, revolver in hand, threatened to shoot crew members if they failed to stand to the guns. "Never mind the fire; go to your quarters!" The fire was finally extinguished, but not before two shots sailed through the bow ports, blowing four men to pieces.[52]

Shore batteries kept up a steady fire. Rebels saw one ironclad drop out of action, then another, and watched shots smash into a third, ripping her iron plating, splintering her timbers.[53]

A shell carried away the tiller ropes of the *Louisville.* Another pierced the thirteen-inch wood and the iron plating of the *St. Louis*'s pilot house. It killed the pilot instantly and showered splinters in all directions. Foote, who had just poked his head inside, caught splinters in the leg. Painfully wounded, he tried to steer the ship, but helplessly he let the wheel spin in his hand.[54] The *St. Louis* drifted down-stream on an erratic course, trailed by the *Louisville*.

Riddled and battered, with four dead and thirty-two wounded, the *Carondelet* caught a shot that jammed the paddle wheel. Another 8-inch shell, fired accidentally from the *Tyler*, burst astern of the *Carondelet* and penetrated her casemate. Leaking badly, she continued to fire, but, seeing the flagship out of commission, she turned to head down-stream. The *Pittsburg*, shipping water from two shots that had smashed into her side, plowed into the *Carondelet*'s quarter and tore off the starboard rudder iron.[55]

Foote, in pain from his wounded leg, smarted too from the repulse. In consultation with Grant, Foote pointed out that his services at Donelson were now futile and said that he would proceed down to Cairo with the *St. Louis* and *Pittsburg*, leaving the *Carondelet* and *Louisville*, still maneuverable but badly damaged, to protect the transports.

Nothing was accomplished by the gunboat attack. The Yankees had fought with twelve bow guns against the thirteen in the shore batteries, planted to give the Rebels the advantage of a plunging fire. But the importance of iron armor was clearly demonstrated. The *St. Louis* was struck fifty-four times, but only one man was killed and only nine were wounded. Catching forty shots, the *Pittsburg* counted only two wounded. On board the whole flotilla, eleven lost their lives and forty-three were wounded—a small number considering the severity of the action.[56]

Grant's guns were silent. When the ironclads attacked, Grant had planned to push his Army around and capture a portion of the enemy's works, cutting off Confederates from their supplies at Dover, driving them back upon the center and left, and preventing their escape. This move was postponed when news spread throughout the Union lines that the gunboats had been thrown back.

Friday night, February 14, passed. Soldiers shivered in the cold. Sleep was impossible on the snow-covered ground, as the Yankees lay listening to the sound of the Johnnies' axes and spades in the trenches only a few hundred yards away.[57]

At Fort Donelson, Rebel commanders realized from the movement of Union troops that the enemy would attack in overwhelming numbers. If the enemy troops could be whipped by hitting them suddenly on the right and center, there was a chance of a Confederate victory. Gideon Pillow was to lead the assault against the Union right; General Simon B. Buckner, third in command, against the center, advancing along the Wynn's Ferry Road.[58]

4:00 a.m., February 15. The woods on the Union's extreme right swarmed with Confederates. Suddenly, the Rebels' left wing under Pillow lunged forward. The Yankees opened up with a murderous fire, but the Confederates kept coming. In the rear of the trenches, Buckner's artillery blazed and two regiments charged. Exposed to a blistering fire from Union guns, Buckner's troops scattered and fell back rapidly.

Pillow's division steadily advanced, and Buckner's force renewed the attack. Pressed in front and on the right flank, the Yankee line was beginning to buckle until reinforcements arrived. The Rebels hurled themselves upon the enemy. Whole companies were annihilated.

There were quick, violent scenes. Cowering from the fire, a Union officer ran from the action. A Yankee sergeant, seeing a Rebel point a rifle at a comrade, dove in front and died.[59] Caught in a cross fire, Union colonels dashed along their ranks, waving their hats, cheering their men on. "Suffer death, men, but disgrace never," cried one. "Stand firm; yield never!"[60] Ordered up as reinforcements, the 25th and 18th Kentucky panicked and fired volley after volley into the backs of their own men. Somewhere a Confederate cavalry officer shouted "Charge!" Horses thundered forward. There were flashes of steel.

For two hours the battled raged. At noon, Grant, who had been away conferring with Foote, hurriedly ordered in fresh troops. Marching into the action to the incongruous tune of "Dixie," the 8th Missouri, the 11th Indiana, and General Lew Wallace's division pushed their way forward on the right and, together with the remnants of the battle-weary veteran forces, assailed the enemy. The Rebels hesitated and retreated slowly within their own lines.

Simultaneously, Grant commanded General Charles F. Smith's division on the Union left to advance. Smith's eyes flashed. He cried out: "Soldiers, that redoubt must be taken!" The 2nd and 7th Iowa and the 25th Indiana led the way, dashing up the hill into the rain of fire. For an instant the Yankees staggered. Smith cursed. "Damn you gentlemen! I see skulkers. I'll have none here. Come on, you volunteers, come on! You volunteered to be killed and now you can be." When his front line shrank under enemy fire, Smith turned to a surgeon and snapped, "Hewitt, my God, if you love me, go back and bring up another regiment of those damned volunteers. You will find them behind the bushes."[61]

General Smith deflected the main portion of his division to the right, thereby engaging the enemy's attention. On horseback, his hat on the point of his sword, General Smith led the storming party to the extreme left, charged, and entered the redoubt.[62]

Night closed in on the field of battle. The guns were still. The Union Army rested on the ground it had gained.

Gideon Pillow, his garrison ringed by the giant force the Yankees had thrown around it, knew that the carnage had not bought victory. Casualties had grievously diminished the fort's defending force, which had numbered 13,000. At field headquarters in nearby Dover, the Confederate generals held a council of war. Pillow, Floyd, and Buckner were there. Others came and went. Scouts returned and reported that the woods were full of the enemy.

The generals, silent, sat by the fire. At last, Floyd said, "Well, gentlemen, what is best to be done? We must do it at once. It is now midnight, and if we retreat, we haven't got a minute to lose."

Pillow insisted on cutting a way out.

Buckner replied that no officer had the right to sacrifice men needlessly. If the Confederates charged through the Union line, three-fourths of their command would be slaughtered.

Pillow responded sharply: "Gentlemen, as you refuse to make an attempt to cut our way out, and as General Buckner says he will not be able to hold his position after half an hour, there is only one alternative left—that is capitulation." General Pillow emphasized that he would never surrender.

Floyd agreed. He would suffer any fate before he would haul down the flag. "I cannot surrender."

"I suppose, gentlemen," said Buckner, "the surrender will devolve upon me."

General Floyd replied that he would turn over the command if he could withdraw his own brigade.

Buckner consented.

Floyd thanked him and said: "General Pillow, I surrender the command to you."

The next ranking officer, General Pillow, replied: "I pass it."

Then Buckner spoke. "I will accept and share the fate of my command. I shall propose terms of capitulation." He asked for ink and paper and ordered an aide to prepare the white flags. Buckner wrote hurriedly to Grant, "I propose . . . the appointment of commissioners to agree upon terms of capitulation . . . and suggest an armistice."

Pillow wished to know if it were improper to escape. Floyd replied that every man must decide for himself. Pillow said quickly: "Then, sir, I shall leave."

Near daylight on Sunday, February 16, Pillow, Floyd, and his brigade slipped across the river and headed for Clarksville.[63]

At Union headquarters, an orderly roused Grant from fitful sleep. General Smith entered, cold and shivering, stamping his feet for warmth. He walked at once to the open fire and turned and faced Grant, who had slipped out of bed and was drawing on his overcoat. "There's something for you to read, General," Smith said, handing him a letter. Smith asked for a drink. Grant's orderly shoved him a flask. Gulping down the whiskey, Smith stood in front of the fire, twisting his white moustache and wiping his lips.

"What answer shall I send to this?" asked Grant.

"No terms to the damned Rebels," retorted Smith.[64]

Grant pulled out a piece of paper, letter size, and began to write. He finished and read aloud: "No terms except unconditional and immediate surrender can be accepted."[65] General Smith whispered something to Grant, then walked out of the room to deliver the reply.

The formal surrender ceremonies took place on board the *New Uncle Sam*, Grant's flagship. Wearing a light-blue jersey overcoat and checked handkerchief, Buckner sat on one side of the table, Grant on the other. As the Rebel general leisurely smoked his cigar, he talked in low, quiet tones, freely giving information regarding Confederate positions and forces.[66] He had lost 2,000 killed and 1,134 wounded.

Out in the river, the Navy held burial services. The subdued voice of Lieutenant Walke on board the *Carondelet* carried through the stillness. "I know that my Redeemer liveth, and that He shall stand at the latter day upon the earth."

There was a pause. The crew heard a voice on the *Louisville*: "I am the resurrection and the life, saith the Lord; he that believeth in Me, though he were dead, yet shall he live."[67]

Nine thousand prisoners boarded the transports. The saloons, cabins, berths, and staterooms were crowded with the wounded of both armies. The prisoners resembled a vast horde of gypsies, some dressed in butter-nut or gray, others in yellow, red, or blue threadbare carpeting, buffalo robes, or patched bed quilts. One Rebel muttered, "Well, I guess we'll have to turn Yankees; damn me if I believe there's any more use of hollerin' for Jeff Davis. Jeff's played out."[68]

"We can whip you even-handed on land," sneered another, "but damn your gunboats."

In Nashville, newspapers still published optimistic bulletins. "Enemy retreating. Glorious results! Our boys following and peppering their rears! A complete victory!" Sunday morning, citizens thronged to church, confident of success. At 11:30 a.m., the news came, and Nashville erupted into panic.[69] Thousands rushed madly through the streets. Hysterical women, half-laughing, half-crying, dragged children behind. Men fired stores and munitions, spiked and rolled thirty-five cannon into the river, and put the torch to the Louisville and Nashville Railroad bridge. Train after train pulled out. Government stores were thrown open. Negro and Irishman, beggar and gentleman toted off piles of Army clothing. Governor Harris galloped through the streets. Finding no parliamentary remedy against invasion, the state legislature adjourned without calling for the nays and, with the governor, boarded a special train for Memphis.

An Alabama newspaper correspondent returning to Nashville Sunday afternoon saw crowds pour out along the turnpike leading to Franklin. White flags flew from the capitol building. Over the wire bridge that spanned the Cumberland, General Johnston's Army rumbled past and took the Murfreesboro turnpike.

Monday, February 17. No enemy gunboats had arrived, as Confederate troops, wet, hungry, and worn out by the long march from Bowling Green, continued to file out of the city. Rumors started that Floyd and Pillow had escaped and that the Army was to make a stand just outside the city. The mayor, who conferred several minutes with Johnston, addressed the crowd at the public square. The Army could not make a stand; Nashville would surrender.

Generals Floyd and Pillow finally arrived that evening.

Pillow proclaimed: "The Federals will be with you only for a time. I pledge you my honor that this war will not end until they are driven across the Ohio River." He left the city immediately. During the night, officials burned two gunboats under construction.[70]

In Cairo, Foote suffered from his infected wound and became increasingly despondent. The Donelson repulse, he was sure, had ruined him professionally. "I will not go near again," he wrote his wife. "You need have no fears about us now, as we will keep off a good distance from Rebel forts in future engagements."[71]

Foote went up the Cumberland River with the *Conestoga* and the ironclad *Cairo*, destroyed the Tennessee Iron Works, and captured Clarksville without firing a shot. He abruptly returned to Cairo to bring up two more ironclads and six mortar boats. Supported by Grant's divisions, he made plans to steam up the Cumberland and assault Nashville.[72]

On February 20, General Halleck learned that Columbus, Kentucky, had been strongly reinforced by Confederate gunboats from New Orleans, which were rumored to be ready to steam on to Cairo at a moment's notice. In Washington, General McClellan, in overall command of Union armies, demanded that Federal ironclads destroy Columbus.[73] But at Cairo only two ironclads and one mortar boat were serviceable; two were on station at Donelson, and the others, lacerated and maimed, were in various stages of repair. Halleck judged the situation inexcusable and commanded the Navy to work day, night, and holidays and send to Cincinnati for more mechanics and carpenters.[74] McClellan wired orders directing the gunboats to strike Columbus.[75]

Unaware of these plans and telegrams, Foote and

Grant readied their force for Nashville. Halleck wired Grant to prevent the gunboats from going beyond Clarksville.[76] Foote was chagrined by Halleck's actions. He and Grant knew they could easily occupy the Tennessee capital. On February 22, Foote, having received no answer from higher authorities, descended the Mississippi River with four gunboats and two mortars, fired a few salvos into Belmont, and returned to Cairo.[77]

Nashville did not have long to wait before the 4th Ohio Cavalry galloped into the city—on Sunday, February 23. Buell's Army tramped into the capital two days later, and the general set up headquarters at the St. Cloud Hotel.

The entire South recoiled. News of the reverses in the West cast a black shadow on the inauguration of Jefferson Davis in Richmond. "The crisis is too serious," commented the Richmond *Whig*, "to mince words . . . The disasters like those of Roanoke Island and the Tennessee and Cumberland Rivers are appalling evidence of inefficiency."[78] On the floor of the Confederate Congress, one senator demanded that the military take the offensive in the West and roundly criticized both the Army and Navy departments. The Secretary of War was asked to resign. Congress voted to investigate the disasters.[79]

The public pilloried those "scoundrels and cowards," Floyd and Pillow, for escaping under fire, circulating a jingle:

> 'Pillow,' says he, 'what shall we do?
> My legs to me have yet been true,
> And I can run as fast as you!
> So call your guards immediately.'[80]

General Simon B. Buckner was branded an Iscariot.[81]

"Johnston has lost caste among the Tennesseans. Oh! How they abuse him," wrote a lieutenant to his wife.[82] Westerners clamored for President Davis to take personal command.[83]

The victories at Fort Donelson and Nashville stiffened the North's spine. Reviewing the first ten months of the war, Gideon Welles was satisfied with naval achievements. At Hatteras Inlet, Roanoke Island, Port Royal, and Fort Henry, the Union's first victories of the war had been won by the Navy, supported by the Army; and at Donelson, by the Army, supported by the Navy. The Navy Department took on a new luster. "I believe all admit," said Welles, "that what has been done by the Navy has been well done, and almost all that has been done by way of advance has been done by our branch of the service."[84] Some generals had done nobly, suggested the New York *Post*, but the Navy alone had shown real originality of talent.[85]

At Cairo, Flag Officer Foote was suffering from battle fatigue; the pressures of the river were beating him down. His wound was still inflamed. "I am in body and mind greatly prostrated," he wrote his wife. "I won't run into the fire again, as a burnt child dreads it." Old Flags clung steadfastly to the fiction that given fifteen more minutes, his gunboats could have obliterated Fort Donelson.[86] He was angry with McClellan and Halleck for cheating the Navy out of the honor of occupying Nashville for the North.

In Washington, Edwin Stanton, who had replaced Simon Cameron as Secretary of War, listened patiently to Foote's grievances and, to placate him, asked McClellan to send 800 more soldiers to the flotilla.[87]

Inspecting the damaged gunboats, naval officers concluded that the battles with the river forts demonstrated the effectiveness of iron plating and that only the bow and stern guns were useful for river fighting. The broadside cannon were serviceable only as reserves to replace disabled bow guns. The ironclads' machinery and steering gear needed additional protection. Shot and shell had passed through the gun ports, but no shot had penetrated the two-and-a-half-inch plating of the forward bulkheads.[88]

6

"I'm Almost Crazy!"

Mud, dirt, and filth cluttered the streets of Columbus, Kentucky, a grubby, drowsy town of 1,000 inhabitants. Effigies dangled from the lamp posts—"Tilghman the Traitor," "Floyd the Runaway," "Lincoln the damned Abolitionist." Perched high on the bluffs overlooking the upper Mississippi, Columbus, the terminus of the Mobile and Ohio Railroad, was an armed citadel—"the Gibraltar of the West," General Polk proudly called it—the first barricade to the descent of the river by Yankee gunboats.[1] Confederate brass ordered Polk and his troops to pull out and abandon the river town, judged now as strategically untenable after the collapse of Fort Donelson. The general hated to leave. For six dreary months amid sleet and rain, his work gangs and roustabouts had shored up the defenses, built barriers, posted cannon to command the river, sown mines, and stretched a giant cable across the turbulent Mississippi.[2]

The Confederate western command faced complex problems. After its defensive line had caved in at Fort Donelson, Nashville, Bowling Green, and Columbus, General P. G. T. Beauregard—charged with the overall command of the Mississippi—bluntly confessed to a Confederate congressman that protecting the river was a

111

herculean task.[3] Richmond authorities demanded fortresses, casemates covered with sod, and hidden batteries at Memphis, Vicksburg, Natchez, Baton Rouge, and New Orleans, but belittled the importance of building gunboats to scour the upper river. The majority insisted that the battle of Fort Donelson had exploded the myth of the Yankee ironclad invincibility.[4]

Confederate telegraphs clacked out pleas to the governors of Tennessee, Louisiana, and Mississippi for manpower. To halt a threatened aggression by gunboats, Beauregard set up new defensive lines at Island No. 10 and New Madrid, Missouri.[5]

At the bottom of a bend in the river, forty miles from Columbus, infantrymen on Island No. 10 girded themselves for a desperate stand. Just above the island, a long straight stretch of river flowed southward. At the island, the river turned sharply right, rolling into a horseshoe turn of 180°, then straightened out, heading south again. This bend formed two narrow peninsulas. Island No. 10, two miles in length, was fixed almost in the middle of the first U-turn. At the top of the curve and north of the island, stood New Madrid. The swift current, the hairpin turn, and the narrow channel made navigation extremely difficult and hazardous.[6]

A few miles below New Madrid, huge swamps occupied both sides of the Mississippi. If a force escaped from Island No. 10, it would have to land above the swamps at Tiptonville, Tennessee, to reach the interior. Above this point the countryside was marshy and, in most places, flooded by water, which would prevent the Rebels from leaving in that direction by land.[7]

On the island, Johnnies hoisted into position twenty-five rifled and smoothbore cannon, placed to fire up-stream by shooting over the low, narrow tip of the first peninsula. To screen the island from invasion, workmen at New Madrid hammered forts to completion, shoveled up trenches, and secured the guns. On the Tennessee mainland, laborers dug eight earthworks, mounted twenty-six cannon—each one protecting the other—and arranged to catch enemy gunboats in a blistering cross-fire.[8]

Beauregard pressed the New Orleans command to send iron-plated gunboats up-river, but the Louisiana military, fearing an invasion from the Gulf, refused support. Impatiently, Beauregard assured Louisianans that the wooden-hulled Union blockaders were too fragile to blast their way up-river to the Crescent City. Ironclads at Island No. 10 were vital to halt the swoop of the predatory gunboats down-river from Cairo.[9]

Instead of ironclads, New Orleans dispatched to Memphis a set of eight converted river steamers—the *McRae, Polk, Jackson, Calhoun, Ivy, Pontchartrain, Maurepas,* and *Livingston,* armed with a miscellany of ancient smoothbores, as well as the floating monstrosity *New Orleans*—the erstwhile Pelican Drydock of Algiers—equipped with six guns and no engines. This flimsy fleet could not weather a collision with Union ironclads. Commodore Hollins, the gunboat skipper, had already convinced himself of the hopelessness of the situation. He could do nothing in a fight; he wanted to pull out and abandon the whole defensive system of Island No. 10. Only two of his steamboats had their engines protected with iron. All were vulnerable to small-arms fire. When eight large-caliber cannon assigned to the flotilla were heisted by the Army midway between Louisiana and Tennessee, the commodore was furious.[10] He resented being pushed around by the military and being subjected to the orders of any and all Army officers, including those of General Beauregard.[11]

At Island No. 10, recruits groused about the wretched duty. They were cut off from the rest of the world—no post office, no newspapers, no letters. Fifteen hundred infantrymen were laid low with bowel disorders. The nights were damp, and wind lashed the island. It was miserable, slushy, and cold.[12]

In March 1862 General Polk inspected the 8,000 men in the sprawling, complicated system of water-locked defenses—the anchor of which was Island No. 10. He was pleased at what he saw and announced that the Mississippi was safe.[13] River folk took these words at face value, but on the eastern front, 1,000 miles away in Fredericksburg, Virginia, men of the 11th Mississippi mistrusted this estimate. Five hundred and fifty out of the 900 comprising the regiment refused to reenlist and demanded the right to return home to protect the river and their firesides.[14] Both they and the western command knew that if Island No. 10 fell, eventual Confederate capitulation along the entire river was certain. To invest the Rebel defenses, the Yankees would first have to capture New Madrid and cut off the island from below.

At Planter's House in St. Louis, General Henry W. Halleck, chewing on a half-smoked cigar, planned to do just that. To mop up the Confederates, he decided to move a ground force down river with the ironclads and obliterate the defensive blockade. To assault and hold New Madrid, Halleck assigned General John Pope and his Army of the Mississippi.[15]

Ten thousand soldiers from Ohio and Illinois paraded through the streets of St. Louis to huzzahs and the beat of drums.[16] At their head was Pope, a confident and energetic little general. At the waterfront, the Army of the Mississippi embarked on transports and stood downriver.

The troops clambered off the steamers at Commerce, Missouri, and struck southward, working their way through deep marshy swamps toward New Madrid, forty miles away. The Army reached a campsite at Hunters Farm the first night. The next day the troops waded eleven miles to Sykeston, a Godforsaken crossroads on the Iron Mountain Railroad, where Union cavalry units flushed out a band of guerrillas hiding in the swamps. That night it rained hard. The Army was mired in mud and slime. By March 3, "Old Pope" was within sight of New Madrid, a day before Foote and his gunboats were to start for Columbus, Kentucky.

Foote's reconnaissance vessels had already steamed into Cairo on March 1 to report that the enemy was evacuating Columbus.[17] Union regiments, commanded by General William T. Sherman, climbed on board transports at Cairo while the ironclads *Cincinnati, Louisville, Carondelet,* and *St. Louis,* the wooden-hulled *Lexington,* and four mortar boats and tugs cleared for action. At dawn on March 4, the expedition cast off lines from the wharves and headed southward. Two miles from Columbus, at Lucas Bend, drums beat on board the gunboats, and crews raced to quarters. Foote maneuvered his flotilla into battle order. On board the *Illinois,* a private pointed to the bluffs and whispered, "I see men behind the breastworks. The Rebels are about to fire. Those immense guns will sink us like an eggshell."

Another yelled loudly, "Let the Rebels fire, and be damned!"

"Beauregard's a cunning fox," retorted a corporal. "He's only waiting to get us under his guns and open on us."[18]

Looking through his glass, Foote noted movement on the bluffs and at the water batteries. Gradually, the flotilla nosed toward Belmont on the Missouri shore. Army scouts clambered into tugboats and moved gingerly toward the Kentucky bank. There was no sign of a Confederate army. The tugs put on full speed, raced toward the Columbus wharves, and disembarked the troops. Yankees swarmed to the top of the bluff and stopped short. Four hundred cavalrymen of the 2nd Illinois had already hoisted the Stars and Stripes after galloping down from Paducah on a scouting expedition.[19]

The town was deserted except for two drunks and a hysterical woman who had "stuck up for the Union." Barracks lay smoldering; railroad tracks and guns were mangled and dismantled.

Hobbling around on crutches, wearing green goggles to shade his eyes, Foote inspected the ghost town and concluded that his gunboat reconnaissance of March 1 had forced the Rebels to abandon this fortified city on the Mississippi. Although he knew that the Union Army of the Mississippi under General John Pope was marching toward New Madrid at that very moment, Foote immediately turned around and headed back for Cairo, complaining that his four ironclads and four mortar boats were impotent to attack the enemy and that his vessels needed repairs.[20] The wrinkled and crotchety veteran refused to cooperate with Pope's Army unless he received clearcut orders from Washington.

In St. Louis, when General Halleck received this intelligence, he raged and wired Foote that the gunboats should not wait for repairs but that an ironclad assault on Island No. 10 was imperative. "I have much better information than you have of the condition of affairs," snorted the general, "and where possible, my instructions should be obeyed."[21]

Pope's forward columns had now advanced to within a mile of New Madrid. Union scouting parties searched the area and discovered two forts garrisoned with 6,000 infantry and equipped with twenty-one cannon. The country was level for miles. The river was so high that Rebel gunboats could peek over the banks. As dusk closed in on New Madrid, the Federals retired to a cornfield two miles in the rear, where they erected permanent camps.

On March 5, the 27th, 39th, 43rd, and 63rd Ohio regiments crept toward the town. The 27th and the 39th moved in upon the enemy forts before the Confederate gunboats opened fire. Through the cannonade the Ohioans drove forward, subduing the Rebel pickets until the guns of the fort caught them in a crossfire compelling retreat. Pope concluded that an all-out assault was foolhardy. He waited uneasily for heavy siege guns and Foote's flotilla.

Peevish at the delay, Pope ordered down his siege guns by land. The 11th Missouri marched to Point Pleasant, twelve miles below New Madrid, and along the bank constructed sunken batteries for a 10-pounder Parrott and other rifled guns to blockade the river from Rebel transports and to cut off supplies and reinforcements from Memphis. Rebel steamers fired away, but their persistent bombardment failed to dislodge the 11th Missouri, which held obstinately to its position.

The heavy siege guns arrived and soldiers wrestled them into position within 800 yards of the forts. Just before daylight on March 13, Union artillery roared, knocking two Confederate gunboats out of commission. Work parties extended Union trenches toward the beleaguered town.

The Confederate command ordered the evacuation of New Madrid to prevent encirclement. Hastily, the Yankees moved in and captured thirty-three pieces of artillery together with thousands of rounds of ammunition. "Nothing escaped except the men," said Pope. The flight of the enemy was so quick, so silent, that they had given no word to their comrades on Island No. 10.[22]

New Madrid had been the weak point of the Confederate defense in and around Island No. 10. Its fall furnished Pope with a base of operations against the island and made its capture only a matter of time. With the exception of the gunboat *Grampus* and the floating battery *New Orleans,* stationed at the island, the Rebel fleet had steamed to Memphis to recoal and get ammunition and were now cut off from the defenders.[23]

From Washington, Meigs wired Foote to push the offensive.[24] In Cairo, the Army pressured the Navy to strike. Halleck badgered Foote to hit Island No. 10. "Why can't Foote move?" stormed the general. "It is all-important. By delay he spoils all my plans."[25]

Foote accused Halleck of harassing him to undertake dangerous operations and tossed up a barricade of excuses. He could attack Island No. 10 only if the Navy Department filled his needs. If the gunboats were repulsed, Cairo, St. Louis, Cincinnati, Pittsburgh, and the entire Northwest would be laid bare to Confederate gunboats. He would not assume that responsibility. He wailed that his gunboats, deficient in steam power, could never return to Cairo once they had gone down-river. The cumbersome ironclads were so sluggish—his advice had never been asked as to their construction—that they could only fight up-stream, bows on. Headed down-stream in the Mississippi River was different duty from battling up the smaller Cumberland and Tennessee, where the boats could be maneuvered into close range and, if disabled, could float away from, not into, the enemy's artillery. The current of the river near Island No. 10 was swift and unpredictable. Under the most favorable circumstances, the gunboats could barely stem the stream and, should an ironclad meet with disaster, she would glide helplessly under the guns of the defenders. Foote could not anchor the gunboats by the stern, as the wheels, placed amidships, caught driftwood in the recess and clogged the paddles. The ironclads could not back up-stream. Foote had expressed apprehension to Meigs about the defects of the gunboats and urged Welles not to build more riverboats with the wheels amidships.[26]

Amid the turmoil, Foote sent off dispatches for anchor chains and Dahlgren rifled cannon. He worked long hours, steadily, catching snatches of sleep at his room in the St. Charles Hotel. With practice he had become nimble on his crutches, but the wound was healing slowly.[27] It was painful and swollen. "Oh, how I long for this war to terminate!" he told a friend. "I have had enough of it."[28] As the responsibility of command drained Foote physically and mentally, he sought comfort in the Bible. He was haunted by thoughts of disaster and would have preferred reassignment. "I would this moment give all I am worth could I have been on the Atlantic," he confided to his wife, "a captain of a good steam frigate, instead of out here under a pressure which would crush most men, and how I have stood it. I can only account for that God has been my helper thus far. All is confusion and I am almost crazy."[29] To his old shipmate and friend, Captain John Dahlgren, at the Washington Navy Yard, he recounted his tale of woe and asked him to inform Welles and Fox about conditions in the flotilla in case he failed before the enemy.[30]

So distorted was the image Foote presented and so well had John Rodgers done the spadework, that Foote was given a vote of thanks by Congress for organizing the Western Flotilla and conducting operations against the enemy. Northwesterners were deceived into regarding him as "the Oliver Cromwell of the Navy," and there was talk of nominating him for the Presidency in 1864.[31]

Foote's flotilla was strewn up and down the rivers. Six vessels lay at the naval base in Cairo, three in battle readiness, three undergoing repairs. One ironclad was cooperating with General Buell at Nashville; two patrolled the Tennessee River; the *Benton* was at St. Louis; two protected Columbus. Badly damaged from the fire at Fort Henry, the *Essex* required a complete rebuilding job, which would take six weeks and cost more than her original price.

The mortar boats were an unknown quantity. The Army and Navy detested the sight of these bastard craft—rafts that could not withstand the jolts of firing 13-inch shells. Carpenters built platforms outside of the rafts' bulwarks for the men to stand upon to avoid the concussion and stretched canvas from side to side to shield the crews from the night air and cold.

Finally on March 12, sailors hoisted battle flags signaling that Foote was ready to move with seven vessels, including the *Benton,* and ten mortar boats. The commander took the dimmest possible view of the venture, and when Halleck sent no troops or transports, he raised such a ruckus that the general reluctantly ordered four regiments from Cairo and Columbus to accompany the naval expedition.[32]

The squadron got under way on March 14. Stopping at Columbus overnight to take on troops, the expedition then slid down-river and arrived near Island No. 10 the following morning. The ironclads stopped, turned, and dropped down stern first to a point within two and a half miles of the target and lined up across the river, all headed up-stream. The mortar boats took station along the Missouri shore. Dead ahead, lookouts saw, through fallen timber and cottonwood trees on the peninsula, the fortifications on Island No. 10 and the floating battery *New Orleans*; to the left, on the Tennessee shore, Confederate encampments and the batteries; to the right, on the Missouri bank, the Union tents in New Madrid.[33] Scanning the shoreline with their glasses, Foote and his commanders viewed the Confederate defenses as stronger and more scientifically placed than those at Fort Donelson and Columbus.

In firing position, the *Benton* unlimbered her artillery at the Tennessee batteries, but the range was too great. The mortar boats shelled the island viciously. They gradually pivoted to pummel the batteries on the far bank. Their first shells fell short, the third struck home. Eight more shells silenced the enemy cannon before the boats swung around to lob more missiles at the island. The flotilla rested for the night.

Foote selected March 17 as the day the fleet would assault the upper battery, on the Tennessee shore. Seamen lashed together the *Benton, Cincinnati,* and *St. Louis,* mounting a lusty bow battery of ten guns—8-inchers, 42-pounder rifles, and 9-inch Dahlgrens. The *Carondelet* and *Mound City* took position on the Missouri shore, just below the mortar boats. For two hours the three iron-clads maneuvered up-stream, testing steering qualities, rechecking ranges.

At 1 p.m. the boats changed course dramatically, pushing their bows down-stream, and charged the upper battery. The fire was severe, the discharge continuous. Sheets of fire flashed from the bows. The air vibrated. The *Mound City,* the *Carondelet,* and the mortar boats threw everything they had at the Rebel position.

Foote dared not close the range. The current was so rapid that the ironclads might become unmanageable. If the Yankee vessels were swept away by the current, it would carry them into the jaws of the enemy guns and expose the bows and quarters—their most vulnerable points—to a murderous crossfire from the Tennessee batteries.

The dense woods behind the Johnnies' cannon made a perfect camouflage. The guns were well placed. Federal shot and shell splashed into the water, sailed over their targets, or fell harmlessly to either side. Mortar shells whined and exploded. Dirt flew in all directions, but no shell hit its mark. All along the line, Rebel artillery were finding the range. Shots hit the water dangerously close to the bows of the flotilla.

The battle wore on. Pacing the deck of the *Carondelet,* which was secured to the Missouri banks, Lieutenant Henry Walke spotted the fire for his gunners. A shell zipped into the river just in front of the enemy parapet. "You damned Rebels," shouted a grimy-faced gunner, "put that in your pocket and never mind the change."

"Look at 'em runnin'," hollered a seaman, clapping his hands and dancing on deck.

The man with the spyglass yelled, "I see their flag yet. Now they're loading their big'un. Watch out! There she goes."

"Get out of the way," Lieutenant Walke sang out from the quarter-deck, "let us pay our respects to that fellow. Lie close." The gunners crouched behind the pilot house. Intended for the *Benton*, the shot zoomed over the *Carondelet* and plopped in the water.[34]

"Here comes another!" cried the boatswain on the *Benton*. The crew dropped to their faces. There was a resounding crash. An eight-inch solid shot smashed the half-inch iron plating and the five-inch timber near the bows, rebounded, danced the entire length of the boat, through the cabin, wardroom, pantry—where it shattered the crockery and landed on Foote's writing desk, crushing the lid.[35]

Dusk was settling before the Navy ceased firing. The gunboats steamed out of range. The *Cincinnati's* engines had been slightly crippled by a solid shot, and the *Benton* had been struck three times. Fifteen officers and men lay on the decks of the fleet, dead.

Foote hoped to renew the attack and destroy the upper batteries. Once these gun emplacements were liquidated, the mortar boats could move to the Tennessee bank, where they and the gunboats could punish the island with a crossfire. But Foote despaired.[36] He fumed that the shells burst prematurely and cursed the antiquated fuses, manufactured for the Mexican War. Two defective cannon had already burst on board the *St. Louis*, wounding fourteen.[37]

On March 18, a bright, crisp day, Union lookouts spotted 500 soldiers moving into the upper battery. In fifteen minutes one mortar boat and the *Benton*, stern down-

river, opened fire with rifled shells. The *Mound City,*
Carondelet, and all the mortar boats secured to the
Missouri shore soon joined in. After an hour of blistering
fire, only one shell had landed in the fort, disabling one
gun. Six additional mortar boats arrived from Cairo in
the tow of the *Pike* and *Dan Pollard.*[38]

The Flag Officer stepped up the daily bombardments.
He refused, however, to close in on the Tennessee batteries and maneuvered his gunboats at a safe distance.
The aging Foote was conscious that the Confederate
river fleet lay below New Madrid, and he was not over-
eager to mix with them. The specter of the Rebels'
"powerful fleet" and its battering rams haunted Foote
day and night.

One way to capture Island No. 10 was to send boats
and transports down-river, past the island, communicate
with Pope's Army, and support this force in crossing the
Mississippi River into Tennessee. Yet to run the forts,
Foote feared, was suicide. Holding one council of war
after another, searching for an easy solution, he breathed
easier when his gunboat commanders concurred that the
enterprise was too hazardous. The plan was shelved, and
the bombardments continued.[39] Impatient with the ridiculous delays and the timidity of the Navy, General Pope
at New Madrid was helpless.[40] He could not cross the
Mississippi without gunboat support, and this Foote refused.

Hour by hour the bombardment dragged on. Each day
the routine was the same. In the morning the shrill whistle
of the boatswain's pipe was answered by the hoarse calls,
"All hands to quarters—stand by the hammocks!" Exchanging shots with the enemy grew monotonous.

Bluejackets read, wrote letters, and napped, and officers, playing cards and chess, scarcely noted the cries of the gun crews: "*Mound City* has just disabled a Rebel gun, torn up the enemy's parapet." "*Benton* exploded a shell in a party of Rebels."[41]

On Sunday after weekly muster, sailors on the *Benton*, dressed in clean blue shirts, assembled on the gun deck for religious services. Hats in hands, they stood in a half circle around Flag Officer Foote who, from behind a high stool draped with the Stars and Stripes, read the prayers. Around the circle, seamen could see the black guns, piles of grape and canisters, rammers, and sponges along the deck. Foote gave a brief sermon on Christian life and duty, after which the men were piped down and dispersed.[42]

After a week the gunboats still remained at the same safe distance, and the effect of their gunfire had been slight. Newsmen with the fleet suspected rivalry between the Army and the Navy and gradually lost faith in Foote and his ironclads. "This gunboat flotilla," commented the *Daily Commercial,* "should be made subservient to the command of the land forces."[43] Reporters were baffled by Foote's refusal to hasten the downfall of Island No. 10, to close in on the batteries, or sweep past them to make contact with Pope's Army at New Madrid. They grew weary of Foote's "non-combative policy."[44] "If these gunboats are not intended to be marched against fortifications, why were they built?" questioned the New York *World.*[45]

Foote was sick and embittered. When he was not walking about on crutches, he was flat on his back in bed. He had lost weight; flesh hung from his body. His wound was no better. His digestion was off. Exhausted, his face thin and careworn, he received the news that his small son had died and that his wife was in failing health.[46] One shrewd gunboat skipper suspected what Foote had already confessed to his wife—that Fort Donelson had done in the veteran, that he was afraid to run the guns, fearful of going under fire.[47] Assistant Secretary of War Scott arrived on board the *Benton* to see what was holding up operations and, after talking with Foote for hours, came away convinced that no matter how many gunboats the skipper commanded, he would not budge from his position.[48]

Flag Officer Andrew Hull Foote was the last man Northerners would expect, from his outward manner, to lack the traditional old-school virtues: courage under fire, freedom from malice, a distaste for bickering—to name no others. Yet Foote lacked them, feared to advance against the enemy, feared he would be defeated, and kept up his prestige among the Administration by hiding behind a camouflage of complaints.

General Pope waited anxiously at New Madrid. Brigades drilled and paraded, privates buffed up the camps and played endless games of horseshoes.[49] The general kept demanding gunboats. With the support of just two, he could cross the Mississippi into Tennessee. Delays infuriated this professional soldier. He pressured Halleck to remove all the sailors, including Foote, from the ironclads and to turn them over to his forces. Pope himself would run the gauntlet.[50]

The Army waited no longer. Pope spat out orders to his engineers to dig a twelve-mile canal across the swampy peninsula from a point above Island No. 10 so that transports, navigating in a man-made ditch, could by-pass the Confederate guns on the Mississippi. Once they arrived in New Madrid, they could embark troops and ferry them across to Tennessee.

From Cairo four steam transports, together with barges loaded with saws, lumber, and one 8-inch Columbiad and three 32-pounders, came down-river to a point near Island No. 8 where Colonel Josiah W. Bissell, Pope's chief engineer, supervised work gangs as they cut into the levee. It was precarious work, but suddenly the river roared through the cut, flooding the cornfields, gouging a wide channel toward the forest beyond. Astride both sides of the opening, gangs wrestled guy ropes into place and warily guided the steamers and barges through the raging waters. Inspecting his handiwork, Bissell decided that it was impossible to scoop out a channel deep enough for the gunboats.

Once past the levee, the four transports moved forward to the edge of the woods. Ahead lay two long, straight miles of heavily timbered forest and ten winding miles of bayous, brush, stumps, and solid earth. The expedition waded into the timber. Three launches inched ahead, cutting and pushing out the underbrush and driftwood, followed by rafts rigged with cutting equipment and by the transports. Sloshing around in waist-deep water, privates cut the trees four feet below the water with hand saws. Workmen ran out two hawsers from the capstan of the *Terry* and hauled off fallen trees by snatch blocks.

Tree by tree the expedition oozed forward. For eight days the Army worked in the slime and brush to clear a passage fifty feet wide. Leaving the woods behind, the fleet entered the bayou country. Soldiers and rivermen— floundering, shoving, sweating—straightened and deep-

ened the small swamp channels. Sometimes it took a
squad of twenty men a whole day to remove a half-sunken
stump. The expedition eased through Wilson's Bayou,
East Bayou, and St. John's toward New Madrid.

After nineteen days of punishing work, on April 4, the
tiny fleet triumphantly steamed to Pope's camp on the
Mississippi River below Island No. 10. These transports
and barges remained in the bayou, concealed from the
enemy and ready to move.[51]

During the delay, the Confederates had anticipated
Pope's plan and dragged guns down the Tennessee shore
and erected batteries to prevent a landing of Union troops.
Through spyglasses, Rebels watched Pope's Army. The
Confederate command on the island knew that its defensive system might collapse at any minute.[52] Its only hope
was the fleet at Memphis. But the fainthearted Confederate naval commander refused to do battle with the
enemy.[53]

With no faith in the Union Navy, General Pope ordered
coal barges brought down the canal and ordered workmen
to fashion a floating battery. Lashed together and bolted,
three barges bore one 8-inch Columbiad and three 32-
pounders. Bulkheaded on all sides with four-foot-thick
timber and protected by hay and sandbags, the middle
barge carried the artillery.[54]

With mounting pressure from Pope, Halleck, Scott, the
press, and official Washington, Foote held daily councils
of war. He asked the same questions and was confirmed
in his decision to do nothing.[55] The stalemate was finally
broken when, as one of the conferences was breaking
up, Lieutenant Henry Walke, commander of the *Carondelet*, astonished his comrades by volunteering to run the
batteries the first dark night.

Preparations to fit out the *Carondelet* began immediately. Sailors tore off planks from the wreck of a barge and covered the ironclad to protect her from plunging fire. All surplus chains were coiled over vulnerable parts of the boat; an eleven-inch hawser was wound around the pilot house as high as the peepholes; gun carriages were taken apart and cordwood was brought up from the hold to construct barricades about the boilers and engine room. Where there was no iron plating on the sides of the vessel forward and aft, carpenters shored up bales of hay, lumber, and chain cables. The black gang adjusted the machinery to permit the escape of steam through the wheelhouse, to avoid the puffing which resulted from its passage through the pipes. Mechanics rigged a hose to the boilers to throw scalding water over any Rebel who might attempt to board. With the hodgepodge of lumber, hawsers, and hay that cluttered the deck, the *Carondelet* looked more like a pigsty than a United States gunboat.

After consultation with other experienced river men regarding the course of the channel, the first master of the *Cincinnati*, a twenty-one year veteran of the Mississippi, boarded the *Carondelet* and relieved her regular pilot. He determined to run the *Carondelet* down the Missouri side.

Foote's ironclads and mortars began a bombardment of that side of the island. Twenty-four sharpshooters of the 42nd Illinois, men who had volunteered to support the sailors in repelling boarders, climbed on board the *Carondelet*, mustered on deck, and strapped on hand grenades.

At 10:00 p.m., April 4, the moon went down. Thickening storm clouds enveloped the sky. In the pilot house,

Walke passed the word to cast off all lines. Thunder saluted the *Carondelet* as she got under way.

Silently, the shadowy figure of the ironclad moved down-river. The first half-mile was passed. Sailors on the gun deck whispered of the possibility of passing the batteries unobserved. Without warning, soot in the stack caught fire and a bright red blaze leapt skyward, illuminating the upper deck of the *Carondelet*. Walke grabbed the speaking tube and bellowed to the engineer to open the flue caps. The flames subsided, but not before the Rebels had seen the grim silhouette. The stacks momentarily caught fire again. Walke stormed, "Why in hell the flue caps are not kept open."

The *Carondelet* was at the upper end of the island. Rockets shot up from the mainland and a cannon roared in the distance. All thought of passing unnoticed vanished. Walke had one chance—give the *Carondelet* full speed ahead and race past the Rebel batteries. The ironclad shot forward.

Vivid flashes of lightning turned night into day. Yankees spotted the Johnnies training their guns. Amid the peel of thunder reverberating along the whole river, rose the voice of Lieutenant Walke. For a split second he saw a mud bank dead ahead. "Hard a port! Hard a port!" he raged. The *Carondelet* was caught in the swift current until she regained the channel.

For thirty minutes Confederate cannon fired, but their aim was erratic. The *Carondelet*, zigzagging, escaping from the shot and shell, ran the guns and arrived off Pope's headquarters near New Madrid. Through his speaking trumpet, Walke informed the startled soldiers that this was the *Carondelet*. A fire was kindled ashore indicating the best landing point. In rounding to, the pilot and the engineer misunderstood signals and the ironclad ran hard aground. Sailors shifted the forward artillery aft, and the ironclad backed off easily into deep water, maneuvering and securing to the river bank.[56]

A jubilant Pope dashed off a note to Foote demanding another gunboat. "I am thus urgent, sir, because the lives of thousands of men and the success of our operations hang upon your decision. With the two boats all is safe; with one, it is uncertain."

Back up-stream, Foote sighed with relief when he learned of the *Carondelet's* success. But he resented Pope's attitude and his intimation that the success or failure of the Army hinged on his decision. He was not responsible for the military, but to the officers and men of his command, and another attempt to run the Rebel guns might be a needless sacrifice.[57] But despite his misgivings, Foote sent the *Pittsburg* to General Pope. With surprising ease, she ran past the batteries.

Bugles sounded in the camps of Pope's Army on April 7, and 10,000 soldiers, bayonets glistening in the sunshine, marched to the transports.[58] The *Carondelet* and the Army steamers got under way and pushed down-river to the enemy's heaviest battery, a 64-pounder and two 64-pounder siege howitzers. The *Carondelet* and *Pittsburg* opened fire and closed the enemy. The Rebels fled. The two ironclads moved down-stream 300 yards, knocked over another 64-pounder siege gun, and steamed up-river to the deserted fortifications. The *Carondelet* signaled the Army. Protected by the ironclads, the transports raced in and landed troops on the Tennessee shore.[59]

Pope's forces tramped inland into the swamps toward Tiptonville, driving the enemy steadily back. At 4:00 a.m., April 8, the Confederates surrendered. Caught in the

Union net were three generals, seven colonels, seven regiments, several battalions of infantry, five companies of artillery— 6,000 men in all—100 siege guns, twenty-four pieces of field artillery, and huge quantities of ammunition.[60]

The island defenders, abandoned by the infantry, sank the Confederate gunboat *Grampus* and six transports, set the floating battery *New Orleans* adrift, and, their hopes of reinforcements gone, surrendered to Flag Officer Foote and the Navy.

Union soldiers and sailors swarmed onto the island and captured two wharf boats—the *J. K. Robbins* and the *J. M. Keith,* loaded with sugar and molasses—righted the half-sunken *Grampus,* and took command of the *Red Rover, Ohio Belle, Mark, DeSoto,* and *Admiral,* transports that the defenders had failed to scuttle. Rummaging about the island, Foote inspected the eleven earthworks with their heavy-calibered cannon. The effect of the mortar and gunboat fire was hardly noticeable, except for plowed-up cottonwood trees and chunks of earth. To protect themselves from exploding shells, the Johnnies had crawled into "rat holes," built of tree trunks and short logs covered with dirt. Under a barrage of questions, a captured infantry officer stated positively that not a single Confederate had been killed by the flotilla's bombardment.[61]

In St. Louis, Frank Boehm's Silver Cornet Band tooted their horns, and throngs shouted "three cheers for General Halleck" as they marched toward Planter's House. Halleck strode to the balcony. There was thunderous applause. "What about Island No. 10? What about Island No. 10?" chanted the crowd.

"We have glorious news today," responded the general. "I have opened the Tennessee and the Cumberland to the commerce of St. Louis and trust it will not be long before the city will have communication with the ocean!"[62] While St. Louisians cheered this optimistic prediction, and the band played "Yankee Doodle," two massive armies, Union and Confederate, were locked in savage battle for control of the Mississippi Valley at Shiloh.

In March 1862, the Rebels under Generals Albert Sidney Johnston and P. G. T. Beauregard had concentrated their strength. Leaving only enough troops to hold Island No. 10, they had drawn in their units from Mississippi and other points and massed them at Corinth, where they planned to move down the Tennessee River to the Ohio. The Rebel Army at Corinth, with 60,000 in its ranks, hoped to strike Grant, whose forces did not exceed 50,000, before General Buell could join him with the Army that had captured Nashville.

Grant's legions had moved southward from Fort Donelson simultaneously with Pope and Foote, on a parallel course. His Army was stationed in a semicircular position three miles above Pittsburg Landing, on the Tennessee, 240 miles from its mouth.

Sunday, April 7, 1862. Around this Union semicircle, the Rebels crept forward. The attack found Grant unready. Although his main Army was at Pittsburg Landing, on the west bank of the Tennessee, he had his headquarters at Savannah, nine miles down-stream on the opposite side. His Army had no line of battle, no defensive works, no outposts to give warning, no recognized head during his absence. The most exposed position, at Shiloh Church, was held by the rawest of troops—men who had just received their muskets and hardly knew how to load them.

At this weak link the Confederates struck at 5:30 a.m. The division of General Benjamin M. Prentiss was nearly overwhelmed at the first charge. Disorganized, it held its ground momentarily, wavered, was forced back. Attacked on both flanks and in the front, the Union line was broken and swept away.

When he arrived on the scene from Savannah, Grant found 5,000 stragglers cowering under cover of the river bluff. His timely arrival led to the adoption of such measures as would put a halt to the flight from battle. But his generalship was of little avail in a situation where the division commanders were left to their own devices.[63]

By midmorning, the whole Union center had been forced to the river, and only two wings were left with their organization intact. The Rebels veered to the left. At 3 p.m. they started to turn General Stephen A. Hurlbut's position and capture the landing, stores, transports —the whole Union Army on the Tennessee.

Union forces occupied a line that extended not more than two-thirds of a mile from the river bank on the right around to the river bank on the left. They were huddled together, surrounded by the Confederate Army and with a deep, swift river behind. There was no chance of retreat.

Since 5:00 a.m., the *Tyler* and *Lexington*—the Tennessee River patrol—had steamed up- and down-river, eager to join the fight, but, receiving no orders from Grant, Lieutenant William Gwin, of the *Tyler*, had impatiently hustled an officer to Hurlbut and asked permission to commence firing. The beleaguered general reported he could not hold his position for an hour and indicated the proper line of fire. The *Tyler* opened up and silenced the

Rebel batteries at that point. She dropped down to Pittsburg Landing and communicated with Grant. He ordered the *Tyler* and *Lexington* to fire at will. Steaming back to within three-fourths of a mile above the landing, they discovered that the Rebel batteries had pressed the Union troops back. The *Lexington* and *Tyler* pounded away. Shells tore into the woods, uprooting trees, falling amidst the Rebel ranks. One observer was sure that the well-directed shots of the gunboats had prevented the Confederates from carrying the Union left. In thirty minutes the Rebel batteries were silenced again, relieving, for a time, Hurlbut's position. By 5:30 the Union lines, caving in, had been forced to the river. The Rebels massed for a final charge.

Between the Union ranks and the Rebels lay a deep ravine. As the climax of the battle drew near, the two gunboats leveled their guns and took position. Colonel Joseph D. Webster of Grant's staff hustled together scattered artillery units and two siege guns, 32-pounders, and placed them where they would play on the left flank of the enemy's line when they charged. For the next half-hour the fate of Grant's Army hung in the balance.

The enemy charged, preceded by a storm of shot and shell from their artillery that swept over the ravine and up to the banks of the river. Rounding to, the *Lexington* and *Tyler* fired broadside after broadside. The enemy swarmed into the line of gunboat fire, into the thunderous hail of shells. Gwin ordered rapid fire, mowing down the advancing Confederate line. Webster's field battery barked on the other flank. The last charge was checked and turned back. In the distance, the advance columns of General Buell's Army arrived. Transported across the river by ferryboats, these reinforcements marched to the

Union's lines and rested for the night. General A. D. "Bull" Nelson sent word to the *Tyler*, asking for a box of cigars and a bottle of wine, and promised the sailors they would soon glimpse "real men-of-war fighting."

The first hours of evening were anxious ones. Rumors spread that the Rebels intended a night attack. The gunboats probed the woods with shot and shell. The whole night through, the *Tyler* and *Lexington* fired shells at intervals of ten minutes in the direction of the Rebels' right wing.[64]

Union surgeons were busy. The wounded lay scattered in all directions. Rain fell from a sullen sky, and devastation was everywhere: mangled bodies, uprooted trees, smoldering wagons, plowed-up earth. An old surgeon declared, "I have been present at both Bull Run and Fort Donelson, but they were mere skirmishes to what I have seen here."[65]

Across the ravine, the same rain dampened the Confederates, who had suffered a severe loss in the death of their commanding general, Albert Sidney Johnston. That night at headquarters, Beauregard dispatched courier after courier. While his men lay in exhausted sleep, interrupted by the gunboat bombardment, he reported that his Army was in no condition to cope with an equal force of fresh troops, well-armed and well-equipped, sheltered by the invulnerable gunboats.[66]

At 5:00 a.m. the next day, Monday, Grant, now reinforced by Buell, moved out upon the Rebel line. By noon the enemy were in full retreat, falling back to their camp at Corinth.

The Army at Pittsburg Landing was loud in its praise of the wooden gunboats. After the battle, when the sailors went ashore, they were hailed and cheered by general and private: "Hurrah for the gunboat-men! Hurrah for the gunboat-men! God bless them, they saved us!" In and around the Union camps it was generally agreed that the arrival of Buell's command at the crucial moment and the fire of the gunboats had rescued Grant's Army from annihilation.[67] Not only from his own observation, but from the questioning of the prisoners, General Hurlbut, whose command was extricated by the fast-firing river craft, concluded that the action of the *Tyler* and *Lexington* was the paramount factor in halting the advance of the onrushing Rebels. Even Grant himself applauded the exploits of the Navy: "Your old wooden gunboats . . . rendered invaluable service."[68]

The South claimed victory. This fight proved, Southerners pointed out, that when Confederate armies battled the Yankees on land, at a proper distance from their gunboats, they roundly thrashed the enemy. "At Shiloh we attacked him," claimed the Richmond *Dispatch,* "and but for the timely aid of his boats would have destroyed his whole Army."[69]

At Island No. 10, Foote collected his gunboats and mortars and, on April 11, cast loose and steamed downriver, followed by the Army transports. The flotilla turned a bend in the river and saw the frowning battlements of Fort Pillow on the heights of Chickasaw Bluffs, midway between Island No. 10 and Memphis. The fleet ran to within a mile of the batteries and secured to the Tennessee shore at Plum Point. Leisurely, Foote surveyed the barricade and the Rebel gunboats and transports, downstream, moving toward Memphis. The mortars moored to the Arkansas shore at Craighead's Point and lofted shells into the Rebel bastion. Pope's transports lay up-stream five miles, at Osceola, Arkansas.[70]

Confederate engineers and 5,000 Negro slaves had started construction on Fort Pillow in April 1861. Planted high on the bluff at a bend in the river, Rebel cannon, ranging from 32- to 120-pounders, commanded the Mississippi. Engineers had erected water batteries at the base of the bluff. Farther up-river, in a ravine, they posted a heavy Columbiad. Toward the top of the bluff, they had hidden a battery of six cannon, while a 10-inch Columbiad occupied a nearby ravine. On the river below Fort Pillow, a ten-gun battery was secured. Excavating into the bluff at the same elevation, gunners had constructed a bastioned work of six cannon, including a 13-inch mortar. Up on the bluff were more Columbiads and other guns, planted in works across ravines. The engineers had blundered, however, because the gunners could not depress this artillery sufficiently, and Yankee gunboats, hugging the shore, could easily evade the Rebel fire except for that from the river battery.[71]

On board the *Benton*, Foote conferred with Army officers. The original plans had called for Pope and his Army to move to the rear of the Confederate forts and attack simultaneously with a gunboat bombardment from the river. This strategy evaporated when Pope, after a quick reconnaissance, discovered it impossible to reach the rear of the enemy works from any point on the river above. Remembering his feat at New Madrid, the general proposed cutting a ditch at Craighead's Point to enable the gunboats and transports to move safely below the enemy artillery.

Secretary Scott visited the *Benton* and communicated General Pope's views. Foote assented. Pope now commanded 16,000 men plus six batteries of artillery and 4,000 cavalry. If the Federals annihilated Fort Pillow, the expedition could move directly upon Memphis and occupy it within twenty-four hours.

Abruptly, these plans changed. Finding that the Confederate armies of Generals Sterling Price and Earl Van Dorn had crossed the Mississippi from Arkansas and had arrived in Corinth, Halleck ordered Pope and his Army to pull out and move immediately to Pittsburg Landing. A handful of troops were left behind with the gunboats to occupy Fort Pillow once Foote and the Navy had captured it. Such movements enhanced the effective force of Grant, but delayed the opening of the Mississippi.[72]

Foote's breakdown was progressive, and he was tormented by fear of defeat. By withdrawing Pope, Halleck had left him high and dry. His force numbered seven ironclads, one wooden gunboat, sixteen mortar boats, and a land force of 1,500. Any action seemed suicidal.[73]

Halleck wired Foote that he wanted Fort Pillow and Memphis captured immediately, but Foote would not run the batteries. Under the weight of responsibility, Foote resigned his command and told Welles he could not continue.[74]

Secretary Scott immediately urged Washington to shake up the entire Western Flotilla, reorganize it, and place it under the control of the War Department. Effective cooperation between the two branches of the armed forces, vital to military movements, had been lacking, especially where commanders were disposed to stand on their rights. Island No. 10 had demonstrated that. To conduct military campaigns successfully, Scott reasoned, the Army and the Navy had to be under one control with an absolute right to require strict obedience to orders.[75] Pope and his officers were of the opinion that if the Navy had been under the military, there would have been rapid progress down-river.

Foote smarted at these recommendations while he waited for his replacement, Captain Charles Henry Davis.[76] Welles ordered Foote not to relinquish permanent command but to go home and recuperate. He was to remain the flag officer of the flotilla, and Davis was to be only second in command. "Your name and prestige I deem important," Welles told Foote, "and therefore do not wish the Rebels to know that you are disabled now."[77]

The bombardment of Fort Pillow continued. Each day the mortar boats were towed down-river to Craighead's Point and spent the day exchanging shots with the Confederates. "It is quite a harmless and innocent game," ridiculed a Northern newsman. "I expect this kind of bombardment will become a fashionable amusement, to be engaged in by citizens of adjacent towns and cities. Shooting galleries will undoubtedly give way to breastworks surmounted by Dahlgrens, to which the public will crowd, willing to spend a dollar . . . in so pleasurable and exciting amusement."[78]

Down-river in Memphis and other river towns it was not regarded as a game. The Navy Department in Richmond wired Commodore Hollins to launch the ironclads *Louisiana* and *Mississippi* and haul them to Memphis to engage the forces of the enemy. Believing his position to be untenable, Hollins asked permission to pull out of Memphis and head for New Orleans. Mallory refused: "Your duty is to do all in your power to resist the enemy's descent of the river."[79]

Steaming rapidly for New Orleans with the *McRae* and *Ivy*, Hollins never received the message. He left the *Maurepas, Pontchartrain, Livingston,* and *Polk* at Memphis. The *Maurepas* and *Pontchartrain* moved into the Arkansas and White rivers, and the *Livingston* and *Polk* steamed up the Yazoo, only to meet disaster later.[80]

Tennesseans hanged Hollins in effigy and demanded a stern policy from Richmond. "What are gunboats made for?" asked the Memphis *Argus*. "Will someone inform us of a single benefit resulting to the Confederacy from the fleet which passed Memphis with pomp and parade before the disgraceful hullabaloo at New Madrid?"[81]

Natchez described Hollins' fleet as one of "make-believe gunboats," and was shocked when they withdrew from Island No. 10 without engaging the enemy. Mississippians blamed the "antediluvian spirit" of the Navy Department, which had corralled worn-out, high-pressure freight boats, installed a few sticks of wood, painted them warlike colors, and sent them off.[82]

General Beauregard eyed Fort Randolph, just north of Memphis. He had no confidence in the Navy and ordered its officers on the upper river to forget about their worthless hulks and to unload their cannon at Fort Randolph.[83] Realizing that the fall of Memphis was only a matter of time, the general in mid-April searched the Mississippi for points between Memphis and Vicksburg sufficiently high for his engineers to fortify. Finding none, he ordered defensive works constructed on the high bluffs near Vicksburg and recommended the fortification of Port Hudson, Louisiana, lying between Vicksburg and New Orleans.[84]

The whole river was imperiled. In New Orleans the editor of the *Daily True Delta* questioned Confederate strategy and asked, "What of our defenses?"[85] Out in the Gulf hovered a Federal amphibious force under the command of Captain David G. Farragut and General Benjamin F. Butler, ready, at any moment, to start its ascent of the river toward the Crescent City.

7

"For God's Sake — We Surrender!"

The decision to launch an amphibious attack from the Gulf against New Orleans was one of the most important of the war. The plans had matured almost five months earlier in Washington, at General McClellan's house. From the moment the high command had decided to attack New Orleans from the Gulf, the Navy Department had gone to work.

The selection of a commander was paramount. The list of naval officers was long. Fifty-seventh on the roster was Captain David Glasgow Farragut. David Farragut had been "adopted" by Commodore David Porter, father of David D. Porter, and had fought in the War of 1812 on board the famous raider *Essex*. In fact he had served under the Union flag as long as old General Scott, having gone to sea at the age of ten. Farragut's foster brother, David D. Porter, who had returned from Gulf blockading duty in November 1861, suggested to Welles that Farragut was the best man for the job. Gideon Welles discovered that Farragut had been residing in Norfolk at the start of the war, but that he had packed up and abandoned the place when Virginia seceded and had taken up residence in New York City.[1] All the secretary had heard or seen of him was to his credit. A capable, energetic seaman, Farragut tended to be generally conservative and prone to look with distrust upon new and untried weapons of war.

Among the Old Regulars of the Navy there was a united opinion. Most of them spoke well of Farragut, but doubted that he was equal to the task. However, none could name a better man for this command. A veteran of Gulf waters, Porter was a possibility, but he was only forty-eight years old, and his position on the Navy List was that of a junior commander.

Neither Lincoln nor his Cabinet had extensive knowledge of David Farragut, who had spent half his career on shore duty. When Senator John Hale, of New Hampshire, heard of Farragut's possible appointment, he gruffly inquired if Welles was certain of his man—Southern born, a former Southern resident with a Southern wife. Several members of Congress closely questioned the Navy Department.[2]

Welles and Fox sent Porter to New York to sound Farragut out. Arriving at the Brooklyn Navy Yard, Porter was horrified to find that the captain had been given that most ignoble of all occupations for an active man—sitting on a naval board examining the fitness of officers for active duty.

In a drab, deserted conference room, the foster brothers talked for hours. The conversation ran first to the old days. Farragut expressed anger with the officers who had gone south to serve with the Confederacy. "Those damned fellows will catch it yet," he wagered.

Porter asked Farragut if he would accept the best command in the Navy—a command such as no officer had ever been assigned. Deep in thought, nervously rubbing his hand over his head, Farragut answered, "I cannot fight against Norfolk."

Then, suggested Porter, "you are not the man I came after, for Norfolk will be the very place to be attacked first, and that den of traitors must be wiped out."

The captain gave Porter many reasons for his objections, among them his inclination to avoid actual combat with his kind. Suddenly, jumping from his chair, Farragut exclaimed, "I will take the command, only don't trifle with me!" Once the captain had conquered his reluctance, Porter told him he would hear within the next twenty-four hours what the command would be.[3]

The next day "Cap'n Davy" arrived in Washington and breakfasted with Fox and Postmaster General Blair. With a winning smile and a jovial, talkative manner, he proved delightfully charming and impressed his hosts.[4] He wore a dress uniform, the coat pulled together by a single button at the throat. Farragut was of medium height, stoutly built and clean-shaven, and tried to hide his baldness by combing the side hairs across the top of his head.[5]

Breakfast over, Fox and Farragut adjourned to the library and settled down to business. The Assistant Secretary emphasized that the Navy Department could not afford a repulse at New Orleans. On the eastern front, General McClellan had committed himself to the tactics of a protracted war. Already the inability of the Federals to match the early military victories of the Rebels had created dissatisfaction with the Lincoln Administration. The failure of the deep-drafted steamers and the slow sailing craft to make the blockade effective was multiplying the Government's diplomatic troubles abroad. Fox underscored that Union success at New Orleans would spell the downfall of Confederate hopes.[6] The Navy had already taken the necessary, but strictly preliminary, step of seizing as a depot Ship Island, in the Gulf to the east of the approaches. Fox roughly sketched out the plan of battle. Farragut approved.

During the next month Fox filled Farragut in on his duties, while Porter and General McClellan pored busily over maps. Lincoln and Secretary William Seward often attended these planning sessions. The President said emphatically that "this is a most important expedition . . . It is not only necessary to have troops enough to hold New Orleans, but we must be able to proceed at once to Vicksburg, which is the key to all that country watered by the Mississippi."

Pointing to McClellan's huge map, Lincoln declared: "Here is the Red River, which will supply the Confederates with cattle and corn to feed their armies. There are the Arkansas and White Rivers, which can supply cattle and hogs by the thousand. From Vicksburg these supplies can be distributed by rail all over the Confederacy. Let us get Vicksburg and all that country is ours."[7] Before leaving one night, Lincoln told McClellan and Porter, "We will leave this matter in the hands of you two gentlemen. Make your plans and let me have your reports as soon as possible."[8]

Army engineers furnished McClellan and Porter with drawings of Forts Jackson and St. Philip, which guarded New Orleans from the Gulf. Perusing these, they were convinced that an ordinary naval force together with mortar boats could bombard and attack the forts and force a passage up to New Orleans. The chief engineer of the Army urged a powerful fleet bearing 400 guns and 10,000 men. He pointed out the advantage of a prompt, bold strike, which would overwhelm the forts before their defenders could ready themselves. To reach New Orleans from Cairo implied the conquest of the whole Mississippi Valley, a complete triumph of Union arms everywhere. To attack New Orleans from the Gulf without waiting for any such problematical result was surer and much sounder strategy.[9]

After eight meetings, it was generally understood that the attack rested with the Navy. The military believed that 10,000 troops were sufficient to subdue and hold New Orleans. The Navy was to follow up the victory with two thrusts, one section of the fleet steaming rapidly to Mobile and bombarding Fort Morgan, another moving up-river to Baton Rouge, Natchez, Vicksburg, and Memphis.

Northward in New England a potbellied military amateur, a political general, paraded around the countryside calling on governors and recruiting regiment after regiment. The high command in Washington had shuttled Benjamin F. Butler to New England to raise and arm a volunteer force for the war in Virginia. "Old Cock-eyed Ben" had met with cordiality except in his home state, Massachusetts, where Governor Andrew was "bitter as hell" over his high-handed tactics.[10] Butler dispatched agents to the seacoast to line up transports: the *Constitution, Idaho, North America, E. W. Farley, Ocean Pearl, Mississippi, Saxon, Undaunted,* and *Fulton.* After months of activity interspersed with fancy dress balls and delightful tea parties, Butler had enrolled 15,000 men.

The ultimate destination of this force was not clear. Butler's original orders called for the New Englanders to move into Virginia.[11] In November Butler contemplated Mobile; in December, an invasion of Texas.[12] He reported to McClellan that 2,000 of his men had already sailed for Ship Island in the Gulf. In mid-January Butler followed as far as Washington.

Confusion gripped the War Department. General Mc-
Clellan had fallen dangerously ill with typhoid fever, and,
when he emerged from his sickbed, he had either re-
considered or forgotten his promise of troops for New
Orleans. All knowledge of this project had been withheld
from the inept Secretary of War, Simon Cameron, who
resigned opportunely in January. Engrossed with his
Army of the Potomac, McClellan announced that Halleck
out West could mop up the Mississippi in short order and
capture New Orleans. He was now lukewarm to the Gulf
operation and lacked faith in the Navy's ability.[13]

An infuriated Fox stormed into the War Department
and caught Secretary Edwin M. Stanton alone in his office. Stanton was astounded to learn that preparations had
been going on for two months. "An attack upon New
Orleans by the Navy?" sputtered Stanton. "I never heard
of it. It is the best news you could give me."[14]

When Butler arrived in Washington, he hurried to
Stanton's home and furnished voluminous reports on his
regiments then training in New England, Governors
Island, Hampton Roads, and Ship Island. Butler sat in
Stanton's library, nervously crossing and recrossing his
legs and adjusting his spats. He suggested an invasion of
Texas, galvanizing the Union feeling there and stopping
the flow of cattle eastward across the Mississippi River.

Abruptly, Stanton asked, "Why can't New Orleans be
taken?"

"It can!" retorted Butler.[15] Stanton immediately countermanded McClellan's orders, which held Butler's troops
on board the transports at Hampton Roads.

The general next visited McClellan, who promised to
beef up Butler's New Englanders with the well-seasoned
21st Indiana, the 4th Wisconsin, and the 6th Michigan,

thus bringing his total command to 15,255. The general-in-chief ordered Butler to reduce all the works guarding the Gulf approaches, strike Baton Rouge, and open communications with the gunboat flotilla moving south. This accomplished, he was to cooperate with Farragut and hit Mobile.[16]

Placed second in command to Farragut, Porter had hurried to New York and Philadelphia to purchase and fit out mortar boats. He had seen varied duty, serving with distinction during the Mexican War, skippering mail steamers in the Caribbean, and, from the outset of the Civil War, commanding a ship in the Gulf blockade. Even now, Porter was a controversial figure. This wiry, muscular-framed man with a loud mouth and a touch of the rowdy, sensitive lest other officers reach the top ahead of him, was liked or hated throughout the fleet.[17] Many called him arrogant, a humbug, an upstart, and worse. Secretary Stanton considered him a "gas bag"; Captain Dahlgren, a liar.[18] Although aware that Porter was a schemer, Welles admired his boldness, energy, and organizational ability.[19]

Porter selected twenty sailing schooners, ranging in tonnage from 125 to 350, and dispatched them to the Brooklyn and Philadelphia navy yards.[20] With drawings in hand, Porter supervised the complicated work of converting them into mortar vessels. To enable the schooners to withstand the shocks of recoil and concussion, carpenters filled them in solid from keel to upper deck with heavy timber. Three inches above the upper deck, they built revolving mortar beds, which ran on tracks. When in position, they lay flat and firm, but ingenious mechanisms permitted the gunners to rotate the mortar guns in any direction.[21] Roustabouts wrestled on board each schooner one 13-inch mortar, cast in Pittsburgh, and two rifled cannon.[22]

Porter searched the New York libraries for material relating to these giant guns. Although he found little, what he did locate he used to write up manuals, which he had printed for the instruction of his men. He opened his own recruiting station and, while the vessels were being refitted, he inducted 1,500 volunteers.[23] To carry stores and ammunition, he bought two vessels and procured the services of the steamers *Owasco, Westfield, Clifton, Jackson, Miami, Harriet Lane,* and *Octorara* to protect and tow the mortar schooners. He hoisted his flag on the *Octorara,* a side-wheeler built, in the Brooklyn Navy Yard, with a rudder at each end to enable her to go up or down the narrow channels without turning around.[24]

The destination of the fleet was secret. The Washington *Globe* facetiously reported that "General Butler's Expedition was off for the Mediterranean."[25] The Navy expected to get the expedition under way in January 1862, but a thousand unforeseeable obstacles hindered operations. Word came from New England that engineers were having trouble installing the machinery on board the new "90-day" gunboats.[26] The 13-inch mortar guns arrived tardily in New York.[27]

Secretary Fox canceled dinner plans one evening to confer with President Lincoln, who wanted to talk over the "mortar mess."[28] Lincoln threatened to take Army matters into his own hands. Confusion in the War Department resulted in a foul-up of orders and the delay of troops to Hampton Roads. Senator James W. Grimes of Iowa snorted to Fox, "Don't wait for the Army . . . Take

New Orleans and hold it . . . The Country looks to the
Navy. You are our only solution, move Heaven and Earth
and do it *at once*."[29]

After extricating the *Hartford* from the ice in the Delaware River, Farragut arrived at Hampton Roads and, in
January, took departure for Key West, Florida, and Ship
Island. In his cabin Captain Farragut reread his orders
from Welles: capture New Orleans and then, if the Cairo
flotilla has not descended, push up-river and assault all
Rebel defenses.[30]

By February he was at Key West. The entire Union
force, numbering forty-eight armed vessels, contained
eight steam sloops, seventeen gunboats, two sailing sloops,
twenty-one mortar schooners, and the Army transports.
This heterogeneous, ocean-going force included deep-
draft, tall-masted, and multi-deck ships—strange-looking
craft for the river.

Butler's force sailed from Hampton Roads; Commander
Porter's mortar schooners, from New York. Two of Porter's
vessels collided in the fog; of these, the *R. B. Forbes* was
beached at Nag's Head, but, the *Clifton* pushing on
through a gale, put into Hampton Roads to repair a leak.
One of Farragut's screw sloops, *Pensacola,* ran aground
off the Florida Keys. The transport *Mississippi,* with General and Mrs. Butler on board, ran into Frying Pan Shoals,
near Wilmington, North Carolina, but was soon rescued
by a naval blockader.[31]

The Confederate Government scoffed at the conten-
tion that New Orleans was more seriously threatened
from below than from above. General Mansfield Lovell,
commanding the military defenses in New Orleans, sent

batches of telegrams to Richmond and, each time, President Davis replied that Foote's ironclads descending the river were more to be feared than Farragut's wooden-hulled vessels from the Gulf.[32] New Orleans was protected from above only by antiquated smoothbore cannon on clay banks and by cotton-clad river steamboats; from below, by two modern forts.

North of New Orleans, General Beauregard struggled to save Tennessee from the onslaughts of Grant's Army. He refused to reroute the troops that Lovell had sent him in November.[33] He needed every man and every gun. To support Beauregard's position, Richmond ordered New Orleans to pour six more regiments of its best troops into Tennessee.[34]

After the losses at Forts Henry and Donelson and Nashville, Richmond revamped its strategy. The Confederacy abandoned the coasts of Florida and Mississippi and left only a small, but effective, garrison at Mobile. Without additional arms, the Davis Government could not hold the entire seacoast.[35]

Yankee armadas were already hitting the Atlantic coast with frequency. With Lincoln's troops occupying and fortifying Ship Island near to the approaches of the Mississippi and with rumors current that additional troops were massing in New York for assaults in the Gulf, General Lovell insisted that he had played fair with Richmond's program of common defense, but now—with New Orleans threatened—he wanted his regiments returned from Tennessee.

The days of the grand reviews and parades in New Orleans had passed. The Hussars, Zouaves, and companies with outlandish names had long since marched to the Tennessee front. Every afternoon around Coliseum Place the flower of the home guard—merchants, bankers, under-writers, and judges—dressed in spotless gray and wearing white gloves, drilled on the harsh turf of the old ball ground. The "old man's band" played polkas, while the drum major twirled his stick majestically. Down on the steamboat landing a body of Creoles paraded in dark blue uniforms, tramping over the white pavement of powdered oyster shells.

Months ago the custom warehouses had been emptied, shut down, their doors bolted. For a while the levee kept busy, but the stir and noise died away. Receipts and or-ders from the interior of Louisiana shrank. The Union blockade had closed like a prison gate. Only the found-ries, the drydocks across-river at Algiers, and the ship-yards at Jefferson City were active. New Orleans, the queen of Southern commerce, was out of business. Decay set in. Streets fell into neglect. The harbor was quiet. Now and then a lone tug fussed in the river, and a steamer or two came and went, but they moved drowsily.

By February 1862 only local volunteers and militia remained in New Orleans to halt the threatened invasion from the Gulf, and, later, a portion of these units were sent northward into Tennessee. The highest authorities adjudged Foote's ironclads to be the true source of danger.[36] "The forces now withdrawn from you," Rich-mond told Lovell, "are for the defense of your command, and the exigencies of the public defense allow us no alter-native."[37] New Orleans was to be defended from above by defeating the enemy in Tennessee.

Angry Gulf residents accused the Davis Administration of a lackadaisical handling of the war effort. Alabama's governor claimed his state was the worst defended in the entire South.[38] Governor Thomas O. Moore of Louisiana was outraged. He had purchased 1,880 rifles from Europe, but this shipment, unloaded on the coast of Florida, had been hijacked by the governor of that state. "In God's name, in the name of my state," he bellowed to Davis, "I ask you to order them to be sent to me immediately."[39] By the time Richmond took action, the guns were scattered throughout the Confederacy.[40]

The New Orleans Committee of Safety sent a representative east to report on the deplorable condition of the Navy.[41] He was assured that the forts below New Orleans would thwart the enemy from the Gulf, and that the *Louisiana* would repel the gunboats from Cairo.[42]

Despite Richmond's complacency, General Lovell strengthened Forts Jackson and St. Philip. He asked for and received $100,000 from the New Orleans City Council. Roustabouts obstructed the lower Mississippi with a raft and schooners anchored and chained together. They prepared and sent down fifty fire rafts loaded with lightwood mixed with cotton, resin, and tar oil.[43] From Memphis, J. B. Cook, an experienced explosives expert, arrived in town and planted mines in the river near the forts, but the powerful current and the depth of the water foiled his efforts. Bled by Beauregard, New Orleans was garrisoned by 3,000 local 90-day recruits called out by the governor and by seasoned units at the forts.[44]

New Orleans had been almost stripped of naval protection. To stem the enemy's assault force, the Confederates depended on the six makeshift gunboats of the River Defense Command; on the *Governor Moore* and *General Quitman,* recently turned over to the Navy by the state; on the unwieldly ram *Manassas;* and on the *Louisiana* and *Mississippi,* still being fitted out at Jefferson City.

When Commodore Hollins arrived in New Orleans from Memphis with the *McRae* and *Ivy*, in mid-March 1862, he was confident of repelling any thrusts from the Gulf. He would have the advantage of going down-stream and, by sending fire boats against Farragut's force, he could scatter it and cause it to become prey to the guns of the forts. The Confederate squadron's cannon were all placed forward, while Farragut's ocean-going sloops would be forced to turn broadside in the river to pivot their guns into action. With the New Orleans fleet, possibly bolstered by the Memphis flotilla, Hollins predicted that all his guns could be trained upon the advancing enemy, while only nine of Farragut's could point up-river except from a broadside position. If Farragut's actions paralleled those of Foote, reasoned Hollins, the Union fleet in the Gulf would not dare run the forts until ground forces could storm them.[45]

Other officers disputed Hollins' theory, believing that nothing the Confederacy assembled on land or in the water could defend New Orleans.[46] Such opinion failed to impress the military commander at the forts, but General Lovell himself perceived their validity.

From Richmond, Secretary Mallory wired Commodore Hollins to return at once to Virginia to become president of a board to examine midshipmen. There was no explanation. Commander John Mitchell replaced Hollins as head of the Confederate Navy in western waters.[47]

Ship Island lay across Mississippi Sound thirty miles south of the Mississippi resort of Biloxi. The barren sand rising slightly above the Gulf waters resembled in shape the hull of a ship with its bow pointed toward New Orleans, sixty-five miles away. To the northeast was Mobile and, farther west, directly astern, Pensacola.

Here, the Union Gulf expedition took shape as transports and gunboats came to anchor. Farragut nosed in the *Hartford* on February 20 and took command of the West Gulf Blockading Squadron, whose responsibility ran from St. Andrews Bay, Florida, to the Rio Grande River.

Desolate and grim, Ship Island inspired a recently arrived, seasick private to exclaim, "Lord, what a wretched place." Nothing met the gaze except sand and water. Flies abounded. Porpoises danced in the sound, attracted by the refuse of the Army camp. Seagulls flapped in the sky.[48] Regiments were wretchedly clad; nearly half of the men were without shoes, many without shirts. They fought mock battles in cotton drawers and fired at the half-sunken wreck on the beach. General Butler and his wife moved into a shack of charred boards as privates brushed away a web of junk—ladders, paint cans, tangles of rope, and moth-eaten curtains.[49]

Transports and cargo ships arrived daily. The *George Washington, Sea Bridge, Young Turk,* and *Daniel Webster* unloaded mess beef, pork, bacon, hams, flour, hardtack, rice, beans, coffee, tea, sugar, vinegar, candles, soap, salt, potatoes, molasses, ice, and hay.[50]

Inside his ramshackle cabin, sitting on a huge French bedstead—a relic from a captured blockade runner—Old Ben and his staff mapped out tactics. Positive that the decisive encounter would be between armies slugging it out in the swamps and bayous of the Mississippi Delta, Butler drilled storming parties and sent to Boston for scaling ladders and siege guns.[51]

Awaiting assembly of the forces, Farragut sent a raiding party to the Biloxi post office and here he learned that Foote had moved down the Mississippi to Island No. 10. The time had come to strike New Orleans.[52]

Without waiting for the slow-moving mortar schooners, Farragut moved his sea-going fleet to Pass a l'Outre and began the work of tugging his vessels across the bar into the Mississippi River.

Upon the arrival of Porter with his mortar schooners, which had proceeded independently under sail from Key West, the commander hurried them into Pass a l'Outre and into the Southwest Pass to fit out at the abandoned and flooded village of Pilot Town. Built on piles, the town's shanties proved invaluable for storing sails, spars, and other gear. Porter's steamers then went back to help the sloops and gunboats over the bar.

To lighten the heavier vessels, sailors toiled night and day sending down yards and masts and hauling off every spare article. After repeatedly running aground, the *Pensacola* was dragged through on her side by Porter's steamers. The side-wheeler *Mississippi* could not be laid over without smashing a wheel. She wallowed through by brute force. Time and time again, the *Mississippi* backed, ran at full speed, keeping in the channel, and plunged into the mud. Then the lighter vessels strove to pull her over. Hawsers parted; tempers flared.[53] It took ten days to prod the *Mississippi* into deep water.

Porter began to have serious reservations about the capture of New Orleans. The obstacles were hazardous and the element of surprise vanished as Farragut used precious days forcing his ocean-going vessels across the bar. Privately, Porter derided his superior for underestimating the difficulties and complained bitterly that no man knew what Farragut wanted because he did not know himself.[54] Out of patience, Porter dashed off a detailed plan of attack to the *Hartford*, suggesting that the mortars open fire first, shelling and leveling the forts before the squadron moved past.[55]

When Farragut's ships finally crossed the bar and secured at Pilot Town, sailors with time now to look about saw a hodgepodge of fighting craft and auxiliaries. Mortar schooners, sloops-of-war, gunboats, beef boats, colliers, barges, ammunition schooners were anchored against a backdrop of shanties and of willow trees and wild cane, which sprouted on the banks of the muddy, yellow lower Mississippi.[56]

A wind storm, whipping down-river, retarded the Confederates who, sensing imminent peril, were hurriedly reinforcing their defenses. The water rose in the swamps. Sharpshooters fell ill from exposure. The regiment guarding the rear of St. Philip was transferred to higher ground on the west bank above Fort Jackson. Snapping their moorings, two fire boats were swept against the chained obstructions, shattering the chains and scattering the hulks. Despite the raging current, the Rebels quickly resecured the barrier.[57]

Once the storm had subsided, Porter towed three mortar schooners up to within 3,000 yards of the forts and let fly a few shells to test the range. Farragut's ships, operating in midstream, diverted the enemy's fire. On the approach of a well-directed shot from the Rebels, "Old Bulldog" Farragut, glass in hand, stood bolt upright on a block, as if defying the enemy, and yelled: "There comes one! There! There!" The shot plunged into the water while bluejackets bobbed and ducked on deck, heedless of their captain's delighted "Ha, too short, too short."[58] Back at Ship Island, Butler's regiments began boarding the transports.

The Union fleet stood in battle array on April 16. Porter brushed aside the squadron's prediction that the bottoms of the mortar schooners would drop out after the tenth shot. The *Westfield, Clifton,* and *Miami* towed the schooners to the lee of a thick wood, where they moored. Camouflaging spars and masts with shrubbery and branches, sailors could plainly see the forts. The head vessel of the first division, *C. P. Williams,* was stationed 2,850 yards from Fort Jackson, 3,600 from St. Philip. The *Para, Norfolk Packet, Arletta, William Bacon,* and *Sophronia* dropped down in a line close behind. Next to the first division, Porter placed the third, consisting of the *John Griffith, Horace Beals, Sarah Bruen, Racer, Henry James,* and *Dan Smith* and the brig *Sea Foam.* The second division, comprised of the *T. A. Ward, Maria J. Carlton, Matthew Vassar, George Mangham, Orvetta,* and *Sydney Jones,* was positioned across the river on the northeast shore, the headmost schooner 3,680 yards from Fort Jackson. Gunners pointed their mortars at a forty-five degree elevation.

Early on the morning of Good Friday, April 18, Porter signaled "Commence firing." The battle for New Orleans began.

The mortars pounded the forts hard. Schooners lurched, careened, shot astern. Hawsers strained. Trees quivered. Windows were broken thirty miles away in Belize. When the mortars fired, the sailors, blackened with powder from head to toe, raced to the stern and stood on tiptoe with mouths wide open to receive the concussion.[59]

The Rebels fired rapidly. They spotted the second division, down-river, and a 120-pound shell smashed into the schooner *T. A. Ward,* tearing through the cabin, damaging the magazine, opening a hole in the starboard side near the water line. The *George Mangham,* the next in line, was viciously drubbed. Porter moved them 200 yards astern.[60]

Searching the ramparts with his glass, a dismayed Porter saw that his mortars had dismounted only a few guns, mashed in one casemate, and riddled the parapets. Inside the forts, where the ground was soft from the rains, the shells buried themselves sixteen feet into the mud and exploded, throwing up nothing but water.[61] But Porter was certain that the mortar fire was undermining Rebel confidence and that within forty-eight hours the enemy would hoist the surrender flag.

A little after sunset, Porter ordered the mortars to secure. Night firing was uncertain, as the wind had freshened. That day the schooners had expended 1400 shells, many of which, equipped with worn-out fuses, had been lost in the air.

The mortars kept hammering away on April 19. The Yankees fired as rapidly as they could load. Although the battering was fearful, the effect of the fire was not what Porter had planned.

The Rebels lined up the Union's second mortar division in their gun sights. Shells ripped into and sank the *Maria J. Carlton.* Their guns swung around to the first division. In a one-hour bombardment, 125 shells fell dangerously close, but failed to damage the mortars beyond hitting the *Para,* cutting up her rigging, and smashing a hole in the deck of the *Norfolk Packet.* Porter's fuses were so defective that he gave up the plan of timing them and put in full-length fuses set to burst after the shells hit the ground.[62]

Easter Sunday, April 20, the firing continued.

That night the *Pinola* and *Itasca,* gunboats of Far-

ragut's squadron, went up-river to examine and remove
the chain obstruction. Unmasted, the low, raking steamers started up-stream and passed unchallenged to the
hulks. Grappling the chains, the two gunboats drew alongside and men jumped over and began dismantling the
obstructions. A rocket shot up. Rebel guns opened. The
Federals quickened their work. Suddenly the *Itasca*, slip-
ping the chains of a hulk and, in the darkness, drifting
toward shore, went aground. The enemy kept firing. The
Pinola gradually tugged off the *Itasca*. Up-river the obstructions, the barrier in which Lovell had placed his
confidence, were now harmlessly strewn along the river
banks.[63]

Porter's bombardment was unending. His men were so
exhausted that they would fall on deck and sleep for ten
minutes, only to wake to fire again. Overcome with
fatigue, with no change of clothes for thirty-six hours,
Porter at one time fell fast asleep on deck as the mortar
on the next vessel flailed away.

The forts still answered. Porter was despairing until
a Confederate deserter struggled out of the swamps with
wild stories of hundreds of bombshells falling into the
fort, broken casemates, burned-out buildings, demoralized troops, a cut levee. Heartened, Porter and his fleet
went to work with renewed vigor.[64]

Farragut's edginess mounted as he began to lose the
little faith he had in the mortar boats. The schooners had
only served to warn the enemy and embarrass the whole
operation. The flotilla had not accomplished what Porter
had promised or expected.

On April 22, Tuesday, the fifth day of the bombardment, Jackson's casemate guns were firing rapidly and
Porter's fleet was running short of ammunition. Farragut

signaled his captains to board the *Hartford*. When he proposed that they pass up-river that night, two older captains argued that they were not ready. Farragut agreed to postpone the passage another twenty-four hours, but no more.[65]

Up-river, New Orleans was in turmoil. On the day Porter had pulled his fleet into position, the ironclad *Mississippi* was hastily launched, and a shocked Governor Moore learned that Richmond had ordered the *Louisiana* to Memphis to battle Foote's armada. In command of the forts, General Johnson K. Duncan was depending upon the *Louisiana's* timely arrival to the south. To send her elsewhere was folly. In a room at the St. Charles Hotel, Lovell and Moore pressured Commander William Whittle to run the *Louisiana* against Farragut. Orders opportunely arrived from Richmond for Whittle to use his own judgment, and he ordered her down.

The ironclad *Louisiana* started for the forts, but her prow was unadjusted, her armament incomplete, and her machinery untested. The paddle wheels were in the middle of the vessel, one just forward of the other. When she pulled out into the stream, the crew discovered that the after paddle wheel, completely submerged by the water churned up by the forward one, splashed uselessly. Next, the propellers failed. Helpless, incapable of stemming the current, the *Louisiana* was towed to the forts.

Moored under the guns of St. Philip, the ironclad served as a floating battery with improperly mounted guns that could only be elevated five degrees. She could not fire her stern guns without menacing the Confederate squadron. Her battery facing St. Philip was useless. She could only engage the enemy when they were actually abreast of Fort Jackson.

The six steamers of the Army's River Defense Squadron acted on orders from the Secretary of War in Richmond and refused to be subordinated to Commander John Mitchell of the *Louisiana*. The captain of the *General Quitman,* the state's gunboat recently turned over to the Navy, wanted to operate independently. It was generally understood that each gunboat would fight unhampered by prearranged signals or tactics and, somehow, keep the enemy under the guns of the forts.

Had the squadron, including the *Louisiana,* been stationed up-river above the forts and strung out across the channel where the Mississippi curved to the right, Farragut's vessels would have been caught in a right-angle crossfire from the forts and squadron. But situated, as the gunboats were, haphazardly along the river banks, packed closely together with no room to turn or strike, they presented an unstable front. If the Yankees could force their way past the forts and arrive at the head of the reach, they would be out of danger.[66]

At 1:45 a.m., April 24, two lanterns shone from the masthead of the *Hartford,* the signal for the fleet to weigh anchor. On the flagship, the crew gulped the last of the coffee and swore at Farragut for not serving grog. Sailors hung cables over the vessel's sides abreast of the boilers, smeared the decks around the guns with whitewash to guide the powder boys in the night, packed a miscellany of shock-absorbing materials, hammocks, clothes, and sandbags in the berth deck over the engine room. Gunners tinkered with the lock strings, filling division tubs with water, placing buckets of sand nearby to be scattered on bloody decks. Doctors swung cots at the main hatch to lower the wounded.

Everyone was tense. Sailors huddled in groups and

talked of their chances; a few sat writing their last testa-
ments. Farragut lounged on a propeller block on the poop
deck, scarcely speaking to his officers.[67]

The Union fleet mustered 192 guns. Divided into two
divisions, the squadron consisted of the sloops *Hartford*,
Pensacola, *Brooklyn*, and *Richmond*, the side-wheeler
Mississippi, the screw corvettes *Oneida*, *Varuna*, *Iroquois*,
and the gunboats *Cayuga*, *Itasca*, *Katahdin*, *Kennebec*,
Kineo, *Pinola*, *Sciota*, *Winona*, *Wissahickon*.

Up-stream, on board the *Governor Moore*, lying near
St. Philip, the watch changed at 2 a.m. The skipper clambered down from the masthead and reported "all quiet"
to General Duncan, who commanded the forts. At the
Fort Jackson water battery, the gunnery officer saw black
shapeless masses, barely distinguishable in the darkness,
moving silently up-river. The artillery was leveled.[68]

General Johnson K. Duncan sent verbal orders to Commander Mitchell to move the *Louisiana* into firing position, down-river, near the enemy. Mitchell reported that
he would get under way in twenty-four hours. "Tell Commander Mitchell," the general snorted, "that there will
be no tomorrow for New Orleans unless he immediately
takes up the position assigned; if he does not do so the
city is gone."[69] The *Louisiana* could not budge.

Farragut's starboard division, led by the *Cayuga* and
the *Pensacola*, churned past Porter's schooners, past the
broken barrier chains, into the glare of the fire boats and
beach fires. Guns flashed. Porter ordered his mortars to
open fire. The Union side-wheeler *Mississippi* shot
through the gap. Behind raced the *Oneida* and *Varuna*.
The *Katahdin*, *Kineo*, and *Wissahickon* brought up the
rear of the first division.

Farragut's second column, the port, immediately astern

of the first division, moved ahead. The *Hartford* started through the gauntlet. The *Brooklyn* ran afoul of a sunken hulk and her nose swung around and bumped into the levee as the *Richmond* veered around and took her place astern the *Hartford*. Their broadsides let go.

On *Hartford*, Farragut paced the quarter-deck, shouting, "Don't flinch from that fire, boys, there's a hotter fire than that for those who don't do their duty."[70] Yankees fired at anything and everything that failed to fly the Union colors.

The Confederate gunboats were already under way, moving down-stream. The *Governor Moore* steamed unaware near the fast-charging *Oneida* and *Cayuga*. Within hailing distance of the Confederate's port beam, the *Oneida*'s captain sang out, "What ship is that?"

The wily skipper of the *Governor Moore* answered, "United States steamer *Mississippi*." This deception miscarried and the *Oneida* raked the Rebel with a starboard broadside.

The *Cayuga* veered to avoid collision with a Confederate tugboat. Mounting the arms chest, the *Cayuga*'s commander bellowed, "Surrender you damn fool or I'll blow you out of the water!"[71]

The *Pensacola*, maneuvering in the wake of the *Oneida*, sprayed shrapnel into the *Governor Moore*, clearing out twelve Rebels at the bow gun. The *Pinola* closed in on the *Governor Moore*'s port quarter and riddled her with broadsides. The *General Quitman* was ablaze at her berth on the east bank, deserted before the Yankees reached her.

Battered, the *Governor Moore* swerved straight toward the oncoming *Varuna*. The *Governor Moore* charged, butted, backed, fired again, and rammed into her. The *Stonewall Jackson*, scrambling to pass the *Varuna* to reach the safety of New Orleans, smashed deep into the *Varuna*'s port gangway. The *Stonewall Jackson* backed clear, steamed four miles up-river, and was beached, fired, and abandoned.

Her deck strewn with fifty-seven dead, the *Governor Moore* turned and again headed into the enemy. With wheel ropes, rudder, and a chunk of the walking beam shot away and her engine room filling with steam, she anchored out of range. The crew set her ablaze, deserted her, and struck out into the swamps.[72]

General Mansfield Lovell arrived from New Orleans in a tugboat and saw seven months of labor swept away. He turned his tug and headed back for the city.[73]

The Union fleet ran straight in mid-channel between the two forts. Guns ran out the ports and recoiled as the gunners sponged, loaded, and fired. The smoke was so thick that Rebel and Yankee shot at flashes. The noise was fearful; the stench of burned powder and flesh, nauseating.[74]

The Confederate bastions, cautious not to hit their gunboats on the opposite bank, fired erratically. Zigzagging into each other's way, without room to maneuver, several Rebel steamers were hamstrung and struck their colors. Seventeen fire boats—neither the Army nor the Navy knew who was responsible—lay alongside the river, unfired.

When the first Union ships steamed through the barrier, all hands on the C. S. S. *McRae* raced to battle stations and fired the port broadside and the 32-pounder on the poop deck. Amidships, the pivot gun exploded after the third round. The *McRae* did not change position until the *Hartford* and *Mississippi* came within range. Rebels cast off lines, but the engines overheated and stopped.

She dropped down away from the *Hartford* and *Mississippi* before she got headway in the current. An 11-inch shot passed through just forward of the engine, seriously wounding the captain and decapitating a first-class fireman. Another shell knocked out the *McRae's* steering gear. She ran in under the guns of St. Philip and grounded.[75]

Tars on the *Louisiana* opened fire, employing the three bow guns and starboard broadside against the Union squadron. An answering volley of 11-inch shells struck her forward, denting and crushing the iron plating.

The U. S. S. *Brooklyn* was in trouble. Athwart the river, her bow grazing the bank, she was caught in a withering fire from St. Philip. She turned to pass up-river.

From out of the smoke, the ram *Manassas* bore down. "The ram! The ram! The ram!" cried the lookouts.

The skipper yelled, "Give her four bells! Put her helm hard-a-starboard!"

The *Manassas,* her lone cannon disabled, her engines out of order, defenseless except for four double-barreled shotguns, butted the *Brooklyn* amidships. A man raced from the ram's after hatch, ran forward along the deck's port side to the stacks to see the damage. He turned and fell, tumbling headfirst into the water, hit by a hand lead from the *Brooklyn.* Yankee guns could not depress, and the *Manassas* escaped in the darkness.[76]

Farragut signaled the *Mississippi* to turn and run her down. The side-wheeler veered and went at her at full speed. When within fifty yards, the *Manassas* put her helm hard aport, dodged her adversary, and ran ashore. The *Mississippi* poured in two broadsides to send her drifting down-river, a total wreck.

The *Hartford* engaged St. Philip at close quarters. A

blazing raft guided by the tug *Mosher* headed for the flagship. Shunning this danger, the *Hartford* ran into a shoal, where shells from the fort set her afire. Flames licked the main rigging on the port side, finally driving the men from the guns. For an instant it looked as if the *Hartford* would blow up. The panic-stricken crew raced around deck screaming. Through the smoke and excited men strode Captain Richard Wainwright, yelling, "Take your places at fire quarters, fire quarters." A shell exploded in the cabin. The fire shifted forward. The *Hartford* was hard aground. Wainwright hailed the engine room, "Are you doing all you can with the engines? You know we are in a bad way if she don't back off."

Chief Engineer Purdy responded: "The throttle is wide open on the engines, sir."

"Is there any way you can increase her power?"

"By reducing her water, which would endanger the boilers."

"Try something to get her afloat," shouted Wainwright.

Purdy ran to the fire room. The ship shimmied from the revolutions of the engines. The throttle was wide open. Purdy forced fires in almost-empty boilers. The *Hartford* backed off. The flames were extinguished.

The battle wore on. Farragut's ships, one by one, eased up-river to safety.[77]

The sky to the east of St. Philip was tinged faintly with gray as the Rebel steamer *Resolute*, her crew crying, "Don't fire, for God's sake!—We surrender!" ran alongside the *Sciota*. The *Iroquois* and *Kennebec* followed the *Sciota*'s wake.[78] Broad daylight prevented only the *Pinola*, *Itasca*, and *Winona* from maneuvering past the forts' batteries.

It was over. A bright sun shone over the green willow

trees that bordered the river. Its banks were lined with burning, sinking hulks, the paddle wheels of some still spinning. The *Governor Moore* lay smoldering. The *Manassas, Stonewall Jackson,* and *Mosher* had been destroyed. The *General Quitman* and steamer *Star* had been set ablaze on the report of the first guns. The tug *Belle Algerine* had been sunk when the *Governor Moore* ran into her. The *McRae, Louisiana,* and River Defense gunboat *Defiance,* with colors still flying, licked their wounds under the guns of St. Philip.[79]

Inside Fort Jackson, a Confederate colonel exclaimed in disgust, "Shut up shop; the old Navy is too much for us; good-by New Orleans."[80] The brick barracks lay destroyed, the parapets and plain were pitted and torn by shells, and the ground was partly flooded. But Forts Jackson and St. Philip still stood, with their magazines safe and with provisions enough for six weeks.

Farragut sighed with relief. His squadron was intact. He had lost only 210 killed and wounded—a small number of casualties considering the holocaust. In his cabin he scribbled off a note to Porter, whose flotilla remained below the forts, suggesting he send a flag of truce to the forts and demand surrender.[81] Porter sent the *Owasco* under a flag of truce to the forts, but the Confederates refused.

Chagrined that Farragut had preceded him to New Orleans, General Butler began landing his troops in the rear of the forts.[82] At noon, April 25, Porter again ordered the Confederates to surrender. Again they refused. At midnight, the troops inside Fort Jackson mutinied, and, seizing the guards, reversed the guns and fired upon officers who tried to check the riot. Many fled out the gates into the swamps only to be picked up by Butler's

Army. General Duncan sent word that the forts were ready to capitulate.[83]

Commander Mitchell charged into headquarters and argued hotly with Duncan. Mitchell insisted that the Confederates should not haul down the flag, but already Duncan had sent a boat under a flag of truce. Back on board the *Louisiana,* Mitchell held a council of war with his officers. During the session, the quartermaster reported enemy gunboats coming up-river with white flags flying. Officers unanimously agreed to destroy the *Louisiana.* In his cabin, alone, Mitchell sat musing, speculating that Farragut's fleet was among the most formidable that ever floated. "I think," he said later, "that any one of the five first-class ships of war could have effected the same destruction of our converted vessels that the whole fleet had accomplished."[84]

Porter's *Westfield* and *Harriet Lane* steamed up to Fort Jackson. To show the Confederates that the Union Navy had not "gone to the devil," sailors mustered in their dress whites, and officers, in blue frock coats and white trousers. They anchored and received the surrender. During the ceremony, lookouts reported the *Louisiana* on fire and drifting down river. She exploded within a few hundred feet of her moorings opposite St. Philip.[85]

The scene at the Tift's boat yard at Jefferson City was chaotic. "Danger is all around," snapped Commander Whittle, wringing his hands, and looking at the half-finished *Mississippi.* "I do not know in the name of God what to do with her."[86]

To tow the *Mississippi* up-river, out of danger, her skipper, Arthur Sinclair, commandeered two steamers,

St. Charles and *Peytona,* and started northward. The huge ironclad, gripped in the strong current, wavered, made no headway, and lost ground. To expedite operations, Sinclair sent his engineer to the *St. Charles,* whose captain stormed, "I don't want any damn son-of-a-bitch of a naval engineer to work on my engines."

A member of the New Orleans Vigilance Committee arrived and promised additional steam power, which never came. Sinclair secured the *Mississippi* to the river bank and went into New Orleans, stationing his lieutenant on board with orders to fire the ship if the enemy hove in sight. At New Orleans, steamboat captains refused him support, tied up their craft, and abandoned the waterfront. Naval officers, later to stand before courts-martial, put the torch to and destroyed the *Pamlico, Bienville,* and *Carondelet.* The *Ivy* escaped to Memphis.

When Sinclair saw Farragut's fleet coming up-river, he started back for the *Mississippi* in the *Peytona* and, rounding the point, saw flames gushing from the ironclad.

The Tift brothers wept, but they did not tarry. An officer reported an angry mob on its way from New Orleans to hang them from the nearest tree. The Tifts stepped on board a boat headed for Vicksburg, where they were arrested, but later released.[87]

General Lovell and his troops boarded a railroad train for Jackson, Mississippi. The forts had been passed, the chain obstructions carried away, the vessels sunk or burned. Without firing a shot, the Union Navy, by shutting off New Orleans' supplies, could starve the city into submission within days.[88]

The sloop-of-war *Hartford* and the gunboats of Farragut's Gulf command stood up-river. The day was damp and drizzly. All along the levee, buildings on both sides of

the river were in flames and, beyond, New Orleans was
hidden beneath the thick smoke. Cotton blazed and
molasses ran in the gutters. One wild-eyed woman, pistols
in both hands, cried, "Burn the city. Never mind us. Burn
the city." The bell on Christ Church kept ringing. Crowds
surged through the streets, shouting, "Betrayed! Betrayed!" The lower steamboat landing, sagging with
sugar, rice, and molasses, was rifled by riffraff. The masts
of the steamer *Washington* were seen tipping, declining,
then sinking down into the river. Fire-gutted merchant
ships loaded with cotton drifted helplessly in the current.[89]

Two officers from the *Hartford* reached the wharves.
Through the holocaust of Common Street, with the mob
screaming, "Shoot them! Hang them! Kill them!" the two
officers, walking abreast and unguarded, looking neither
to the right nor to the left, reached City Hall. Up on the
roof, an hour later, stood a Federal commander, ready to
haul down the flag of Louisiana. In the street below
gleamed the bayonets of the United States Marines. Two
howitzers were loaded and aimed at the mob. Rioters
hooted, jeered, and pointed cocked pistols at the man
on the roof, as Mayor John T. Monroe, fearful of violence
and bloodshed, came out of City Hall, stood before the
howitzers, folded his arms, and eyed the gunners. Down
came the flag. There was solemn silence.[90] New Orleans
was still. The Queen City of the South, the richest and
most garish city of the Confederacy, had fallen to the
United States Navy, April 26, 1862.

She fell because she deserved to fall. The Army and
Navy had acted autonomously; commanders were not
sure who controlled what. Richmond had given command
to officers unfamiliar with the river and had been nig-

gardly with arms. A lack of vision had forced New Orleans to depend upon fire boats, river obstructions, and fixed batteries. Instead of letting contracts to seasoned ship-builders, the Confederate Navy had been hoodwinked by fast-talking operators. The demands of Beauregard, try-ing to stem the tide in Tennessee, held part of the Rebel fleet at Memphis and kept Louisiana and Mississippi troops in the front line. The pressures from the Cairo flo-tilla and the Gulf squadron were slowly sapping the life out of the Confederacy all along the Mississippi River.

At Amite, Louisiana, two old maids sat gloomily by the fire and tried to believe that the fall of New Orleans was a false rumor.[91] In Jackson, Mississippi, the governor called out the state militia.[92] Near Corinth, a private threatened to desert to defend New Orleans.[93] To charges of draining Louisiana, Beauregard argued that if his Army had been routed, New Orleans might have capitulated sooner.[94]

Newspapers throughout the Confederacy fired a bar-rage of invective at Richmond. The *Norfolk Day Book* considered the defeat the most deplorable tale ever told in North America; the Atlanta *Intelligencer* prepared for the worst; the Alexandria *Democrat* asked all states to quit sending troops for the defense of Richmond; the Richmond *Dispatch* charged apathy in high places.[95]

Mallory did not sleep for three nights. The shock of New Orleans almost killed him. On the floor of the House of Representatives, a Confederate congressman from Mississippi moved to abolish the office of the Secretary of the Navy.[96]

Officially, the defeat at New Orleans was blamed on Mallory. When the Union recaptured Norfolk and the Navy Yard, and the crew of the *Virginia* destroyed her to

prevent her capture, public indignation grew to fever
pitch. The Confederate Congress called for a full-dress
investigation of the Navy Department. After a thorough
examination, however, Mallory was exonerated and even
praised.[97]

The Confederate loss had serious repercussions abroad.
In France the *Presse* reported that the "fate of the rebellion . . . is now . . . an accomplished fact."[98] A French
Cabinet member whispered to a Confederate agent that
if New Orleans had not fallen, the South's recognition
would have been assured.[99] Even the London *Times,*
sympathetic with the Southern cause, intimated for the
first time that it saw little chance for the South.[100]

State officials and municipal authorities, New Orleans
bankers and Louisiana farmers believed that Richmond
had sold them down the river. The Confederate Army
had retreated in shameful fashion. "How much longer is
Louisiana to be considered beneath the consideration of
the Confederate Government?" blustered Governor
Moore, who had set up headquarters at Opelousas. From
now on, he threatened, all arms bought with Louisiana
money would remain in the state.[101]

On May 1, General Butler and his Army arrived in
New Orleans. Union troops paraded through the streets,
led by the 31st Massachusetts and the band of the 4th
Wisconsin. The New Orleans mob surged along the pave-
ments on either side of the marching troops, struggling
to catch sight of General Butler, crying, "Where is the
damned rascal?" "There he goes, God damn him!" Cake
stands overturned. Tin coffee pots rolled in the gutters.
General Butler concentrated upon keeping in step with
the music. In Canal Street the parade broke up. The 31st
Massachusetts occupied the vast, unfinished Custom

House. The 30th Massachusetts bunked in the Odd Fellows Hall, while other regiments lodged at the Mint, Lafayette Square, and Lyceum Hall and at a boarding house on Poydras Street.[102]

At the point of a gun, a hackman drove General Butler, Mrs. Butler, and her hairdresser to the St. Charles Hotel, which was boarded up and shut tight. In loud, harsh tones Butler gave the proprietor his choice: to open up and receive Union officers willing to pay or to have the hotel turned into a barrack. The hotel keeper relented, and Butler and his staff moved in. A regiment was drawn up around the hotel, and four howitzers were placed on the street corners.[103]

At once Butler issued proclamations to deal with the problems of banks, consuls, refugees, cotton, and prisoners, while his soldiers flushed out Rebels hiding in the bayous.

Farragut's follow-up attack stalled. The Army and Navy had no adequate, predetermined, well-coordinated plan to push the victory, to capitalize on the enemy's initial shock. The Navy lacked ships of suitable draft to steam up-river; the Army, sufficient troops to move beyond New Orleans. For their short-sightedness, the Union was to pay dearly.

General Butler insisted that an expedition should start for the mouth of the Red River and cut off Confederate supplies moving eastward.[104] But even with scant know-how of river navigation, Farragut understood that if deep-drafted, ocean-going steamers ascended the Mississippi, they probably would never return; the current was too swift, and the shoals were too hazardous. He determined to strike Mobile, although Porter begged him not to leave the river. In Washington, Fox announced that the rebellion was caving in and that the Navy could easily capture the entire Gulf coast. Welles hoped that Farragut already was in Memphis.[105]

On board the *Hartford,* moored to the New Orleans wharf, Farragut reiterated that Mobile presented the best target. He ordered Porter to move his schooners to Ship Island and await the sloops and gunboats.[106]

Throughout May, Porter lingered in the Gulf. To keep his mortars in fighting trim, Porter and his schooners sailed off to Florida and captured defenseless Pensacola and took soundings and laid buoys near Mobile Bay in anticipation of the attack. Back at Ship Island, he was convinced that his mortars, four gunboats, and 6,000 shells could liquidate the port.[107]

Porter was outraged when he learned that Farragut was steaming northward for Vicksburg without the mortar boats. The commander angrily asserted that Farragut would jump the mud bars and attack Vicksburg in balloons inflated by his own hot air, by gas generated at the capture of New Orleans.[108]

Farragut was acting against his own judgment; he had received confidential orders from Fox to push up-river and meet the western flotilla. The Navy Department considered the Mississippi River more important than Mobile. If Farragut could reach Memphis, Beauregard would be cut off from escape into the trans-Mississippi West.

8
"They Send Us All the Rubbish"

In Washington, D. C., at the Navy Department, Gideon Welles's desk was flooded with letters suggesting devices and schemes for combating the enemy afloat: waterclad vessels, India rubber monitors, land monitors, submarines equipped to bore holes in ships' bottoms, systems for blowing Benzine into wooden gunboats, men-of-war without crews mechanically controlled by sailors five miles away.[1] Engineer Charles Ellet, Jr. bombarded the Navy Department with letters on how to demolish ironclads like the *Virginia* with steam rams.

Absorbed with the task of building monitors for Atlantic and Gulf duty, Welles had no time to sift the practical inventions from the crackpot. Receiving no sympathy from the Navy, concluding that Welles was "weak-minded," Charles Ellet, Jr. hurried off to the War Department.[2]

Every morning in his reception room, Secretary Edwin Stanton gave an hour to the public. With a quick step he came through the door and took his stand behind a high writing desk, which reached to his shoulders. His eyes, large and piercing behind steel-rimmed glasses, darted over the waiting petitioners. He had an hour to give, and no more.

At one of these sessions, Ellet warned Stanton that the Rebels were massing iron-sheathed rams to strike Union vessels and destroy the blockade at sea. He proposed fast-charging rams, unarmed, unprotected, depending upon speed alone, to attack Confederate ironclads roaming around Hampton Roads.

When Stanton learned from General Henry W. Halleck that the Rebels were building ironclads along the Mississippi to raze Foote's flotilla and hold the Northwest at bay, he remembered Ellet and ordered him West to convert steamers into rams within twenty days. Haste was paramount.[3]

Commissioned a colonel in the United States Army, Ellet took the train from Washington. In Pittsburgh, after registering at the Monongahela House, he met with shipping bosses, threatened to seize vessels if they held out for exorbitant prices, and bought three powerful tow-boats, *Lioness, Samson,* and *Dick Fulton,* and two smaller but extremely powerful craft, *Mingo* and *Horner,* to act as tenders.[4]

Supervised by Ellet, work gangs cleared off the upper cabins and fitted each hull with three solid timber bulk-heads secured by iron rods, arranged to make each craft almost immune from longitudinal shock. As a sole defer-ence to defense, laborers shored up the boilers with a double tier of oak planks and plated the pilot house. The colonel refused to arm the rams or drop the boilers into the holds or sheath the hulls. Surprise, speed, and strength formed the backbone of Ellet's aggressive tactics. Once past the Confederate forts, the rams could make no re-turn. They would either control the Mississippi or be sunk in the attempt.[5]

To avoid the implication of favoritism and to marshal

the entire industrial energy of the Ohio Valley, the colonel extended his operations from Pittsburgh to Cincinnati, Ohio, and New Albany, Indiana. Although wined and dined by high-pressure delegations eager to peddle second-rate vessels, the discerning and systematic Ellet carefully chose only four additional steamers: *Queen of the West, Monarch, Switzerland,* and *Lancaster.*[6]

Along the waterfront, United States Navy inspectors jeered at these apologies for men-of-war and watched, dumbfounded, as ordinary house carpenters worked on the rams. Two leaked so badly that roustabouts pumped day and night until they were patched up.[7] Fleet Captain Alexander M. Pennock, from Cairo, snapped, "I am glad that the Navy is not responsible."[8]

Ellet searched the cities for crews. Stanton promised prize money for captured vessels and an extra month's pay for every fortified Rebel position that the fleet passed.[9] Except for a few volunteers from the Ellet family—son Charles, aged nineteen, and brother Alfred, an officer in the 59th Illinois—the colonel manned his boats with daring river men, pilots, engineers, and deck hands. When the rams were ready for combat, in May, 1862, Secretary Stanton committed a serious military blunder by instructing Colonel Ellet to operate in the rivers independent of Foote's command.

General Halleck, meanwhile, had purchased the side-wheelers *Lafayette* (ex-*Alex Scott*) and *Choctaw* (ex-*Nebraska*)—1,000 tons each—and gave the job of converting them into ironclad rams to David D. Porter's cousin William Porter, who, still suffering from burns received at Fort Henry, prided himself on pioneering in building a river navy.

On the *Choctaw,* Porter constructed a stationary "war

dome"—"like the Dome on the Court House in St. Louis,"
pierced it with four ports, and mounted two guns. Workmen protected the turret with armor designed by Porter
composed of two layers of iron and one inch of vulcanized
India rubber cushions supported by two feet of oak
timber. The *Choctaw* and *Lafayette* were armed with
Parrott rifles, Dahlgrens, and 24-pounders and carried
platforms amidships for two 12-inch mortars.

Porter also shouldered the responsibility of refitting
the *Essex,* disabled at the battle of Fort Henry. He
stripped her to the water line, chopped off the bow, added
forty feet to her length, and completely rebuilt her.[10]

River men accused Porter of insanity. The Cincinnati
Daily Commercial growled that Washington had assigned
a salt-water sailor to do a river man's work.[11] Meigs questioned the propriety of rebuilding a rotten ferryboat, as
the probabilities of opening the Mississippi before she
was finished seemed excellent.[12]

Disregarding advice, oblivious to criticism, Porter
plunged into debt, complained of Washington's niggardly
allotments, and, by mid-June 1862, announced that the
Essex was ready.[13]

On her first trial run, accompanied by twenty guests
including General John M. Schofield, the *Essex* left the
St. Louis wharf at the foot of Carr Street, stood out in the
river, and steamed against the current, her engines working well.

Her casemates were much higher now, higher than
those of any gunboat in western waters. Her hull was
entirely buried in the water. Carpenters had set her
wheels in a recess at the stern, bombproofed the roof, and
built false sides and watertight compartments to prevent
an effective blow by an enemy ram. Mechanics had pro-

vided her with two engines and three boilers—newer and larger—placed below the waterline. She carried three 9-inch Dahlgrens, one 10-incher, and one 42-and two 50-pounders.

As the *Essex* passed the *Tyler* and the Eagle Foundry, sailors and mechanics ashore cheered and waved Union flags. Moving up-river five miles, the *Essex* turned and charged down-stream. In the spacious wardroom, guests toasted Porter with champagne and were impressed with his "apartment," which was furnished with heavy Oriental rugs, ornate chairs, tables, and a bed.[14]

The Cairo command inspected the half-finished *Eastport*, captured after the collapse of Fort Henry, and predicted that she could easily be put into fighting trim. Her side timbers and machinery were already complete, the boilers had been dropped in the hold, and her hull appeared sound.[15] But by the first of April, upon close examination, inspectors discovered that the *Eastport* was far from ready.[16]

She had grown from hull to gunboat without elaborate plans or specifications. To her sharp bow, laborers secured a wrought iron ram weighing 5,700 pounds, crossed and bolted together into a compact mass and extending back thirty-four feet from the bow. Launched in July 1862, readied in August, her bottom deteriorating by September, the *Eastport* was returned to Cairo for complete rebuilding in October.

Authorities in Washington, haunted by phantom Confederate ironclad rams, noted Foote's difficulties at Island No. 10 and Fort Pillow and decided to build more gunboats.[17] Stanton asked contractors for plans and promptly turned them over to the Navy, who now, after months of official bickering, took the responsibility of constructing river gunboats.

Welles received reams of advice. General Meigs urged impregnable vessels; the War Department, craft with drafts less than six feet; William Porter, side-wheelers, not propellers.[18]

A board of naval experts in Washington, men ignorant in the ways of a western river, swayed by the exploits of John Ericsson's monitors, paying scant heed to Foote's insistence upon maneuverability, steam power, and protection from plunging shot, recommended turreted vessels and signed contracts with James Eads, Joseph Brown of Cincinnati, Tomlinson and Hartupee of Pittsburgh, and the Bestor brothers of Mound City for the *Winnebago, Milwaukee, Kickapoo, Chickasaw, Marietta, Sandusky, Ozark, Chillicothe, Indianola,* and *Tuscumbia* and for two paddle-wheel iron monitors, *Osage* and *Neosho.*[19]

At the Carondelet Marine Railway and Dry Dock Company, Eads erected mammoth frame sheds to house the hulls and a machine shop equipped with fourteen forges and machinery for punching and bending the iron plates. Mechanics swarmed into the shipyard, fastened and fitted the side armor, secured the rudder skegs to the sterns, cut holes for propeller shafts, laid and riveted the iron deck, fitted hatch combings and transom beams, trimmed the bulkheads for turret machinery, and worked on engine keelsons.

Iron from the Maumee River was rolled by Gaylord and Son at Portsmouth, Ohio, and freighted to Carondelet. Mechanics heated the plates in the long furnace, then raised them by block and tackle and, hauling them by crane to the press, forced the top block down hard and squeezed the mass of iron into the desired shape. In half an hour the plates acquired a permanent set and, when they were taken out, mechanics punched holes in them for the bolts, planed the edges, and laid and riveted them on the ways.[20]

Eads ran headlong into trouble. Mechanics left to enlist in the Army or serve with commercial steamboats or were caught in the state of Missouri's crackdown to enroll men for the militia. Workers in Illinois, Indiana, and Ohio would not step foot in Missouri. Transportation lagged. Every light draft boat on the river worked for the government, and mill owners were reduced to using slow-moving barges. To dislodge the logjam and rush the boats to completion, Eads paid enormous wages and finagled from Welles the steamer *Bostona* to haul iron from Portsmouth to Carondelet.[21]

Eads's experimental monitors, *Osage* and *Neosho*, iron rafts each with a single revolving Ericsson turret armed with two 11-inchers, were light draft stern-wheelers fitted also with propellers. The large houses for the paddle wheels, turret, and tall thin stacks were the only things visible above the water line.

When the *Osage* left Cairo in May 1863, she grounded. Two days later, testing her cannon, gunners fired two rounds and disabled the turret. Too unwieldy to steam up-river, she had to be hauled in by tug. The *Neosho*, barely stemming the current, would neither turn or handle properly. Contractor Eads set about altering both monitors to meet the demands of the river war.[22]

Laborers pounded away on the ironclads *Chickasaw*, *Kickapoo*, *Milwaukee*, and *Winnebago*, larger in dimensions than the monitors, each carrying two revolving turrets—one designed by Ericsson, the other by Eads—

and mounting two 11-inch Dahlgrens. Eads boasted that his turrets were superior to those of John Ericsson as the guns were placed on movable platforms, enabling the crews to load them in the safety of the hold. Only nine men were needed to handle both guns, compared with the thirty-six required on the sea-going monitors.[23]

Inspectors entertained grave doubts as to the fighting qualities of these Eads ironclads.[24] Could their hulls withstand the severe battering, the plunging shot of the enemy? Except for their batteries of 11-inch guns, these ironclads could not measure up to the Pook turtles or to the *Benton*, the best fighter in the flotilla.[25]

In Cincinnati, Joseph Brown struggled with the side-wheeled, flat-bottomed, turreted ironclads: *Tuscumbia, Indianola,* and *Chillicothe*. The hull of the *Chillicothe,* the smallest of the three, was too unsteady to hold the massive decks and, when engineers installed the boilers, the bottom sank ten inches. Assured that the boilers would go through the bottom at any minute, the naval inspector grimly observed, "I have never met with a more complete failure." With eighteen tons of iron hanging on it, the bow pulled away from the deck. The accommodations were terrible: no ventilation, no space, no light. The crew cursed the excessive heat in the engine room and could not remain below decks longer than twenty minutes. A general came on board and went below only to explode up the ladder, bellowing that he was suffocating. He suggested that the *Chillicothe* be abandoned, and that all work be stopped. The commanding officer protested about his ovenlike cabin and asked for immediate transfer.

Brown installed iron rods running fore and aft under the deck to draw the bow and deck together, secured hog chains, added to the *Chillicothe's* depth of hold to give head room to the crew, lengthened the hull to make room for the machinery, and poured heated cement to run under the iron plates to seal the leaks.[26]

On her trial run from Cincinnati to New Albany, the *Chillicothe*, entirely iron plated and furnished with steam capstans to haul her over mud bars, performed admirably. Clambering off, Brown boasted that the *Chillicothe* was so watertight that even the bilge water smelled.[27] But when Lieutenant Commander John Walker took the gunboat in October 1862, he pronounced her a "cumbersome scow."[28]

Mechanics bungled the ironwork on the *Indianola* and *Tuscumbia,* both of which lacked accommodations for officers and crew. Brown dismantled the iron plates on the bow to make them fit more snugly and built stern casemates.[29] On their trial trips they worked well and in February 1863 the *Tuscumbia* and *Indianola*—"She is worth the whole fleet at Cairo," bragged Brown—were in commission.[30]

At Mound City the Bestor brothers readied the *Ozark*. With the blessings of the Cairo command, Isaac Whittaker, engineer and inventor of sorts, installed an apparatus for firing torpedoes under water.[31] Wary inspectors watching carpenters build fore and aft bulkheads in the hull and mount a submarine battery feared that the *Ozark* might trim at the bow.[32] Their concern prompted Washington to suspend work and order the invention removed. But even without it the *Ozark* trimmed badly, her engines lacked power, she leaked, her machinery was faulty, her turret failed, and she required an enormous quantity of coal, more than any other ship in the entire United States Navy.[33]

For patrol in the Tennessee and Cumberland Rivers, the command purchased light draft steamers and plated their casemates with a thin sheet of iron.[34] Armed with two guns apiece, these boats were known as tinclads, a misnomer. The first of these tinclads—*Brilliant* and *St. Clair*, stern-wheelers from Pittsburgh—took station in August 1862 and were joined by the *Marmora*, *Signal*, *Glide*, *Cricket*, *Silver Lake*, *Romeo*, *Rattler*, *Linden*, *Hastings*, *Silver Cloud*, *Champion No. 4*, *Springfield*, *Duchess*, *Mary Miller*, *Florence*, *Forest Rose*, *Juliet*, *Covington No. 1*, *Queen City No. 3*, *Argosy*, *Key West*, *Thompson*, *Kenwood*, *Fanny Barker*, and *Exchange*. The captured Confederate gunboats *General Pillow*, *Fairplay*, and *Robb* were converted and sent to the Tennessee River.

Yet ships are useless unless maintained, provisioned, and manned. The Western Flotilla added auxiliary vessels. The *Swallow* was fitted up as a floating blacksmith shop with forges, drills, and lathes. The tugs *Restless* and *Resolute* were pressed into service to tow gunboats up-stream. The *Great Western* and *Judge Torrence* served as ammunition schooners; the *Red Rover*, as a hospital ship.

The duties of Fleet Captain Alexander M. Pennock and the officers of his command at Cairo were extensive. All munitions, all stores, all recruits, upon which the gunboats depended, were funneled through the southern Illinois depot to be distributed down-river. The flotilla experienced serious interruptions in this flow of supplies. But the resources of the North were so superior to those of the South that Union sailors were amply provisioned in contrast to the men who served on the Rebel gunboats. The Union flotilla overcame deficiencies by borrowing from the military and, frequently, the War Department ordered it to draw subsistence from the Army directly, when engaged in joint military and naval expeditions.

Vital to the squadron's efficiency were the hundreds of tons of coal a month that moved southward, towed in barges, to feed the ironclads. Cairo advertised for bids in newspapers and awarded contracts to bidders who offered the lowest and most acceptable propositions. While the fleet was fighting within a hundred miles of Cairo, the coal problem was one of getting prompt deliveries, but as the war advanced the gunboats began steaming out of easy reach of the colliers, and they turned to burning cordwood and fence rails.

Month by month Northern industry overcame the lag that sudden demand had occasioned. The flotilla's ordnance officer came to rely less and less upon the Army. Once industry rolled into high gear, the gunboats never lacked ammunition and guns. The Army's antiquated 42-pounders, which burst if fired too frequently, were rolled into the Mississippi as soon as the new 8-inch shell guns arrived.

The Navy's biggest headache was manpower. Not a vessel left Cairo with a full complement of officers and men. Cairo reported that the *Eastport* lacked 150 sailors, the *Tyler* was short 105, the *Lexington* and *Conestoga* lacked thirty each, and forty per cent of the *Benton's* men were either sick or wounded.[35]

Naval officers journeyed eastward from Cairo, printed circulars and posters, and opened their own recruiting station at 346 Water Street in New York City. They posted handbills in all post offices on the railroad line from Chicago and Cairo and appointed businessmen in towns and hamlets to act as agents.[36]

The Navy experimented by hiring contrabands, Negroes who were former slaves, to serve in the western command.

Swarms of Negroes flocked to the protection of the Union flag and volunteered for duty, not as seamen, but as boys with a wage of $8 per month plus one ration.[37] Some skippers had serious misgivings over fighting alongside the contrabands. There were occasional incidents. In a display of vicious cruelty, Acting Master's Mate Frank Love kicked two Negroes, thrashed them with his fists and a capstan bar, and swore that he would shoot them and "any damned officer that took their part."[38]

Volunteers from the Army filled some vacancies. By the spring of 1863, 800 soldiers and 600 contrabands were fighting in the gunboats on western rivers.[39]

The castoffs from Eastern ports and the rowdy river men appalled Regular Navy officers with their lack of discipline. "They send us all the rubbish here," complained the flag officer.[40] Troublemakers abounded. The most notorious ruffian in the flotilla, James Brandon, resisted the boatswain when discovered tampering with the drug locker, hurled a spittoon at the executive officer, struck the guard with a shovel, pushed an invalid overboard, and escaped from the brig before he was finally clamped in the Cairo guardhouse.[41]

Most officers and men wanted transfer to Atlantic duty. The Western service tore them down, physically and mentally. "I am worn and weary," testified a lieutenant. "I weigh 20 pounds less than I did when I came to the West, and have not had one day's rest from duty since."[42]

Crews stifled in the low, unventilated "Federal bake ovens" of the ironclads, with the steam and fire of the engine rooms below and the intense rays of the sun above. Oftentimes the temperature pushed 110° F. in the shade. To escape the smothering humidity, all hands swam in the limpid, sluggish waters of the rivers. The mosquitoes, flies, varmints, and bugs grew worse as the squadron moved south.[43]

Surgeons reported cases of heart palpitation, scurvy, measles, brain tumor, bronchitis, rheumatism, diarrhea, dysentery, subtropical fevers. The sick and the halt reported to the hospital ship *Red Rover* or to the Mound City Hotel, rigged up to accommodate 250 patients.

Liquor was the curse of the squadron. Officers and men drank freely, and many suffered kidney diseases aggravated by the "Cairo rotgut." Lieutenant Fyffee arrived in Cairo drunk, reported for duty drunk, and stayed drunk.[44]

When the gunboats arrived in Cairo for repair and overhaul, Navy courts were jammed. Individual officers and men were charged with such offenses as neglect of duty, gross inefficiency, desertion, theft, pillaging the homes of peaceful citizens, conniving with the enemy, sleeping on watch, and rape. Punishment was quick and severe. Seamen who deserted were sentenced to be shot. Richmond Cornelius, Negro, was found guilty of mutinous conduct and striking an officer and was hanged.[45] For insubordination, sailors were whisked away to prison for four years. Seaman John Walker of the *Tyler* was given ten years for calling his captain a "God damned Dutch son-of-a-bitch" and telling him "to kiss my arse."[46] Farragut claimed that many officers acted insubordinately to insure being transferred or sent home.[47]

Patrol duty on the rivers was irksome at best. In between gun drills, reconnaissance missions, and forays after Rebel guerrillas, gunboatmen swabbed decks and performed other chores. In the evenings, on the fantail, men played cards or sang snatches of homely songs.

Oh, give me the girl with the blue dress on,
  The white folks call Susanna;
She stole my heart and away she's gone
  Way down to Louisiana.[48]

Richmond stepped up the manufacture of underwater mines. Mississippians and Louisianans dumped demijohns filled with powder into the streams and creeks. Engineers set adrift "guerrilla torpedoes," mines secured to logs bearing bales of cotton to attract attention.[49]

The Confederate Navy Department looked to the defense of the Red River and authorized Lieutenant Jonathan Carter to construct ironclads at Shreveport.[50] The Louisiana Legislature appropriated $1,000,000 for additional rams.[51] Boatswain Chester Condon hurried to Houston, Texas, to collect iron to plate the sloop *Missouri,* building at Shreveport.[52] The 650-ton wooden steam ram *Webb* lay moored at Alexandria on the Red River.

At Memphis, Constructor John Shirley was building the ironclad rams *Arkansas* and *Tennessee.* When Foote's armada passed Columbus and Island No. 10 and began hammering at Fort Pillow, desperate Rebels scuttled the partly built *Tennessee* and moved the *Arkansas*—her woodwork completed, her hull covered with iron to the main deck—to Greenwood, Mississippi, on the Yazoo River.[53]

When Commander Isaac Brown took command of the *Arkansas,* guns and machinery lay scattered about her decks. The timber for the gun carriages was still growing in the woods. Only one blacksmith shop was geared to Brown's demands. In two days Brown moved the *Arkansas* to Yazoo City, rigged up steam drills, brought iron in wagons from the railroad twenty-five miles away, corralled fourteen forges and 200 carpenters, called on planters for slaves and overseers. Changing the original specifications of the *Arkansas,* which called for a solid bow and stern, he mounted two 8-inch Columbiads in the newly cut bow ports; two 9-inch Dahlgren shell guns, two 6-inch rifles, and two 32-pounders in broadside; and two 6-inchers astern. Machinists installed two low-pressure engines, Memphis-made, and two propellers and secured the boilers beneath the water line.[54]

The *Arkansas* resembled a cross between the flat-bottomed river boats and the keel-built ocean-going steamers. Her bow was sharp, her stem tapered, the center of the hull broad, her sides perpendicular, the bottom nearly flat. Mechanics arranged iron armor to form a nearly solid mass, about three inches thick, backed by timber and compressed cotton bales. Dovetailed together, the ordinary railroad iron ran horizontally along the sides; the boiler iron sheathing for the quarters and stern, vertically. "What she was designed for, no man probably knows," exclaimed an observer, who, after inspecting her, termed her a "two-sexed monstrosity."[55]

To battle enemy ironclads and tinclads, mortar boats and rams, ammunition schooners and supply craft, Farragut's squadron and Foote's flotilla, the South was forced to depend upon the *Arkansas,* a handful of cottonclad rams and gunboats at Memphis, and a few vessels up the Red River. In war no sudden signal tells men that their cause is lost. For a long time on the river, the Confederacy had been short of matériel, workmen, equipment, boats, and guns—the machinery of war. A sense of defeat grew slowly, month by month, year by year, until the defenders were standing on the edge of emptiness and had, in spirit, accepted disaster as inevitable.

"We Will Chaw Them Up in Just an Hour"

Off Fort Pillow on May 9, 1862, Flag Officer Charles Henry Davis—Boston born, Harvard bred—boarded the flagship *Benton,* saluted the quarter-deck, wended his way to Foote's cabin, and found him in bed. Davis was shocked at the sight of this pale, emaciated man.[1]

Talk centered on the war. The Union blockade at sea was tightening. On the Eastern front, the vast Army of the Potomac—112,000 strong—was on the Peninsula with a firm hold on its base at Fort Monroe. Yorktown, Virginia, had fallen to McClellan's troops on May 4. Here on the Western front, the Shiloh campaign was stalemated. General Beauregard's Army stood fast at Corinth, and Fort Pillow was impeding the Union flotilla's descent of the river.

Foote rambled on about the campaign, but his conversation with Davis was interrupted by the whistle of the boatswain's pipe mustering the crew on the lower deck. The invalid emerged from the cabin on crutches supported by Davis, Lieutenant Phelps, and two sailors. In words hardly audible to the crew, Foote muttered: "Farewell, you will be victorious. The Mississippi will be open to all men—all nations—before ten days. God bless you. Good-by!" Exhausted from the ordeal, he slumped into a chair for several minutes. Regaining his strength and with seamen carrying his trunk, Foote limped off the *Benton* into the *DeSoto* for the trip back to Cairo and a Northern tour of convalescence.

That evening over the wardroom table, discussing future operations with his lieutenants, Davis decided to continue Foote's tactics—the tedious, long-range bombardment of Fort Pillow—and to await developments. Dinner over, the conversation at an end, Davis retired to his cabin and, despite the smells, noises, and heat, slept soundly.[2]

That same night, down-river beyond Craigshead Point, Captain Montgomery, C. S. A., of the River Defense Command, and his men met on the flagship *Little Rebel*. They had assembled eight fast cottonclad rams, left over from New Orleans, and were ready to engage the lone Union ironclad, which stood guard as the mortar boats lobbed shells into Fort Pillow.[3] In a corner of the dimly lit cabin sat Jeff Thompson, skipper of the *General Bragg*, Brigadier-General of the Missouri State Guards. Jeff was a legend along the river, the Missouri Swamp Fox who fed on ramrods and packed a bowie knife stuck perpendicularly in his belt.[4]

The next day at 6:30 a.m., the sun was already turning hot as the mortar boats were towed into firing position, convoyed by the *Cincinnati*. Scarcely had they moored and the gunners hoisted the shells, when the ram *General Bragg* darted around the point, black smoke gushing from her stack, guns blazing at the *Cincinnati*. One ram, two, then six more came into view. The *Cincinnati*, with hardly enough steam up to turn a wheel, slipped her cables, ponderously swung out into the stream, and tried to maneuver below the enemy to fight up-river, bow on. She was an easy target. On came the *General Bragg*. The *Cincinnati* fired a broadside. Cotton bales shot into the air. Splinters flew, but the *General Bragg* steamed on, firing, her shots thudding against the iron sides of the *Cincinnati*. The bow of the ironclad spun around. The two boats crashed together. "Give'r another broadside, boys," shouted the *Cincinnati's* commander. The men let go a salvo at pointblank range. The Rebel, hurt severely, hauled off, disabled, her tiller ropes severed.

The second ram, *General Price*, charged at the ironclad and crushed three feet into her fantail, demolishing the rudders. The *Cincinnati's* stern swung crazily toward the oncoming *Sumter*. "Haul down your flag and we will save you!" cried the Confederates.

"Our flag will go down when we do!" answered the Yankees. The crash came. Water poured into the *Cincinnati*. The black gang stood waist deep in the engine room. Magazines flooded. Sharpshooters on the *General Lovell* sprayed the *Cincinnati's* decks with musket fire. *Cincinnati's* commander Roger Stembel drew his pistol, took aim, fired, and killed the *General Lovell's* pilot. Seconds later, Stembel was felled by a Minie ball in his month. First Master William R. Hoel rushed down the gun deck and sang out: "Boys, give 'em the best you've got!"[5] The guns of the *Cincinnati* thundered for the last time. She rolled first to starboard, then to port, gave a convulsive shudder, and went down bow first near the mud bank.

By this time, the *Benton, Carondelet, St. Louis,* and *Mound City,* moored three miles up-river, were under way. The *St. Louis* bore down on the enemy and hit the wooden hull of a ram amidships. The Rebel sank, her crew clinging to the sides of the *St. Louis*. The *Carondelet* opened fire on two rams, exploding the boilers of one. Ramming at full speed, the Rebel *Van Dorn* collided with the bow of the *Mound City* and sank her. The *Benton,* mauling the enemy with shellfire, moved toward two rams and gave them a blast; then, as she wheeled to starboard, her stern guns discharged. Again and again the *Benton* circled, delivering a withering sheet of fire. Enemy rams tried to reach her, but were beaten back.

The *Beauregard, General Lovell, Jeff Thompson,* and *Little Rebel* pulled away from the ironclads and peppered them with shot and shell. The water was too shallow, and their guns were too inferior, for the rams to cope with the full flotilla of ironclads. In ten inmutes, the issue was settled. The rams withdrew down-stream to the protection of Fort Pillow.[6]

The Yankees had been caught napping. Davis had sent no picket boat down-river to warn against a surprise. Not even the *Cincinnati* had sufficient steam up to protect herself. The rams had struck quickly and retreated as planned. In this fleet collision on the upper river, the first full day of Davis's command, Confederate cottonclads had sunk the ironclads *Cincinnati* and *Mound City.* Her steam pumps hissing, the auxiliary craft *Champion* raised and floated the two hulks, which were towed back to Cairo for repairs. Visibly shaken from this ordeal, Flag Officer Davis demanded that the Army unit form a protective cover by establishing batteries on the Arkansas shore, and he ordered deck hands to hang extra railroad iron on the bows and sterns of the gunboats.[7]

Colonel Ellet and his rams arrived for active duty. The careful, defense-minded Davis immediately squelched the plans of this daredevil. He refused to hazard another encounter with the Rebel fleet and vetoed Ellet's plan to rush the batteries. To the conservative and unimaginative Davis, the ironclads and rams bore the same relationship as heavy artillery and light field pieces.

Antagonizing Davis, Ellet responded that the risk was greater if the ironclads lay back and let the cottonclads pick them off one by one as they had the *Cincinnati* and *Mound City*. Ellet was painfully blunt. He was acting on orders from the War Department in Washington, not the Western Flotilla in the Mississippi. His rams were built to hurtle into the enemy and sink them. Delay would be fatal. Incensed by Davis's inaction, Ellet decided to run the batteries alone.

On June 3 he readied the *Queen of the West* and *Monarch* to round Craigshead Point and smash into the enemy lying under the guns of Fort Pillow. The captain, two pilots, the first mate, all the engineers, and the deck hands, sensing danger, deserted the *Queen of the West*. Hastily recruiting a makeshift crew from the other rams, Ellet took personal command.

The Rebel steamers slipped their lines and escaped down-river before the *Queen of the West* and *Monarch* reached them. An angry Ellet wrote Stanton, deriding Davis for his weak-kneed tactics.[8]

Unknown to either Davis or Ellet, General Beauregard had withdrawn his Army from Corinth and ordered the evacuation of Fort Pillow. He fell back to Tupelo, Mississippi, and pondered. The Confederates would make a last-ditch effort to hold the Mississippi River at Vicksburg. For awhile, he opined, Vicksburg would stand against the enemy, but she, too, would fall like so many other positions for want of men, guns, and matériel.[9]

The fifth of June dawned hot, cloudy, humid. Colonel

Ellet had moved down during the night for reconnaissance and, finding no enemy, landed that morning and hoisted the Stars and Stripes above Fort Pillow. The battlements were in good condition, and the guns but indifferently spiked. After the arrival of the Navy, Lieutenant Phelps of the *Benton* realized that Foote and Davis had blundered and wasted a whole month. Inspection of the casemates and bluffs revealed that the Confederates could not have depressed their guns, that the Yankee ironclads, by clinging to the banks, could easily have passed unscathed.[10]

Leaving a small force to occupy the fort and the *Pittsburg* to guard it, the entire expedition headed down-river for Memphis. The night was clear and mild. Spyglasses scanned the shores to catch the first glimpse of the river port. "There's Memphis! Don't you see the lights on the bluff?" exclaimed Master Bates of the *Benton*. Two miles north at Island No. 45, Phelps asked: "How is the water? Can we anchor here?"

Pilot Dan Duffy nodded: "Yes, sir, there's plenty of water."

"Then round the *Benton* to."

The anchor went down and Davis's tug, *Jessie Benton,* snorted off to notify the other gunboats and transports. Gleefully, officers boasted that they would be drinking mint juleps in the Gayoso House the next day.[11]

In Memphis, the city council resolved never to surrender voluntarily. Jeff Thompson talked of an easy victory. "We will chaw them up in just an hour."

"Are you sure of that?" questioned a friend.

"Certainly I am, there is no doubt of it."[12]

The night passed and dawn came, mild and clear with a brilliant sun. Yankees on the morning watch saw Memphis in the distance spread before them, elegant buildings with graceful domes and steeples. The steamboats *Hill, New National, Victoria, Kentucky,* and *Acadia* bobbed at the wharf. Sightseers with picnic baskets crowded the bluffs and levees to witness the fight.

All hands were drummed to quarters. Sailors hauled up anchors chanting the familiar "Heave ho! Heave ho!"

"Drop down toward the city, sir, and see if you can discover the Rebel fleet," Davis advised. To a staff officer: "Let the sailors have breakfast." Davis took his on deck— hardtack, a slice of "that salt junk," and coffee.[13]

The Rebel fleet rounded the point. The *General Bragg, General Price, Sumter, General Van Dorn, General Lovell, Jeff Thompson, Little Rebel,* and *General Beauregard* advanced in a double line.

The *Benton* neared the Tennessee shore trailed by the *Carondelet, St. Louis, Louisville,* and *Cairo.* On board the *St. Louis,* the skipper descended to the gun deck and passed from crew to crew cautioning them to be deliberate, not to fire without taking sure aim. "Here is a chance to distinguish yourselves," he said calmly, "and to sustain the fair reputation of the *St. Louis.*"[14]

The *Little Rebel* arrived opposite the upper end of the city and fired her bow gun, the shot passing over the Federal fleet. The *Benton's* cannon boomed.

Unaware of what was happening until he heard the shots, Ellet and his rams cast off and steamed boldly down-river, through the ironclads. "It is hardly possible that these rams will survive the action," Ellet cautioned his brother, "but they are sufficiently strong to take with them when they go down any enemy vessels of greater strength."[15]

The ram attack was unexpected and sudden. The

Queen of the West and *Monarch* tore into the enemy. The *Queen of the West* missed the *Beauregard* and crushed into the *General Lovell,* whose stacks careened dangerously over the bow of Ellet's ram. In less than thirty seconds, while the *Queen of the West* was still locked with the *Lovell,* the *Beauregard* struck the *Queen of the West* on the starboard side, damaging the tiller ropes. The *Queen of the West* broke loose. The *General Lovell,* her side caved in, sank. Her crew dove for the water, swimming, grasping for sticks of wood to stay afloat. Ellet, horror stricken, watched a Confederate, his left arm ripped off by cannon shot, beckon those on shore. The *Benton* launched a yawl in the thick of the fight to rescue the drowning Rebels.

The crippled *Queen of the West* was beached on the Arkansas shore. Ellet lay wounded on deck. The *Monarch* sped between two enemy rams. The *Beauregard* and *Price* missed the *Monarch* and plowed into each other. The *Beauregard* cut down the *Price* to the water line and tore off her port wheel. Locked together, they received a withering fire from the ironclads. The *Price* disencumbered herself and drifted toward shore. The *Benton's* shells blew up the *Beauregard.*

The other Union rams, *Switzerland* and *Lancaster,* moved about gingerly. The pilot of the *Lancaster* froze at the wheel and rang for reverse instead of full speed. She shot astern, plowed into the bank, and stuck fast. The *Switzerland,* confused and unsteady, failed to swing into action.[16]

From the Arkansas shore, Confederate musket balls mauled the *St. Louis.* The Masters Mate sang out: "Sharpshooters in the woods. Rake them with the broadside."

Volumes of white smoke belched from the *St. Louis*, felling trees, branches, and Confederates.[17]

The battle became a free-for-all. The fleets were enveloped in smoke. A shot lodged in her steam chest, the *Little Rebel* made for shore. The *Bragg, Sumter, Thompson,* and *Van Dorn* backed down full, turned, and sped down-stream, pursued by the *Monarch* and the ironclads. At President's Island, the *Bragg* and *Jeff Thompson* ran into the Arkansas mud, their crews escaping into the woods. The *Sumter* was captured. Only the *Van Dorn* fled to safety.[18]

A Yankee newsman described the victory as extensive, decisive, speedy, and effectual.[19] The *Lovell* had been sunk, by the *Queen of the West*; the *Bragg*, blown up; *Little Rebel,* disabled; *Jeff Thompson,* set on fire by Yankee shells and burned to the water's edge; the *Price* and *Sumter,* abandoned; the *Beauregard,* obliterated.

The South's River Defense Squadron, weaker in firepower and manned by military officers, had been helpless against the rams and ironclads. The cumbersome Union fleet had proved so easy a victim in the first engagement, that Montgomery had risked his cottonclads to save Memphis. But without the element of surprise the Rebels were unequal to the effort.

The battle at Memphis wiped out Confederate naval power on the upper Mississippi and opened the river as far as Vicksburg. Only the *Arkansas* and the Red River rams, operating singly, and the guns of Vicksburg stood between Davis and the open Gulf.

The mayor of Memphis surrendered the city at 3:00 p.m. and Federal troops tore down the Confederate flag from atop the Commercial Hotel. In the deserted telegraph office, soldiers found a note: "I leave this office to any Lincolnite successor, and will state that, although you can whip us on the water, if you will come out on land, we'll whip you like hell."[20]

Along the levee thousands of Negroes milled about the Federal ironclads. One correspondent asked a Negro what he thought of the battle. "O massa," was the reply, "I tinks a good deal of it. Uncle Abe's boats mighty powerful. Dey go through our boats just like dey was eggshells."[21]

News of the shattering victory raced northward. In Cleveland, Foote wrote Welles, "The grand object of my mission has been virtually accomplished."[22] Privately, Foote considered Davis extremely lucky—he had been in two fights, won the glory of capturing Memphis, all within a month.[23] At Cairo, Charles Ellet died of his wounds, and the command of the ram fleet was assumed by his brother, Alfred.

The river trade flourished. Two weeks after the melee, the Mississippi crawled with steamboats descending from St. Louis, Cincinnati, and Pittsburgh, their holds stuffed with cheese, butter, coffee, tea, flour, candy, soap, and luxury items. Memphis wharfs sagged beneath the weight of cotton and sugar awaiting shipment north.

The Gayoso House overflowed. Southerners cornered Cincinnati merchants and tried to prove that the welfare of the Northwest was inseparably connected with that of the unconquerable South. They described the Indiana troops in Memphis as mere instruments in the hands of New England fanatics. A few Tennesseans predicted that if the war lasted another year, the entire Northwest would be arrayed on the side of the South.[24]

Davis had little time for the joys of Memphis. Dispatches from the Navy Department and General Halleck, then with the Army in Mississippi, ordered the flotilla down-river. It was to steam up the White River to Jacksonport and rescue General Samuel R. Curtis, hard pressed by the Arkansas Rebels.[25]

The *Mound City*—recommissioned—and the *St. Louis, Lexington,* and *Conestoga* and the transports *New National* and *Musselman,* with Colonel Graham Fitch's 46th Indiana, turned into the White River—a narrow, crooked ditch—on June 16. Dense forests stood along the swampy banks dotted with persimmon and pecan trees and intertwined with canebrakes. Rarely did the sun sneak through into the dusk. Clouds of mosquitoes swarmed about the ironclads. From reliable sources, the Yankees learned that the Confederates were at St. Charles, but they found no St. Charles marked on the map or set down in James's *River Guide Book.*

At 8 a.m., June 17, the expedition spotted dead ahead a barricade of sunken hulls—the *Maurepas, Eliza K.,* and *Mary Peterson*—athwart the river. Up on the bluff, just below St. Charles, two 42-pounders and two 9-inchers commanded this bend of the river. For an hour the ironclads and gunboats shelled the woods. The *New National* and *Musselman* landed Fitch's Indiana farm boys. The *Mound City* steamed up and silenced the lower battery and headed for the second, two hundred yards away.

Captain Augustus Kilty and Mr. Nixon, the White River pilot, stood in the pilot house of the *Mound City.* In the wardroom, Mr. Gunn, the purser, played cards aimlessly. On the port side, forward, Emmanuel Stokes, Walter McClain, Jack McClintock, and J. P. Lee trained their Dahlgren. Masters Mate Dominey, forward on the starboard spar deck, shouted orders to the men.

A Confederate 42-pounder shot hurtled through the port side forward, burst the steam drum, and lodged in the pantry. Stokes's right shoulder and McClain's chest were carried away. McClintock and Lee were cut in two, just above the hips. Captain Kilty had just raised the trap door to pass orders below when steam exploded in his face. Nixon fell to the deck below, suffering a horrible death. Gunn jumped through the port of the wardroom to the fantail, hesitated, dashed back for his money, and died.

Distorted, scorched bodies were strewn on deck. The badly burned, shrieking from the excruciating pain, tore off clothing. "Help! Help—water, give me water, water, save me. Oh God! Save me, save me. Oh, kill me, shoot me. Oh! End my misery."

Mate Dominey pulled off his coat, covered his head, and screamed to the men not to jump overboard. Sixty sailors failed to heed his warning. Rebel sharpshooters shot and killed thirty struggling in the water.

Dominey raced to the stern and waved his handkerchief for the gunboats below to tow the disabled ironclad out from under the enemy's fire. Quartermaster McKean and a coal heaver were shot down as Dominey pulled them out of the water.

The St. Louis was a boat's length astern. Captain Wilson McGunnegle dispatched rowboats to pick up the water-logged survivors from the river. McGunnegle could hear Dominey yell: "Come and tow me down; we are all lost; we are all lost!"

McGunnegle ordered him to shut up as the Mound City would soon drift into a position where the tug Spiteful could render aid. The Conestoga, full in the face of the enemy fire, passed a line to the Mound City's stern and pulled her to safety. Confederates tried to storm the stricken ship, but were cut down by the tug *Spitfire's* guns.

Sailors turned the *Conestoga's* wardroom into a receiving station. The purser, knife in hand, tried to keep from vomiting as he cut off the clothes of the scalded and deluged their bodies with oil and flour and covered them with raw cotton.[26]

The *St. Louis* and *Lexington* pummeled the Rebel battery. Colonel Fitch signaled to cease fire. Reaching the top of the bluff in the rear amid a storm of bullets, Fitch's right wing wheeled sharply and took the Confederate guns.

Captain Kilty, seriously burned, along with the other wounded, was transferred to the *Musselman* for the trip back to Memphis. Only twenty-three men from *Mound City's* crew of 175 had escaped injury.[27]

The *St. Louis* and *Lexington* and the transport *New National* left the scene of battle, maneuvered through the barricade of sunken hulls, and stood up-river. Progress was slow; the river twisted with hair pin curves, and the water was falling rapidly. At the village of Clarendon, Fitch called a halt. Jacksonport and Curtis's Army could never be reached, and the possibility was fading fast of ever navigating the shallow waters back to the Mississippi. The expedition turned, steamed down-river, took the *Mound City* in tow, and entered the Mississippi.[28] At this moment, in Memphis, Davis read urgent dispatches from Farragut. He was at Vicksburg.

"For Twenty Minutes It Was Bang-Bang-Bang"

In the distance men in Farragut's squadron saw the Mississippi bend to the northeast for five miles before it flowed beneath the bluffs. Here it turned abruptly to continue its course northeastward, leaving a narrow tongue of land a mile wide opposite the city. At the sharp crook, perched on the Walnut Hills, stood Vicksburg, 400 miles by river from New Orleans, 350 miles by river from Memphis, forty-five by land from Jackson, Mississippi.

Peering over the breastworks at the Union squadron below, Brigadier General M. L. Smith was confident that the 4th, 5th, 8th, 20th, 27th, and 28th Louisiana volunteers were sufficient to hold the town. Guns from Pensacola and Mobile ringed the bluffs, arranged to bear on enemy gunboats as soon as they came within range, to fire directly into them as they passed the city, to rake them again as they steamed off up-river. The Confederates had packed the water battery with two rifled 32-pounders and four 42-pounders; mounted three 8-inchers, one 9-inch, and an 18-pounder at the highest point on the bluffs at the bend in the river; spotted fifteen other cannon along the crest of the hills above and below the town.[1]

The gunboat *Kennebec,* with Flag Officer Farragut on board, closed in on the Rebel batteries. Her fire could not reach the crest, gunners could not elevate the Dahlgrens sufficiently, but a single, plunging shot could sink the gunboat. The distance from one end of the batteries to the other was three miles. The current in the river ran at three knots. The speed of the ships was not over eight. Farragut calculated that each gunboat would need three quarters of an hour to pass the works and another twenty minutes to reach safety beyond the upper batteries.

Farragut met with General Thomas Williams, who commanded the 1,500-man assault force. Supplies were almost exhausted. Coal, food, ammunition had to be towed 400 difficult miles from New Orleans.[2] The long supply line, the almost impregnable fortifications, and the rumors of fifteen Rebel ironclads up-river forced commanders to conclude that "the place is not worth the trouble."[3] Immediately, rumors scurried about the squadron: Farragut was refusing to fire into Vicksburg because of his Southern sympathies.[4] One newsman reiterated that Vicksburg and Memphis should have fallen earlier and flayed Farragut for scattering his mortar schooners and for delays.[5]

Flag Officer Farragut left the *Iroquois, Oneida, Wissahickon, Sciota, Winona,* and *Katahdin* off Vicksburg and started for New Orleans with the *Brooklyn, Richmond, Hartford,* and Army transports. Guerrilla bands, concealing light batteries in the woods and behind levees along the river, bushwhacked the squadron. At Grand Gulf, Confederate shells ripped into the transport *Laurel Hill.* With disabled boilers and steam escaping, she drifted down-stream with the current. The *Brooklyn* and two gunboats hove into sight. Captain Thomas T. Craven of the *Brooklyn* boarded the stricken transport and saw the wounded and dead on the deck below. "This is awful, General Williams! What would you advise?"

"I would shell the town."

Regaining the deck of the *Brooklyn,* Craven signaled the gunboats to commence firing. Shells from thirty guns crushed frame buildings into kindling, brick houses into heaps of debris.[6]

At Baton Rouge, Chief Engineer James B. Kimball of the *Hartford* started for shore with a boat party. Twenty guerrilla horsemen galloped down to the wharf and fired two volleys, wounding him. The boat escaped back to the *Hartford,* which blasted broadside after broadside over Baton Rouge. The mayor rushed on board and implored Farragut not to shell the city. Farragut, in a towering rage, threatened that if such an assault occurred again, the squadron would demolish any city, any town, any village, any plantation where the offense was committed.[7] Farragut left two gunboats and General Williams's force at Baton Rouge and returned to New Orleans.

Dispatches from Washington awaited the commander. President Lincoln was distressed over rumors of his retreat, and Fox pressed for the squadron to steam back up-river.[8] Hurriedly Farragut answered Fox and wrote a lengthy letter to Welles. Navigation in the Mississippi was beyond anything he had ever encountered; he had seen more anchors lost there, more vessels shaken up than he had seen in a lifetime. Not one third of the Union steamers were fit for duty; half the men's enlistments were up, and they were clamoring to go home.[9]

At the St. Charles Hotel, General Benjamin F. Butler insisted that the Navy subdue Vicksburg.[10] Farragut argued that his guns could not reach the heights.[11] He recalled David Porter and his mortars from Ship Island and Butler ordered General Williams—his force strengthened by the 30th and 31st Massachusetts, 7th Vermont, 9th Connecticut, and 21st Indiana—to cooperate with the gunboats and storm the batteries.[12]

It was with bitterness that Farragut reascended the river. "I am now up the Mississippi again," he complained, "and when I will go down, God only knows."[13]

Two miles from Vicksburg, Porter stationed nine of his mortars on the starboard side of the river and seven on the port. At 2:00 a.m., June 28, the mortars began their dull, heavy roar, shaking the earth and river.[14] The squadron got under way in a double battle line; the sloop *Richmond* led, the *Hartford* coming next, followed by the *Brooklyn.* The gunboats formed another line, headed by the *Iroquois* and *Oneida* on the port bow of the *Richmond,* to bombard the upper forts without interfering with the sloop's fire. Next came the *Wissahickon* and *Sciota* on the *Hartford*'s port bow, the *Winona* and *Pinola* on the *Brooklyn*'s port bow.[15]

Captain Craven openly opposed the attack as "fool-hardy."[16] When the squadron approached Vicksburg, Porter's fleet stepped up the bombardment. Inside the city, shells tore into houses, stables, vacant lots, orchards, scattering fragments far and wide. Explosions rocked Vicksburg to its foundations. Civilians rushed into the streets and hurried for the country and safety. The military feared enemy landings.[17]

General Williams and his men, instead of storming the battlements, watched from the strip of land across the river. Union guns, everything from 13-inch mortars to muskets and rifles, roared at the bluffs. Guns in the Confederate water battery, guns midway up the slopes, guns atop the hill, guns in the streets answered. The Rebel batteries were so scattered, so camouflaged that the Yankees lost the range every few minutes. The Confederates fired erratically.[18]

Farragut handled the attack badly. Instead of slowing the engines, taking careful aim, and knocking out the water batteries, the fleet sped by the bluffs, each ship acting independently. But Craven, on the *Brooklyn,* flustered by Farragut's offhand, verbal orders, thought he was to silence each battery as he passed. The *Brooklyn,* faltering, did not move up in line, but kept blazing away at the lower batteries with her forward guns. Strewn haphazardly across the river, Porter's steamers forced the *Brooklyn* to stop her engines. Rebel cannon caught her in a cross fire. To Craven's surprise, he saw nothing of the *Hartford* or the others ahead. Unsupported except by the *Kennebec* and *Katahdin* astern, sure that it was impossible to reduce a single hilltop battery, Craven muted his guns and dropped down-river.[19]

Up-stream, Farragut's gunboats and sloops arrived safely above Vicksburg. Raked severely, the *Hartford* had taken a 50-pounder in the shell room, an 8-incher in the poop deck, shells through the rigging. Casualties numbered seven killed, thirty wounded.[20]

After the engagement Farragut breakfasted with Alfred Ellet of the ram fleet and sent a blistering censure to Captain Craven, who asked to be relieved.[21] This request was promptly granted.

A grumpy Farragut calculated the next move. Hulls had been injured by frequent collisions and groundings, and many engines needed repairs. During the summer months, the water in the Mississippi would be at its lowest, and the possibility of being stuck for a year loomed large—"A beautiful prospect," he joked, "for the 'hero' of New Orleans."[22] The Government would keep him in the river until all his vessels and reputation rotted. "Fighting is nothing to the evils of the river," he told his wife, "getting on shore, running afoul of one another, losing anchors. I am worked to death."[23]

Farragut's officers questioned his judgment and accomplishments before Vicksburg. Recriminations, hard feelings, and petty quarrels racked the squadron.[24] An officer from the *Kennebec* charged that Farragut had botched the attack by not silencing the batteries and asked a congressman to order his ship out of the river.[25] Throughout the fleet, men knew that the Old Man had no heart for river fighting.

Vessels steaming north from New Orleans reported fortifications at Grand Gulf and Port Gibson. "We are now virtually prisoners," a correspondent wrote sourly, "hemmed in on all sides, and can only be relieved from our uncomfortable situation by the arrival of Halleck's Army."[26]

Farragut eyed that neck of land opposite Vicksburg occupied by Williams's troops. A canal, diverting the main channel of the Mississippi, would make Vicksburg an inland town and permit gunboats to pass up and down with safety.[27] Williams impressed 1,200 Negroes, rounded up from neighboring plantations, and set them to work from morning to night, shoveling, chopping, "digging the grave of Vicksburg."[28]

The job took three weeks, but the Mississippi shot right by the cut, leaving only a trickle in the ditch. Sternwheelers, their paddles churning, endeavored to force

water into the canal, but they failed. Fatigued, deci-
mated by sickness, Williams's men abandoned the
project.[29]

Flag Officer Davis and his flotilla joined Farragut four
miles above Vicksburg at the mouth of the Yazoo River.
July weather scorched the squadrons. "I never can de-
scribe to you that heat," Davis fretted, "the succession of
still and breathless days—long, long, weary, red-hot, gasp-
ing days."[30]

It was accepted that neither wooden sloops nor ironclads could defeat the Rebel Army at Vicksburg. The
mortars could possibly destroy the city, the gunboats
might silence the batteries, but the situation demanded
a concentration of infantry and artillery to force the Confederate military into submission. Farragut hurried a dispatch to Halleck for troops, but the general denied his
request.[31] Then Halleck, reaping the credit for the western advance down-river, was recalled to Washington and
made General-in-Chief of the Armies. Grant was given
command of the forces in western Tennessee and northern
Mississippi, with authority over General William S. Rosecrans, who had succeeded Pope as commander of the
Army of the Mississippi, and Buell, commanding the
Army of the Ohio. David Porter and his schooners were
reassigned to Virginia waters.

Far up the Yazoo the Confederates readied the *Arkansas* for action. Commander Brown, with orders to
steam into the Mississippi, harass the Federal fleets, and
speed for the Gulf, moved the ram down the Yazoo to
Haynes Bluff on July 14.[32]

That night two Rebel deserters arrived at the *Essex*,
in the Mississippi, and informed the Yankees that the
Arkansas would strike early the next morning. At first

Farragut and Davis pooh-poohed the story, but, moved by the persistency of the deserters, decided to send out an expedition at daylight.[33]

At the first streaks of dawn, Commander Brown cleared the decks of the ram *Arkansas* and reminded the crew that they must win or perish: "Should they carry us by boarding, the *Arkansas* must be blown up. On no account must she fall into the hands of the enemy. Go to your guns!"[34]

Stripped to their waists and with handkerchiefs tied around their heads, sailors sanded the decks, filled fire buckets, strapped on cutlasses, loaded rifles, readied bayonets, threw open the shell rooms and magazines. Surgeons furnished division commanders with tourniquets.[35]

The *Tyler, Carondelet,* and *Queen of the West* moved up the Yazoo River. Officers of the *Tyler* had just sat down to breakfast when lookouts sighted a strange craft dead ahead. Captain Gwin sprang from the table and out on deck. Sure that his wooden-hulled gunboat could never cope with the ironclad, Gwin signaled the *Carondelet,* half mile astern, and ordered the *Queen of the West* to destroy the *Arkansas.* The Ellet ram ignored orders and raced in the opposite direction. The *Tyler* rounded to, her stern gun sputtering.[36] Zigzagging into position, the *Carondelet* fired a salvo. For thirty minutes the antagonists, *Carondelet* and *Arkansas,* fought it out at close quarters. In the heat of battle, Commander Walke of the *Carondelet* erred in judgment. Had he kept head to the enemy, he might have sunk the *Arkansas,* but, suddenly, to escape being rammed, his guns partially disabled, Walke turned the *Carondelet* and ran off among the willows and shallow waters of the bank, where the iron behemoth dared not follow. All opposition had ceased.[37]

The *Arkansas* turned and chased the fast-flying *Tyler*, which was hastening to warn the Yankee fleets in the Mississippi. Engineers passed word to Commander Brown that the temperature in the fireroom was 130°. Steam, which at the beginning of the melee registered 120 pounds, now had dropped to sixty. Fighting the *Arkansas* as a ram was now out of the question. Nearing the Mississippi, the Confederates saw sloops-of-war, ironclads, and mortar boats hugging the river banks. The odds were enormous. An Irishman stuck his head out of the port and exclaimed, "Holy Mother, have mercy on us, we'll never get through there!"[38]

Again the Yankees were caught with their boilers cold. Farragut had heard firing up the Yazoo River, but it did not occur to him, as he lay at anchor, that the ram might come out fighting. The *Arkansas* steamed courageously into the Mississippi. "For twenty minutes it was bang-bang-bang," recalled a Rebel lieutenant.[39] Farragut, dumfounded, dressed in his nightshirt, rushed out of his cabin. The *Hartford,* her machinery torn down for repairs, was helpless.[40]

Passing along within a cable's length of the enemy, the *Arkansas* fired ahead, astern, to port and starboard. One Union broadside tore away the *Arkansas*'s breechings to the boilers, destroying the draft. Flames licked the gundeck. The *Kineo* squared off with the ram, firing her heavy 11-inch Dahlgren and two 12-pounders. The Rebel sailed past heading for the *Louisville*. The Union ironclad gave her a full blast from the broadside and bow guns. Solid shot bounced off, shells shivered into a thousand fragments.

The Federals—*Hartford, Iroquois, Richmond, Sumter, Oneida, Sciota, Wissahickon, Winona, Cincinnati, Benton* —took aim and fired. One shot hit the *Arkansas* abreast the bow gun, another whistled through and exploded cotton bales, yet another ripped in—showering iron and wooden splinters—killing twelve. Riddled, her stack resembling a "nutmeg grater," her decks a slaughter pen, the *Arkansas* continued to fire. Stationed on the ladder of the *Arkansas's* berth deck, Quartermaster Eaton superintended the passing of shells. "A 9-inch shell, five-second fuse. Here you are, my lad, with your rifle shell; take it and go back, quick. What's the matter that you can't get the gun out?" He sprang from his station, threw his weight on the side of the tackle, and the gun shot out the port.

"What are you doing here wounded? Go back to your gun, or I'll murder you on the spot. Here is your 9-inch shell."

To another wounded man, he was solicitous: "Mind, shipmate, the ladder is bloody, don't slip, let me help you."[41]

Shells from the *Arkansas* holed through the *Hartford, Iroquois, Richmond,* and *Benton.* The ram *Lancaster* maneuvered across her path. Confederate gunners loaded five-second shells into the bow guns and fired, slashing the *Lancaster's* drum, emptying hot steam and water into the barricaded engine room. Crew and sharpshooters poured up the scuttles, tore off their clothes, and dived into the river. The *Arkansas* sailed through the Federal fleet and arrived at Vicksburg amid the shouts and huzzahs of the defenders.

Farragut was in a white heat. "Damn it," he bellowed, "what will be said of us? Let a little boat like that escape the whole fleet! It's disgraceful. We must wipe out the disgrace, if it takes every man's life in the fleet. We must do it, by God!"[42]

The "Old Bulldog" stormed on the *Benton,* hellbent to destroy the *Arkansas,* and demanded that every sloop, every ironclad, every gunboat, every mortar move at once for Vicksburg.

That night at twilight, the *Benton, Cincinnati,* and *Louisville* hotly bombarded the upper forts. Tense, confused, the Gulf squadron wasted an hour getting under way, and it was not until darkness that all the gunboats were moving. Lookouts found it impossible to locate the exact position of the *Arkansas,* lying as she did under the shadow of the bank. The Gulf fleet hammered away into the night. It passed down-stream below Vicksburg.[43]

Obsessed by the exploit of the *Arkansas,* Farragut swore that he would steam back that same night and cut her to pieces. The squadron was to continue the attack until the monster was sunk. Davis delayed and refused to jeopardize the Western Flotilla in an attempt at Vicksburg.

In his cabin, three men fanned themselves and charted tactics. The steward brought in a decanter of sherry. Davis and William Porter of the *Essex* helped themselves; Farragut stuck to tea. The black-bearded Porter sprawled out in a chair, dangling a gold watch fob and talking rapidly. Farragut was tired. In the undress blues of a captain, he looked plain and unassuming. The scholarly appearing Davis, who affected a long, sweeping mustache, sat upright and fumbled with the gold ring on his left little finger.[44]

A plan for destroying the *Arkansas* matured. At daylight, the *Essex,* commanded by Porter, and the *Queen of the West* were to hit the ram; the Western Flotilla was to cover them at the upper batteries; the Gulf squadron, from below.[45]

At dawn, the *Benton*, *Cincinnati*, and *Louisville* slid down river and blazed away at the upper batteries. The *Essex* and *Queen of the West* got under way. The Confederate batteries opened fire. Amid a hail of shells, the *Essex* and *Queen of the West* sprinted for the *Arkansas*. The *Essex's* 11-inch bow guns exploded shells, hammering the ram's armor, splitting the breech of the starboard gun, killing eight. The *Arkansas* let go her bow line, swung into the current, stern on. The oncoming *Essex* grazed the *Arkansas* and ran into the mud, where she lay for ten minutes, subjected to the close-range firing of the shore batteries and the *Arkansas*. As the *Arkansas* passed the *Essex*, Porter muzzled his guns, backed hard on the engines, and nudged off the bar. Disabled by a shot in her engines, the *Essex* floated down-stream, unsupported by the lower fleet three miles away.

The ram *Queen of the West* pitched into the *Arkansas*. The vessels shuddered. Backing full, the *Queen of the West* ran afoul in the mud. Dented and blackened, hit twenty times, she finally escaped. The *Arkansas* limped back to the dock.[46]

Porter arrived below Vicksburg in a fury and turned on Farragut. Davis blamed the Gulf squadron for lack of cooperation.[47] "The whole thing was a fizzle," reported Phelps. "Things have happened that will create talk."[48]

Farragut now broke time-honored tradition and consulted the enlisted men. All hands mustered on the *Hartford's* quarter-deck. Farragut stood to one side as Captain Wainwright addressed the men and outlined the alternatives. To depart down-river without destroying the *Ar-*

kansas was dangerous. To pass the batteries and attack Vicksburg was dangerous. Which should they choose? Hurrahs rang from the quarter-deck. "We will follow you anywhere!" "We go to Vicksburg!" Crews whistled and cheered as Wainwright and Farragut disappeared into the cabin.[49]

The next day the squadron received welcome orders from Washington to proceed down-river, strengthen the blockade, and conduct operations in the Gulf.[50] Eager to leave, but lingering while General Williams and his men packed up, Farragut secured the services of the *Essex* and the ram *Sumter* from Davis's flotilla.

On the passage southward, Farragut tarried at Baton Rouge. For the first time, sailors had a chance to inspect the state house of Louisiana, with its Gothic architecture. They saw the Hiram Powers statue of George Washington, the broad staircase, the American flags clustered about an eagle painted over the Speaker's chair. Sightseers meandered out to the state prison on the outskirts, which, before the city's surrender, had been used as a barrack. Mattresses, bedding, tables, benches, chairs, whiskey bottles, boots littered the cells. On a greasy table, a sailor turned up a deuce of clubs and on the back found the message: "You God damned sons-of-bitches, if it were not for your gunboats we would see you in hell before we would give up this place. E.E.S."[51]

Farragut withdrew to New Orleans, leaving Williams's force to occupy the town. The operations of the squadron now extended along the river, up the navigable tributaries, and out into the Gulf. A series of annoying skirmishes was executed—expeditions that seemed small in themselves but which, in the aggregate, cut off important channels of communication. The destruction of salt works, the smashing of illicit trade centers in the bayous, the capture of small steamers were insignificant compared to an important battle, yet these actions consolidated the victory. General Beauregard blamed sickness in the ranks for the evacuation of Corinth, weakness brought on by the lack of fresh beef. Cattle no longer moved from southern Louisiana to Mississippi.

Stung by the loss of New Orleans and Baton Rouge, their vital Red River supply line threatened, the Rebels planned desperate measures. General Braxton Bragg succeeded Beauregard as commander of the forces between Virginia and Mississippi. He transferred his Army to Chattanooga and left the defense of Vicksburg and the operations in northeastern Mississippi to Generals Earl Van Dorn and Sterling Price. Strong military reason dictated the protection of the Red River and a blockade of the Mississippi between Vicksburg and Union-held Baton Rouge, insuring the safety of Confederate supplies and communications between west and east.[52]

According to plan the ironclad *Arkansas* got under way from Vicksburg for Baton Rouge. Passing Bayou Sara, her engines failed and she floated down-stream to within fifteen miles of the city, where she moored. After engineers completed repairs, she was restarted, but her starboard engine broke down again.[53]

Acting in concert with the *Arkansas,* Confederate General John C. Breckinridge marched down the state of Mississippi toward Baton Rouge with 5,000 picked men and added an additional 1,000 from Camp Moore, Louisiana.

At dawn on August 5, the Rebels struck General Williams's center—the 14th Maine, 21st Indiana, and 6th Michigan—at the intersection of the Greenwell Springs Road. The attack pressed forward. General Williams motioned his lines to fall back. A lieutenant colonel rushed up and yelled out, "For God's sake, General, don't order us to fall back! We'll hold this position against the whole damned Rebel Army."

"Do your men feel that way, Colonel?" snapped Williams.

Turning to his regiment, the colonel commanded, "Fix bayonets."[54]

The 14th Maine advanced into a solid fire, retreated, then surged forward. Williams fell, mortally wounded.

Breckinridge listened in vain for the guns of the *Arkansas*. He saw around him weary men, exhausted men, men who had had no water since leaving the Comite River. Union batteries commanded the approaches to the arsenal and barracks. He ordered his regiments to pull out.[55]

William Porter's *Essex* steamed northward from Baton Rouge, neared the stranded *Arkansas*, and opened fire. The Rebel, her engines barely working, slipped her lines and aimed at the *Essex*. Wavering in the river, the *Arkansas* crept 300 yards before her starboard engine failed completely. According to William Porter's statement, the *Essex* poured in a hot fire, and Yankees saw several Confederates abandoning ship and heading for the woods. Smoke engulfed the *Arkansas*. Suddenly flames hit her magazine and she blew up.[56] Porter's jubilation was short-lived, for Farragut refused to commend the *Essex*, asserted that "the moral influence" of the wooden-hulled sloops had sunk the *Arkansas*, and jealously banished Porter from the squadron.[57]

At 5:30 p.m., August 13, David Glasgow Farragut hauled down his flag from the mizzen and raised it on the mainmast of the *Hartford*, announcing to the fleet at New

Orleans that he had been elevated to the rank of Rear Admiral. A salute was fired, and that night crowds serenaded him at the St. Charles Hotel.[58]

With the destruction of the *Arkansas* less than two weeks after Farragut's withdrawal from Vicksburg, there remained afloat no threat to the Union's domination of the entire Mississippi River. The failure at Baton Rouge induced Confederate General Van Dorn to marshal more troops and guns at Port Hudson, Louisiana. Holding two strongly fortified points on the Mississippi, Vicksburg and Port Hudson, the Rebels now controlled only the 200 mile stretch between them, but beef, bacon, lard, troops, and ammunition from Texas still flowed eastward unmolested via the Red River.

After Farragut departed for the Gulf, the Western Flotilla near Vicksburg moved northward to Helena, Arkansas. "There is no knowing what crazy project the Department may have in view or how this move of mine may be taken," Davis confided to his diary, "but it seems to me that the only course now . . . is to yield to the climate and postpone any further action at Vicksburg till the fever season is over." Sickness and death haunted the flotilla. A hundred gunners of the mortar fleet and forty per cent of the gunboat crews were ailing and off duty. The hospital ship *Red Rover* overflowed with patients.[59] The Rebels erected batteries at Carolina Landing and Greenville, Mississippi, which surprised and destroyed the *Sallie Wood* and *Swallow,* interrupting temporarily the flow of supplies and ammunition between Cairo and Helena.[60]

Judged from one viewpoint, Davis was justified in ordering his fleet to a more temperate region for the summer. His attack force was reduced to three ironclads,

220 Battle Flags South

one ram, and the *General Bragg*. The remainder of his command patrolled the river and its tributaries, protecting the Army's lines of communication, halting the activities of guerrilla bands, seizing Confederate transports and cargo steamers. Shifting these gunboats would weaken Davis's position in the rear to bolster his front.

From a strategic viewpoint, the Western Flotilla should have prosecuted the campaign at Vicksburg while Farragut's squadron blockaded in Gulf waters. It was paramount to station a naval force below Vicksburg to prevent the transportation of supplies and divert a portion of the Confederate Army.

Davis's fundamental nature revolted against the hazards confronting him at Vicksburg. He failed to display the initiative that wins campaigns and renown. "I saw enough to convince me," David Porter remarked, "that Davis . . . desires to lose his command." [61]

During the summer of 1862 gloom blanketed Washington. McClellan had been beaten back on the Peninsula. Lincoln recalled General Pope from the West, put him in command, and reduced McClellan to a subordinate position. The Confederate Army under Lee and Jackson defeated the Federals at the Second Battle of Bull Run. Demoralized and crippled, the Army of Pope retired toward Washington in disorder, thousands of stragglers clogging the roads. Streets and avenues once more resounded to the rumble of Army trains. One citizen on Pennsylvania Avenue proclaimed, "Everything is just as it was before the Army of the Potomac marched for the Peninsula—only more so."

The nation was restless, and men spoke of a "brainless

war." They complained of battles without results, of campaigns without battles, of promised action and distressing inaction. Semiofficially, Washington had assured Northerners that decisive movements were at hand, that Rebel armies were to be surrounded, that cities were to be captured, rivers opened—that the industrial energies of the North would crush the rebellion.

The Administration circulated predictions that the war would end before ninety days, before the leaves fell, before the winter set in, before Christmas, before some appreciable point of time just ahead. "A thunderbolt was forever being forged, but never launched," blustered the Cincinnati *Daily Commercial*.[62]

The situation at Vicksburg was discussed in the Cabinet, and Congress transferred the responsibility for the Western Flotilla from the Army to the Navy.[63] Over at the Navy Department it was business as usual. Secretary Gideon Welles recalled Flag Officer Charles Henry Davis from the West and assigned David Dixon Porter to command the Western Flotilla with the rank of Acting Rear Admiral.[64] Before Porter left Washington, he visited the White House and talked with President Lincoln for over an hour. The next day he was on a train heading for Cairo.[65]

11

"Hammer and Tongs"

Porter arrived in admiral's regalia. He was never to forget crawling through the mud in his full-dress uniform to take his first look at the "Emporium of the Mississippi Valley"—Cairo. The excitement that had accompanied the battles of Forts Henry and Donelson had long since faded away. Cairo had relapsed into a state of commercial and military torpor, and only a handful of gunboats—moored to the wharf—and the provost guard denoted war. Townsfolk worried about Negro refugees quartering in Army barracks and, during the "shaking season" of October, took to tossing down quinine cocktails to ward off the fever and ague.[1]

Porter quailed at the sight of the Western Navy. Three Pook turtles; a hospital ship; the worn-out *Lexington, Tyler,* and *Conestoga;* the ram *Eastport,* damaged after plowing into a mud bank; a wharf boat with ammunition; a floating blacksmith shop—these were the visible signs of naval supremacy.[2]

At his offices on the waterfront, Porter tore open a dispatch from Fox: "The opening of that river is imperative."[3] Determined to put the flotilla into battle trim, no matter what the cost, driving himself day and night, the admiral demanded and received 300 guns; purchased and altered into gunboats fifty-four light-drafted vessels; hounded the Cabinet into turning over the semi-independent ram fleet to his command; visited St. Louis and Cincinnati to spur the completion of the *Choctaw, Lafayette, Chillicothe, Tuscumbia,* and *Indianola;* condemned and retired the Fremont mortar boats and ordered replacements; printed orders by the hundreds on his portable printing press; restored to operation the machine shops in Memphis. Circumventing regular channels, Porter annoyed the Navy Department, and Fox accused the admiral of currying favor with the President.[4] Secretary Stanton lost his temper. Alfred Ellet called Porter a "fool" bent on empire building.[5]

The admiral reorganized the squadron, detailing specific gunboats to specific areas, and adopted stringent measures against Confederate guerrillas and against illicit trade. The *Robb, Fairplay, Brilliant, St. Clair* and *General Pillow* rampaged up the Ohio River to seek out and destroy the enemy. The *Carondelet* roved the White River to ferret out Rebels. The *Baron DeKalb* (ex-*St. Louis*), on a sortie, landed twenty-five men who, after a nine-mile chase near Memphis, seized a band of renegades.[6] When the steamer *Gladiator* was ambushed, 300 Indiana troops mopped up Confederates hiding in the Arkansas brush and reduced a town to ashes.[7] The Rebel steamers *Lottie, Blue Wing,* and *Lady Pike,* hauling contraband, were captured. Helena, Arkansas, became the forward base for the Western Flotilla.

On a bright fall day, John A. McClernand, classical scholar and political general, visited his former Springfield neighbor in the White House. Lincoln entered the

East Room dressed in an ill-fitting black suit resembling an undertaker's.[8] The general wanted to recruit in the Northwest and raise his own Army to capture Vicksburg.[9] The Army at New Orleans, strengthened by 10,000 additional troops and under a new commander, General Nathaniel P. Banks, could go up-river to meet his Army coming down.

Gaining Lincoln's approval, McClernand hastened to Springfield with orders that posed so many contradictions that neither Lincoln nor Stanton knew how to explain them to General Halleck. They ordered the general to recruit troops in Indiana, Illinois, and Iowa and station them at Memphis,[10] where, technically, they should have been under General Grant, who commanded the Department of the Tennessee. Met with cordiality by state governors, McClernand rounded up forty-nine regiments of infantry—mustering upwards of 40,000 men—and sent them to Memphis.[11]

Anxious to grasp the initiative and launch a campaign against Vicksburg, Grant was upset by the increasing persistency with which newspapers carried stories of an independent command under McClernand. At Oxford, Mississippi, General William T. Sherman and Grant met in an abandoned house. By prompt, rapid movements, Sherman was to move down the Mississippi with 40,000 men, land on the banks of the Yazoo River, and invade Vicksburg from the north. Grant, with his forces at Oxford and Holly Springs, would cooperate, his actions depending upon the enemy.

General Sherman hurried back to Memphis to assume command of the troops—McClernand's troops and those of General Curtis at Helena.[12] Unaware of such movements, McClernand tarried in Springfield, gathering up the last dregs for his Army.

In Cairo, David Porter was confused by so many conflicting reports from so many military commands.[13] In December, Porter finally met with General Grant on board a gunboat. The admiral had never seen him before. Grant, dressed in a worn civilian coat and dusty gray pants, seemed out of place among the elegantly attired naval officers.

Porter and Grant took a small table apart from the rest of the company. Grant came quickly to the point. "When can you move your fleet?"

"Tomorrow, or whenever you wish to start."

"Then I will get off at once," Grant replied. "Sherman will meet you at Memphis on the 20th with forty thousand men, all embarked on transports. I will leave Holly Springs about the 18th and march on Grenada with all my force. This will draw off the Rebel Army now at Vicksburg to contest my advance, and you and Sherman can get possession of the place, as you will meet with inferior numbers. I will be in with the Rebels if they fall back on Vicksburg."

Talk then centered on General McClernand. Grant warned of complications and wanted to seize Vicksburg while McClernand loitered in the Northwest.[14]

Arriving at Memphis several days later, Porter sought Sherman at the Gayoso House. An orderly ushered the admiral into the reception room, where he waited an hour, two hours, for the general. Sherman finally bustled in and seemed surprised to find Porter.

Sherman poked the fire as he told Porter all that he had done, all that he was doing, and all that he intended to do. After arranging the final details of the expedition, Porter headed northward to pick up his squadron.[15]

He dashed off a note to Welles. "Don't be astonished at the lists of niggers I send you," he scribbled as he signed on contrabands. "I could get no men, so I work in the darkies. They do first rate and are far better behaved than their masters."[16]

In Springfield, McClernand grew restless. On December 12, he notified Washington that he was ready to take command of his Army in Memphis.[17] A day passed, another, without an answer. The 15th, 16th, and 17th of December slipped by.[18]

New orders sped from Washington to Grant. He must divide his command into four Army Corps and place the one headed down the Mississippi under McClernand. Grant wanted to concede nothing to this political general. Already he had worked out strategy with Sherman. The order giving McClernand a corps command reached Grant on December 18, and confirmation was sent to Sherman and McClernand, but a Confederate cavalry raid cut the telegraph lines. On December 22, McClernand read the message—the first communication, direct or indirect, from Halleck.[19]

Two days earlier, Sherman's force, on board forty-five transports convoyed by gunboats, stood down-river from Memphis.[20] That first night the task force tied up to the river bank. Neither sleeping nor eating, the general was absorbed in the work before him, poring over maps, interrogating deserters. It took four days to reach Helena, where General Frederick Steele's division joined the expedition.

The Confederate telegraph clacked out the message: a Federal expedition—transports, ironclads, mortars, and gunboats—was on the move. General John Pemberton, who had succeeded Van Dorn in overall command, grimly read the dispatches. A West Pointer who had seen service at twenty different military posts, Pemberton was a slender man, austere, stern, tough.

His line of defense was anchored at Vicksburg, the right resting on Haynes Bluff, a strongly fortified position on the Yazoo River, twelve miles from the city; the left, on the Mississippi, at Grand Gulf, sixty miles below. Military units and 6,000 Negroes had bolstered the defenses by filling the batteries with heavier and better ordnance, cutting down trees to impede the enemy's progress, digging rifle pits. Throughout the fall and early winter, the Army at Vicksburg had prepared for the Union thrust.[21]

Yankee gunboats probed the Yazoo River. The *Cairo, Pittsburg, Queen of the West, Marmora,* and *Signal,* taking soundings and shelling the woods, rounded a point and ran into mines, demijohns crammed with powder linked to logs filled with shot.[22] The *Marmora,* 100 yards in advance of the *Cairo,* stopped dead in the water. Commander Thomas O. Selfridge, Jr. nosed the *Cairo* ahead, ran close into shore, and backed down full. Two quick, violent explosions rent the air. The *Cairo's* bow shot skyward, shuddered, and plunged into the river. In two minutes water was over her forecastle. Selfridge shoved the *Cairo* into the bank as sailors manned the hand and steam pumps, but it was no use. The *Queen of the West* ran alongside and hauled off the crew. In twelve minutes, the *Cairo* was submerged out of sight except for her stacks.[23]

At Helena, Porter accused Selfridge of disobeying orders. Selfridge reported on board the *Black Hawk*: "I suppose you will want to hold a court." Porter had no time for courts and, on second thought, praised the commander for gallantry and assigned him command of the *Conestoga*. Selfridge left the flagship with the feeling that he would go through "hellfire and water" for a man like the admiral.[24]

At Milliken's Bend, down-stream from Helena, the expedition rested, primed for the assault up the Yazoo River. To toughen up his corps, Sherman sent 7,000 men inland to Monroe, Louisiana, to rip up thirty miles of railroad track. General Nathaniel Banks, with an overwhelming force, it was understood, was ascending the Mississippi from New Orleans. At last account, Grant's Army was approaching the Yallobusha near Grenada. Lieutenant Gwin on the *Benton* took an expedition up the Yazoo to sweep mines and secure a landing area.

All Christmas Day, officers and men suffered from boredom. There were a few ineffectual attempts at Christmas festivities, but Yuletide staples were nonexistent, and the day dragged. Sherman met with naval officers. The Yazoo River was complex, dreary, desolate, its banks dense with cypress trees, its water brown and sickly. Forking into two, sometimes three and more branches, its basin subdivided by bayous, the northern portion of the watershed was the Coldwater, which joined the Tallahatchie and, after receiving the Yallobusha from the east, became the Yazoo.

Morning dawned overcast on December 26. The expedition entered the Yazoo at noon, the transports in a single line led by a tinclad, ironclads, and the *Black Hawk*. Off in the haze stood smouldering ruins—a brick house, steam sawmills, a sugar refinery, cotton gins, machine shops—rumored to be the plantation of Rebel General Albert Sidney Johnston, killed in action at Shiloh.

At a place called Johnson's Farm, the transports and soldiers disembarked, hacking their way through the willows, brier, vines, and live oak. Rain fell. Darkness came. Confusion was everywhere. Companies separated. A. J. Smith's division delayed, not arriving until the 27th.[25]

Johnson's Farm was an island, separated from Vicksburg by swamps, lagoons, bayous, and quicksand. The Union right rested on a bleak bayou, Old River; the left, on narrower Chickasaw Bayou.

A Negro visited the *Black Hawk* and reported that Mrs. Jefferson Davis and her servants were living in Vicksburg and that the President himself was there.[26] President Davis had in fact arrived on the scene, and was conferring with Governor John J. Pettus at Jackson. At the State House, a dilapidated affair with broken windows and mildewed interiors, Pettus chatted with Davis as strangers and friends wandered in and out. That afternoon Davis addressed the Mississippi Legislature and stated that the Confederate blockade of the Mississippi was ruining the Northwest.[27]

Up-river, General McClernand reached Memphis. Where, asked the general sternly, were his troops? They had gone south with Sherman. McClernand hastily started down the Mississippi in search of his Army.[28]

On December 27 Sherman's Army had moved out to their positions—Steele's division above the mouth of Chickasaw Bayou; George Morgan's with Frank Blair's brigade below the same bayou; Morgan L. Smith's on the main road to Vicksburg, with orders to bear left; A. J. Smith's on the extreme right.

Porter's gunboats puffed up the Yazoo to draw off a portion of the enemy. Nearing heavily fortified Haynes Bluff, the *Benton's* guns blazed. The channel was too narrow for support vessels, and the sturdy *Benton* bore the brunt of the attack. For two hours the ironclad and the enemy on the bluffs slugged it out. Shots, mostly 64-pounders, bounced off the *Benton*'s pilot house and side armor, but crushed the unprotected decks.[29]

Sitting in his cabin on board the *Black Hawk*, talking with Sherman, Porter saw the *Benton* limping downstream. The admiral boarded her in time to comfort the wounded Gwin who, two hours later, died in Porter's arms. But Gwin's death did not prevent the admiral from blaming him for the repulse.

Silence shrouded the area on the night of December 28-29. No fires were lighted. The trees dripped miserably from heavy rains. Confederates continued to dig rifle pits and throw up additional breastworks. In the Union camp, soldiers asked the whereabouts of Generals Grant and Banks. One recruit wrote home: "On Vixburge they have One of the strages fortifiication. We will have the hardest Batel that was ever recorded in history. You thir at home no more bout than we do here."[30]

At headquarters, Sherman planned a direct assault into Vicksburg, through Chickasaw Bayou and up the hill, which glowered with rifle pits and batteries, arranged to mow down an advancing Army. Morgan's division was to attack the hill, while A. J. Smith's and M. L. Smith's divisions were to cross the bayou on the sand bar and wipe out the levee parapet and the first line of rifle pits, preventing the enemy from concentrating on Morgan. Steele was to hold the road leading to Vicksburg.

Monday, December 29. Sherman launched his attack. All along the line, Yankee artillery roared. Viciously, the Rebels replied. Federals emerged from the woods at noon.[31]

General David Stuart of M. L. Smith's division started to cross the bayou at the sand bar. Opposite the bayou, the levee parapet stood eighteen feet high. To ascend it was impossible without digging a road, which would have to be done under a double cross fire from the enemy. Stuart detailed the 6th Missouri for the job. Under a hail of bullets, two companies of volunteers, crouching, crawling, inched forward across the sand bar to dig at the bank. Once under the protection of the overhang of the bank, they started with pick and shovel.

Morgan prepared to assault the hill, supported by Blair's and Thayer's brigades. The entire division was to carry the hill and sweep into Vicksburg. Frank Blair, who had stumped Missouri for Lincoln and then resigned his seat in Congress to fight, swung his brigade over the bayou bridge first. Sherman saw him push to the foot of the hill. The signal for Stuart's brigade to cross the sand bar was to be the heavy firing from Morgan's division.

Blair led his men to the first line of rifle pits, guarded by the 28th Louisiana and the 42nd Georgia. After a brief hand-to-hand struggle, Blair drove the enemy into their second line. Blair rushed on. Suddenly, the enemy, from behind masked batteries, opened a withering fire. The ground was covered with Blair's dead and dying—645 Yankees. The survivors recoiled and fell back.

Heavy firing from Morgan's division, the signal to launch the all-out attack, was never heard. Thayer's brigade, which might have supported, lost its direction and didn't cross the bayou. Nor did Morgan in person. His first report to Sherman was that his troops were not discouraged at Blair's repulse and that he would move out, but his assault never came.

Sherman prodded A. J. Smith to open his diversionary

attack. The 54th Ohio, charging the bridge, met a murderous fire. Momentarily, they stood their ground, fighting against superior numbers. In the heat of battle, a Union battery poured shells into friend and foe alike. The Rebels fled from the field, and the 54th Ohio, collecting their dead and wounded, retired.

The volunteers of the 6th Missouri, still pinned down by the sharpshooters of the levee parapet, sheltered themselves the best they could and waited. But the day was hopelessly lost, and, at dark, they retreated.[32]

Night closed in. The Union stood on its original ground, but had suffered a severe repulse. During the night it rained hard. Sherman, his rubber shawl wrapped around him, stepped on board the *Black Hawk*. In Porter's cabin, he slumped into an armchair and, leaning his head on his hand, was lost in thought. He was unaware that Grant had been forced to retreat and that Banks lay in New Orleans, prostrated by a flare-up of old injuries sustained at Cedar Mountain.

At length, Porter asked, "Why General, where are all your spirits tonight? What's the matter with you?"

"My spirits are on Chickasaw Bayou," he retorted acidly. "Admiral, I never was so cut in my life. This has been a dreadful disaster to us."

"Why, General," Porter replied, "I am astonished to see you regarding it in that light. How many men have you lost in all?"

"Seventeen hundred."

"Well now, General," Porter replied, "it is my opinion that any man can bear up and be jolly after losing one. God almighty is fighting the battle in his own fashion, and for some good purpose he don't intend us to be successful now. We will win in the long run, and you may bet on that."

Cheering slightly, Sherman said, "Admiral, there's a good deal of sense in that remark. No doubt it's all for the best, so if you will let your steward make me a toddy to warm me up, I will think more about the matter. But, as we have to give this affair up for a short time, what shall we do next?"

"Anything you please," Porter answered.

"Then, let us go and lick those fellows at Arkansas Post. It's dry land there and the boys, who are a little disheartened, will get set up again."[33]

The admiral proposed one last try at Vicksburg. Move 10,000 men up to Haynes Bluff, bombard, and seize the batteries. Such actions would give the Federals domination of the Yazoo River and place them in communication with Grant. Sherman agreed.

Porter started out in a tug to hunt his gunboats. He had seen fogs before, but never like the one that blanketed the Yazoo River that night. Maneuvering in the narrow stream, he barged into Steele's flagship, broke his rudder, and awoke the general from a sound sleep. At daylight the fog was still heavy, thick, maddening. Nothing moved. Poised, ready to commence the attack, Sherman was disheartened. It began to rain again and it rained hard.[34]

The expedition to Haynes Bluff was abandoned. Sherman pulled out his troops and headed out of the Yazoo to Milliken's Bend.

January 1, 1863. The North continued to be rocked by reverses. Sherman had abandoned Vicksburg. On the banks of the Stone River in Tennessee, soldiers of Rosecrans's Army were burying 1,677 dead and caring for 7,543 wounded after fighting the Rebels to a standstill. Burnside's Army of the Potomac, around its fires on the Stafford Hills, opposite Fredericksburg, Virginia, was beaten, demoralized after a bloody defeat by General Lee. In the Gulf, Rebel cottonclads wiped out a section of Farragut's blockading squadron and recaptured Galveston, Texas. Whether Halleck or Stanton could survive the storm of abuse was problematical. Senator Grimes of Iowa termed Grant a thickheaded, stupid dog.[35] The Cabinet quarreled among themselves.[36] Newspapers lambasted Sherman. "We want McClellan," cried the Cincinnati *Daily Commercial*.[37]

At Milliken's Bend, Sherman was in a temper. In the combined movement against Vicksburg, he alone had been present and on time. Grant had failed, as had Banks. Sherman blamed the Chickasaw Bayou defeat upon his untested and inexperienced troops.[38]

Porter had asked, "What next?"[39] Sherman had two alternatives. First, intrench at Milliken's Bend, cut inland toward the Red River, disrupt the trade to Vicksburg, and await renewed movements by Grant and Banks. Second, clear out Arkansas Post and Fort Hindman on the Arkansas River, the key to Little Rock. Already, detachments from that fort had captured the *Blue Wing* and annoyed Union transports and mail vessels.[40]

General McClernand arrived at Milliken's Bend, where Sherman suggested a plan for capturing Arkansas Post. McClernand informed Sherman that Grant was not coming, that his depot at Holly Springs had been captured by the enemy and he had been forced to withdraw to La Grange, Tennessee. The next day a disgruntled and outranked Sherman handed the overall command to McClernand.

Preparations advanced for the assault up the Arkansas River. Fort Hindman roosted on a horseshoe bend high up on the bluffs, fifty miles from the Arkansas's mouth,

117 from Little Rock. Fourteen guns—8- and 9-inchers, Parrott rifles, and howitzers—commanded the river approaches. The garrison, commanded by Brigadier General Thomas J. Churchill, C. S. A., numbered 3,000.

The Union expedition rendezvoused at the mouth of the White River and, on January 9, entered what seemed hardly more than a bayou. There were no houses, no farms, only emptiness, swamps, and wilderness, which echoed the progress of the fleet, the hoarse puffs of escaping steam, the rattle of machinery, the snatches of bawdy songs. A few miles from the mouth of the White River, the expedition veered into a cutoff and passed into the Arkansas.[41]

Sailors on board the *Rattler*, the lead boat, sounded the river with two lead lines. The tinclads *Romeo* and *Juliet* followed, their guns trained forward, fuses cut to one second. Next, ahead of Porter's flagship *Black Hawk*, steamed the *Louisville, Baron DeKalb,* and *Cincinnati* and the tinclad *Marmora,* sounding the river. The transports trailed, with the *Lexington* bringing up the rear.[42]

The gunboats slackened speed. The troops, McClernand's 13th Corps and Sherman's 15th, disgorged themselves from the transports. In the darkness, soldiers camped around fires, heating huge coffee kettles and eating roast pork slices and crackers. On the *Black Hawk,* Porter and Sherman diagramed tactics. Porter marked the positions he intended to occupy and the Navy's line of fire so that Sherman knew exactly how far he could advance without running into it.

At dawn, drums rolled "fall in."[43] The advance column, the 8th Missouri, followed by Giles A. Smith's division, turned into the woods. Rebels, behind earthworks protected by logs, lashed out at the Federals. Steadily, uphill, sometimes crawling, sometimes running, the Yankees advanced, the Confederates retreated.

Toiling through the woods for two hours, the Federal units arrived at the swamps and bayous. Deeper and deeper into the marshes the Army waded. In mud up to their arms, the soldiers sloshed forward.[44] They halted, wheeled around, and doubled back on another route.

Outflanked, General Churchill ordered his men to fall back to the inner line of intrenchments.

Out in the stream, the ironclads checked their ranges. At 5:30 p.m. word came from McClernand to assault. The *Louisville, Baron DeKalb, Cincinnati* advanced. Three smoothbores, eight rifle cannon roared from the forts. On the *Baron DeKalb,* the lead vessel, gunners yelled to the captain for permission to fire. Each time the answer shot back: "Keep cool, I will tell you when." At a range of 400 yards, the skipper sang out: "Let go."[45] Guns from the *Baron DeKalb, Louisville,* and *Cincinnati* opened fire. The bastion shuddered and ceased firing. The Army assault failed to come off. Sherman was not yet in position.

The gunboats dropped down-stream in the evening. A simultaneous attack by the flotilla and troops was planned for the next afternoon.

At 1:00 p.m., Porter ran alongside the *Baron DeKalb* in a tug and yelled, "Captain Walker . . . attack the batteries." Sherman's field artillery and Porter's naval cannon erupted. Fire from the ironclads plowed up enemy casemates, knocking out gun emplacements, shattering the fort to pieces. Iron rails tumbled down. Timber was blown up. Guns flew in the air. The tinclads and the ram *Monarch* darted past the fort under fire, up-river to cut off a possible retreat.

Inland, Sherman's fire enfiladed the road that led to

the fort. Yankees lunged forward only to reel back from the Rebel fire. Rallied, they assaulted again, but paid dearly. The cannonading was furious. Hemmed in on all sides, the fort's guns disabled by ironclad fire, the Texas and Arkansas troops, replying only with muskets, refused to yield. Amid a torrent of bullets, General Churchill waved his hat and shouted, "Boys, we are driving them," and, dashing forward, bellowed, "Come on!" He turned and saw the 24th Texas Dismounted Cavalry displaying white flags.[46] The Yankees took the advantage, crowded the lines, and forced surrender. One hundred and ninety Confederate reinforcements arrived just in time to be caught in the Yankee net.[47]

Porter rushed into the fort, and his marines took possession. It was a horrible sight. "Shellproof casemates," log houses reinforced with iron bars, resembled a slaughterhouse for cattle. In a bombed-out hospital, wounded Colonel John W. Dunnington's first words to Porter were: "You wouldn't have got us had it not been for your damned gunboats."[48]

Porter was jubilant. "Arkansas has now nothing but some fieldpieces," he wrote in a letter to Senator Grimes.[49] To a friend in Washington, he rejoiced, "After three hours of hammer and tongs, the landlubbers were whipped out of their boots."[50]

Sherman found McClernand in the cabin of the Tigress, repeating over and over, "Glorious! Glorious! I'll make a splendid report."[51] Officers and men, burning the barracks and rummaging for booty, thought McClernand had shown good judgment in keeping out of the way and letting Sherman direct the fighting.[52]

Casualties, Union and Confederate, numbered 1,000. Thirty men lay killed and wounded in the flotilla. Two thousand prisoners were brought in. Fort Hindman, while not a great victory, was yet an inspiring change from the blunder at Chickasaw Bayou.

In Memphis, Grant was angry that McClernand had gone off on a "wild-goose chase" up the Arkansas River.[53] He ordered him to reassemble his troops on the Mississippi River for an assault against Vicksburg with Bank's Army, daily expected from New Orleans.

Porter went down-stream to Milliken's Bend. His forces were now spread thin. At Helena stood the *Black Hawk, Louisville, Chillicothe, Rattler, Glide, Linden, Baron DeKalb, Cincinnati, Signal, Romeo, Forest Rose, Marmora,* and *Juliet* and the rams *Monarch, Horner, Queen of the West,* and *Lioness.* The *Carondelet* was at Island No. 10; the *Lexington,* convoying prisoners from Fort Hindman to Cairo. The *Bragg* and *Conestoga* were undergoing repairs at Memphis, while the *Fairplay, General Pillow, Brilliant, St. Clair,* and *Robb* were patrolling the Tennessee River. The *Little Rebel* and *New National* were moored at Cairo. The *Eastport, Lafayette, Choctaw, Indianola,* and *Tuscumbia* were fitting out.

A frontal attack upon Vicksburg was impracticable. Haynes Bluff on the Yazoo prevented an Army from passing to the rear of the city that way. Eastward were earthworks, batteries, trenches. Pemberton and 35,000 men stood guard, while another strong arm was being organized by General Joseph E. Johnston to halt any flanking action. No Union vessels operated below Vicksburg to ferry the Army across for an attack from the rear.

This was the situation in January 1863, when General Grant arrived at Milliken's Bend.

12

"Everything Is Going to the Devil at Railroad Speed"

When Grant took personal command, the men in the ranks rejoiced. But the general, surrounded by water and mud, his soldiers shadowed by death, was wary. On the west side of the river, floods deluged most of the countryside. Camping on dry spots, the Army was strung out for sixty miles. It could not move except by boat. The January nights were freezing. Only tents sheltered the soldiers, except for the fortunate few who were able to rig rough log cabins or burrow deep into the side of the levee. Racked by sickness, the Army numbered 58,000 on paper, but could muster only 28,000 for duty. Mobile hospitals were jammed, and men died daily. The levee was a huge graveyard where fatigue parties piled the dead in heaps with little ceremony. Above Vicksburg, the east bank had not enough dry land to quarter an Army, let alone to permit an assault against the city.[1]

Yet the flooded terrain introduced possibilities to cut a canal into Lake Providence, which was linked with the Mississippi via the Tensas, Washita, and Red Rivers, or to enlarge the old Williams's canal across Young's Point enough to slide transports through to below Vicksburg.

On his flagship *Magnolia*, Grant huddled over a table, slowly inhaling his cigar. He calculated the risks involved in these ventures and also considered the possibility of cutting through the levee at Delta, six miles above Helena on the east bank, to push an expedition into Old Yazoo Pass, which bypassed Haynes Bluff.

To deepen Williams's ditch, mud machines, arriving from Memphis, scooped up ooze as 4,000 soldiers and 2,000 Negroes drilled stumps and demolished them with heavy charges of powder. Rebels mounted the rifled gun, "Whistling Dick," on the bluffs and fired from across the river into the diggers. Heavy rains and winds whipped at the work details. Then the head of the canal suddenly gave way, and soldiers tumbled into the torrent, but were rescued by the tug *Swallow*. After the entire lower half of Young's Point was flooded, the work was abandoned.[2]

General James B. McPherson's Corps, waist deep in water, sawing down trees and digging up stumps, cleared a canal through to Lake Providence. Coal barges towed by a steamer mushed through, but the Mississippi failed to cut a permanent channel, and the military deserted the project.

Porter and Grant pursued their scheme to flood Old Yazoo Pass, a dry river long since forgotten. They hoped to send gunboats and transports through the Tallahatchie to the Yazoo River above Haynes Bluff, where they could raze the enemy's transport fleet at Yazoo City, cut communications, land an Army, and attack Vicksburg from the rear. A detachment of diggers shoveled and blasted the levee at Delta. Water surged through the cut, sweeping everything before it, engulfing the Yazoo Basin, forging a channel eighty yards wide.[3]

The admiral detailed the *Chillicothe* and *Baron De-*

Kalb and the tinclads *Rattler, Romeo, Forest Rose,* and *Cricket* and gave Commander Watson Smith leadership of the naval forces. Porter conceived the initial operation to be naval and was indignant when Grant assigned 6,000 men under General Leonard Ross and twelve transports to accompany the gunboats.

The expedition penetrated the cut on February 24. Moving only in daylight, the troop carriers—the best Grant could find—frequently broke down, and the ironclads, hauling three coal barges apiece, advanced lethargically through the narrow, tortuous channel. Instead of moving out at dawn, Smith never got under way before 7:30 a.m. The gunboats and transports stopped along the way for a leisurely lunch. General Ross advised the ironclads to cast off the coal barges and speed ahead of the slow-moving transports, but Watson Smith continued to crawl along with the Army.

The alerted Johnnies had time to fortify. Vicksburg dispatched General John C. Moore's brigade and two 8-inch naval guns into the area, while Major Minor Meriweather, from Yazoo City, constructed earthworks at Fort Pemberton, Greenwood, Mississippi, near the mouth of the Yallabusha.

Smith's gunboats and Ross's transports neared Fort Pemberton on March 11. A short, quick bend in the river brought the *Chillicothe* face to face with the enemy's batteries. The Confederate guns opened fire. In seven minutes Rebel shells blew out the turret's ports and crippled her. Damaged and helpless, she backed downriver, where mechanics patched her up.

At sun-up the next morning, the *Chillicothe* and *Baron DeKalb*, piled high with cotton bales for added protection, started for the fort. At a thousand-yard range, the channel was so crooked that they could only lie abreast of each other, their sides touching, their sterns made fast to the bank. The Confederates pummeled the *Chillicothe's* hurricane deck and bent down the grating to disarrange the steering wheel, while the *Baron DeKalb* suffered six hits in the forward casemates. Firing erratically, the gunboats retreated.

Two more days, two more meaningless exchanges. Informing Smith that reinforcements were on the way, General Ross demanded that the Navy continue the bombardments. Commander Smith retorted that the channel was too narrow to maneuver in, his ammunition and rations were low, his officers and men fatigued. Lieutenant Colonel James H. Wilson, chief topographical engineer, privately censured Smith for lack of backbone. Army scouts picked off Confederate snipers, but found Fort Pemberton surrounded by swamps and bayous inaccessible to ground assault.

On March 18, Watson Smith fell ill—"softening of the brain," Porter later claimed—and started back to Helena. After consultations with General Ross, Lieutenant Commander James P. Foster, second in command of the gunboats, decided to stop the attack. The expedition filed back into the Tallahatchie, only to meet Union support troops under General Isaac F. Quinby.

Amid driving rain, the ironclads returned to lob shells sporadically toward Fort Pemberton. A week passed, but the Army failed to budge from the warmth of their transports. Diffident in a command situation, operating without orders that covered such circumstances, Foster chose retreat. General Quinby realized that if he remained, 200 miles of unprotected communications would lie between him and Grant. He decided to retreat with Foster.[4]

Lincoln termed the action in the Tallahatchie ridiculous, and Gideon Welles scored Porter for sapping the flotilla's strength on tomfool by-plays that promised no results.[5] At Helena, Porter accused Smith of disobeying orders and blistered shipbuilder Brown for constructing such an enfeebled monstrosity as the *Chillicothe*.

Porter was worried over the whereabouts of the attack force he had sent to police the Mississippi between Vicksburg and Port Hudson. After dawn on February 2, twenty days before the Yazoo Pass Expedition headed into the bayous, Colonel Charles Ellet, aged nineteen, commanding the ram *Queen of the West* and the *DeSoto*, had got under way. The youthful Ellet had hauled 12-pounders on the *Queen of the West* and fitted up the armed steam ferryboat *DeSoto*. Porter promised to send the ironclad *Indianola* as soon as he found a crew.

The sun was high in the sky when Ellet's force rounded the point toward Vicksburg. Rebel guns opened fire. A 7-inch shell lodged in the cabin of the *Queen of the West* without exploding. Despite the Confederate hammering, Ellet decided to destroy the steamboat *Vicksburg*, moored at the wharf. The *Queen of the West* circled slowly, then lunged forward with such force as to penetrate twenty feet into the *Vicksburg's* port quarter, cutting away the cook house and demolishing the cabin. The ram's incessant stream of shot ignited the *Vicksburg*, while Confederate shells set the ram's cotton bales ablaze. With dense smoke suffocating the engine crew, Ellet was positive that the *Queen of the West* would sink if she attempted to butt again. Nimbly, the ram turned, headed downstream, and passed the stronghold.[6]

The fire extinguished, the *Queen of the West* sped by the guns at Warrenton, Mississippi, giving a "don't-carea-damn snort on her whistle."[7] The ram and *DeSoto* passed Natchez and Ellis Cliffs and arrived fifteen miles below the mouth of the Red River. She captured the enemy cargo steamer *A. W. Baker* and the *Moro*, loaded with 110,000 pounds of pork, 500 hogs, and quantities of salt; destroyed 25,000 pounds of meal awaiting transportation; took the *Berwick Bay*, with 200 barrels of molasses, ten hogsheads of sugar, 30,000 pounds of flour, forty bales of cotton. Gingerly, Ellet pushed up the hazardous channel of the Red River. Standing on the gundeck inside the casemate, Ellet, who could not see the river, barked at Pilot T. W. Garvey for steering erratically.[8]

The ram and the *DeSoto* reached the mouth of the Atchafalaya River. They burned their prizes, and the *DeSoto* remained there to guard the coal barges while the *Queen of the West* explored the Atchafalaya. That evening, as the ram was returning to the *DeSoto*, an organized band of plantation overseers hid behind the levee and attacked with double-barreled shot guns. Captain James D. Thompson, Ellet's sailing master, was hit, his knee badly shattered. The *Queen of the West* continued on course and anchored at the mouth of the Atchafalaya for the night.

The thirteenth of February was another calm blue day. The ram started up the Atchafalaya to avenge the night attack. She stopped at the first sugar plantation, razed the mansion, the outbuildings, everything. At the next manor, Ellet set fire to the houses, steam mills, and Negro huts. The *Queen of the West* retraced her steps, hooked up with the *DeSoto*, and rambled up the Red to the mouth of the Black River.

The next day, after steaming fifteen miles up the Black, the *Queen of the West* surprised and captured the Red

River packet *Era No. 5*. From the passengers, Ellet learned that Fort Taylor protected the river at Gordon's Landing. Leaving his prize and the coal barges astern, the ram and *DeSoto* moved up-river and neared Taylor in the evening.

The Confederates held off until the ram rounded a sharp bend; then, at a range of 300 yards, they fired with everything they had. The first shot barely missed. A Northern newsman exclaimed, "If that is the first, watch out for the second. They won't miss much next time."[9]

Shots flew thick and fast. Ellet ordered Pilot Garvey to back down. The *Queen of the West* fouled in the mud. The Yankees failed to respond to the Confederate fire, since only the unprotected bow gun bore on the fort.

The enemy found the exact range. Hardly had the chief engineer reported that the escape pipe had been shot away, when an explosion rocked the *Queen of the West* and a rush of steam enveloped her.

Ellet ran aft of the pilot house and fell on deck, face down. Then, jumping up, he raced to the forecastle, spewing abuse at Pilot Garvey and crying, "The boat is gone." Frantic, he ordered the men to toss cotton bales over the side. The colonel was the first to abandon ship. Leaping astride a cotton bale, he led the escape down-river to the *DeSoto*.

Sailors leaped into the river to drown or to scramble on board cotton bales and follow the colonel to safety. When Pilot Garvey reached the *DeSoto*, he found Captain Asgill Connor on his knees and Ellet yelling to Lieutenant J. E. Tuttle not to run the *DeSoto* under the enemy's guns.[10]

There was no hope for those still on the ram. They dared not blow her up, as they could not move the wounded Captain Thompson. The Confederates kept firing, raking the cabin, plunging shot through the deck.

At dark a thunderstorm shook the countryside. Three volunteers from the *DeSoto* attempted to board the ram and blow her up, but were captured. Ellet did not dispatch another party, but retreated down-river in the *DeSoto*. She grounded, backed off, grounded again, found the channel, and reached the *Era No. 5* at 11 p.m. Ellet scuttled the slow-moving *DeSoto* and got under way in the *Era No. 5* at full speed.

The packet raced down the Red River and headed out into the Mississippi. Hugging the shore, opposite Ellis Cliffs, the *Era No. 5* hit a mud bank. Ellet exploded, accused Garvey of disloyalty, and clamped him in irons. The *Era No. 5* finally backed off and hastened up-stream.

The *Indianola* was steaming leisurely past Natchez. Her skipper, Commander George Brown, sighted a strange craft moving northward. He fired a warning shot across her bow.

"Who are you?" Brown yelled.

"We are friends," responded twenty voices.

"Where are you from?"

"From the Red River. We belong to the ram fleet."

"Where's the *Queen of the West?*" demanded Brown.

"She's blown up."

"Where's Colonel Ellet?"

"He's on board," answered the *Era No. 5*.[11]

The *Indianola's* gig went alongside. On the ironclad, Commander Brown and Ellet conferred and decided to steam southward and search out the Confederate gunboat *Webb,* rumored to be in the vicinity. Near Ellis Cliffs, Ellet, from the deck of the *Era No. 5*, saw smoke rising in the distance. In a few minutes the *Webb* was visible. With whistles shrieking, *Era No. 5* wheeled and fell back toward the onrushing *Indianola*. The whistles alerted the *Webb*, which turned and barged down-river. The *Indianola* fired twice, both shots missing.

Ellet returned up the Mississippi to Vicksburg without a convoy or escort. With bales of cotton loosely piled on the lower deck, the *Era No. 5* passed Natchez unmo-lested, escaped the fire from Grand Gulf and Warrenton, and arrived inside Federal picket lines.[12]

An outraged Porter berated Ellet for disobeying orders, and stormed, "My plans were well laid, only badly exe-cuted."[13] The ram skipper retorted, "Everything is going to the devil at railroad speed," and, privately, gibed that Porter was "too mean to live."[14]

The *Indianola* continued to blockade the mouth of the Red River, but dared not enter for want of a river pilot. Rumors circulated that the Rebels were massing an offen-sive force composed of the refloated *Queen of the West*, the *Webb*, fitted with a ram, and the cottonclads *Dr. Beatty* and *Grand Era*.

Awake to the danger, Brown changed his plans and, on February 22, the *Indianola* started northward. Her full coal bunkers could take her to Vicksburg, but Brown, afraid that additional coal might be needed, towed two cumbersome barges alongside. Progress up-river was slow.

On the same day, the *Queen of the West, Webb, Dr. Beatty,* and *Grand Era,* under the command of Major Joseph L. Brent, C. S. A., rendezvoused twenty miles below Gordon's Landing and started out after the iron-clad.

Hampered by her coal barges, the *Indianola* barely made three knots up-stream. The pursuers quickened the pace once they reached the Mississippi. Brent learned that his quarry was far ahead in miles, but not hopelessly out of reach in hours. The night of February 22-23 wore on.

The dawn brought no Federal reinforcements for the *Indianola*. She moved past Natchez and was observed from shore. When the Rebel flotilla arrived at that river town, Brent discovered that his prey was only half as far ahead as she had been earlier. He became certain that he could overtake her.

The *Indianola*, hauling her barges, continued to crawl forward. She passed Grand Gulf at noon. Vicksburg was within striking distance. The Confederates reached Grand Gulf only four hours behind. Running more than two miles to the *Indianola's* one, Brent calculated that he could overhaul the fleeing Yankee at 9:40 p.m. just above New Carthage at the foot of Palmyra Island.

In the late afternoon, Brown spied heavy smoke astern. He was positive that he was being hunted, but continued to steam slowly up-river.

A veil of clouds partially obscured the moon that night. At 9:30 p.m., near New Carthage, Brown sighted the Rebels three miles astern. The chase was reaching a climax. Thirteen miles ahead lay the Federal batteries on Young's Point, but Brown swung the *Indianola*, barges and all, down-stream toward the enemy. The distance between the assailants closed.

At point blank range the *Indianola's* guns barked twice. Two misses. The *Queen of the West* rammed her bow into a coal barge. The *Webb* hurtled into the *Indianola's* bow, just forward of the second barge. The *Queen of the West* maneuvered off into the murk, out of sight, to get up steam for the next attack.

The ironclad's guns fired sporadically. With only half

a crew—Porter had sent out the *Indianola* undermanned—Brown could not work both batteries. The forward cannon kept discharging, but there was no precision to the Yankee fire.

As night came on the *Webb* began circling, and the *Indianola* swung laboriously around to meet the assault. They clashed together and quivered. The *Webb* veered off the bow, cutting a barge adrift. The *Queen of the West* loomed up. Again, the bow of the ironclad swerved, and a blast from her 11-inch cannon scored a hit on the *Queen of the West*, which kept coming.

Engaged in his first combat, Brown charged along the deck brandishing his revolver. He went to his knees at the grating on the main deck to see if the engineers understood the pilots' signals. He snapped out orders to the helmsman, to the engineers, to the gunners. Once he loaded, aimed, and fired one cannon himself.

The *Queen of the West* came at the *Indianola* from astern. A Yankee shot struck the *Queen of the West*, knocked off some cotton bales, and caused her to list. Another whistled through the ram's forward port and destroyed a brass 12-pounder. But the ram crunched into the *Indianola's* starboard quarter abaft the side-wheel and wrecked her rudder. Her starboard engine crippled, her side leaking badly, the *Indianola* was in a precarious position. After the collisions, the *Webb* and the *Queen of the West* steamed off for another run. The *Webb* assailed at full speed as the *Indianola* pulled away and let go with a 9-inch shell. It missed. The *Webb* cut into the *Indianola's* weakened stern. Water flooded in and Brown realized that if she were struck again, the ironclad would sink so fast that few, if any, lives would be saved. The *Queen of the West*, staggering and listing, and the

Webb, her bow almost torn off, bore down again. The cottonclads *Dr. Beatty* and *Grand Era* closed in for the kill. Brown bellowed, "Surrender!" The *Webb's* crew threw out lines, and the ram towed the stricken vessel ashore. A Confederate colonel stepped on board and accepted Brown's sword. One hundred sailors were taken prisoner; four others jumped overboard and escaped in the underbrush. Casualties in the ninety-minute scrap numbered only six for the *Queen of the West*, one for the *Webb*, two for the *Indianola*. The jubilant Rebels announced plans to repair the *Indianola* and put her in commission.[15]

Early on the morning of February 24, a steamer came up the Mississippi and anchored in front of the Confederate river town Warrenton. Through his spyglass, Porter saw that she was the *Queen of the West*. Where was the *Indianola*? he worried. The fate of the ironclad was discussed throughout the flotilla. When definite news of the capture of the *Indianola* arrived, Porter was highly critical of Commander Brown.[16] The admiral's fleet now lay scattered up-river, and he had nothing to send past Vicksburg except the Pook turtles.

In Washington, Lincoln read the distressing reports and sent for Gustavus Vasa Fox.[17] Knowing that the *Indianola* threatened Farragut, Welles wired Porter, "She is too formidable to be left at large and must be destroyed."[18]

Porter did not hesitate. Carpenters converted a coal barge into a dummy ironclad. They increased her length by adding log rafts, raised false casemates and a pilot house, stuck in five "Quaker guns," slapped mud together to resemble furnaces, piled up pork barrels for stacks, and burned tar and oakum at their base. This "fearsome-looking monster" cost Porter twelve hours of work and $8.23.

Unmanned, the phantom sailed off in the current, which piloted her perfectly through the heavy bombardment of Vicksburg's shore batteries. The *Webb, Queen of the West, Dr. Beatty,* and *Grand Era* hurried down-river ahead of the "Black Terror." In the confusion the *Queen of the West* rammed the *Grand Era.*[19] In Jackson, Mississippi, General Pemberton ordered the half-repaired *Indianola* blown up.[20] Receiving this dispatch, watching the *Webb* and *Queen of the West* scoot by, the lieutenant in charge of the salvage party ignited the powder and exploded the *Indianola.* The dummy ironclad passed the blazing guns of Warrenton. Gradually, the Confederates detected the hoax, and desperate telegrams went out countermanding previous orders.[21] But it was too late. Porter's decoy hit a mud bank and was captured.

Amid the pungent odors of the river town Helena, Porter could now turn his attention to squadron business. Loaded with ordnance, provisions, and stores, the *General Lyon* and *New National* arrived every few weeks from Cairo. Insisting that his monthly coal allowance was not enough, Porter stockpiled 160,000 bushels. To feed the squadron, the admiral called for twenty bullocks a week together with chickens and eggs for the hospital ship, *Red Rover.*[22]

Accidents and surprise attacks plagued the squadron. With inexperienced firemen, the *Eastport* left Cairo, lost steam, foundered on a bar, and returned to the dockyard for a $25,000 repair job.[23] A fire started by Negroes in an ashcan completely gutted the tinclad *Glide.* Concealed in the brush, guerrillas surprised and disabled the ram *Dick Fulton* and the Army steamer *Hercules.*[24] The drunken captain of the *Lily* went berserk, steered the tug crazily, hoisted white handkerchiefs, and headed for Vicksburg. Disaster was averted when the ironclad *Louisville* headed her off, but the ill-starred *Lily,* with a new skipper, accidentally rammed the *Choctaw* and sank.[25]

Porter's gunboats scourged the upper river to halt illicit trade—the bartering of Confederate cotton for contraband and Union gold. Trade was authorized only in the territory occupied by Federal troops, but the temptation to amass fortunes induced traders and United States Treasury agents to resort to deception. Ironclads arrested the *Home, W. A. Knapp, Chippewa Valley, White Cloud,* and *Rowena* with contraband goods. The *Monarch* and *Juliet* seized 250 bales of cotton along the river banks, and the *Rattler* took the *Rose Hambleton* and *Evansville,* loaded with bales. The *Tyler* confiscated seventy bales hidden in the outbuildings of Dr. Duncan's plantation and twenty-two more at the Pringle place. In the White River, the *Conestoga* impounded sixty bales and, at Cypress Bend, the *Monarch* secured forty-two. In one twenty-day period, the flotilla sent to Cairo for adjudication 388 bales valued at $139,000, and held on to 259 for use in the squadron.[26] The admiral discovered one of his tinclads, *Forest Rose,* engaged in the contraband trade. Acting Master Hentig of the *Curlew* was found guilty of speculating in cotton and placed under arrest.[27] "Cannot we stop this cotton mania?" asked Porter.[28] Grant stripped General Willis A. Gorman of command when he was detected dealing illegally.[29]

On the Cumberland and Tennessee Rivers, Union tinclads skirmished daily with a hidden foe who attacked, inflicted damage, and disappeared into the woods. The tinclad patrols maintained General Rosecrans's lines of communication to Nashville, destroying skiffs and rafts, rescuing refugees, convoying transports, extricating Army units entrapped by the Rebels.

Porter scrutinized his maps. The levee cut at Delta had flooded the entire countryside and every creek, old water course, bayou, and morass offered navigable waterways. An expedition, by cutting its way through the inundated woods, might enter Steele's Bayou, Black Bayou, Deer Creek, Rolling Fork, the Big Sunflower River, and reach the Yazoo above Haynes Bluff.

To discover this route's feasibility, Porter and Grant made a reconnaissance in a tinclad up Steele's Bayou and, sounding five fathoms of water, steamed into Black Bayou and a dense forest. It was a curious sight to see a tinclad and tugs gliding through the woods, crashing by trees, shaking loose a menagerie—coons, snakes, rats, and mice, which landed on deck to be swept away by sailors manning the brooms. By removing the trees, Porter and Grant believed that an expedition could push through. Satisfied with their work, they returned to Helena.

Porter decided to lead the attack himself and ordered the *Louisville, Cincinnati, Carondelet, Mound City,* and *Pittsburg,* four mortar boats, and four tugboats to get under way. Sherman and troops from Stuart's division boarded the *Silver Wave* and *Diligent,* to follow the ironclads and determine the practicality of sending the whole Army.

Porter's fleet filtered into the willows of Steele's Bayou on March 15. In the morning dawn, the whole forest was filled with a milky mist and a heavy moisture—a sort of white resplendence that lifted and fell. During the afternoon the expedition oozed into Muddy Bayou—wider, freer from projecting trees—and sloshed thirty-one miles to Black Bayou. The ironclads bulled their way through wild eglantine, grapevines, willow and cypress trees cloaked with Spanish moss. A foraging party brought back chickens, hams, eggs, and butter.

By 2 p.m., March 19, the fleet passed Moore's plantation and was within range of Rolling Fork and Deer Creek. In the tug *Fern*, General Sherman and a contingent of soldiers overtook the ironclads. Astern, the wooden transports with 6,000 men were being switched fearfully by the willow trees. At the intersection of Black Bayou and Deer Creek, Sherman waited for his transports while Porter went above to explore the route.

In Deer Creek—narrow, twisting, thick with willows—the squadron wiggled along making one mile an hour. Yankees burned cotton marked "C. S. A." and razed corn and pork stored in warehouses, awaiting shipment to Vicksburg.

The ironclads penetrated the very heart of the Yazoo Valley before the Confederate military learned of the squadron's existence. Vicksburg sent three regiments under General Winfield S. Featherston, and General Samuel W. Ferguson struck out from Fort Pemberton with a battalion of infantry and six field pieces.

Porter reached a point seven miles below Rolling Fork, which connected Deer Creek with the Big Sunflower. To pin down the ironclads, Rebels—military and civilian—chopped down trees ahead and astern. The tug *Thistle*, followed by the *Carondelet* with Porter on board, steamed ahead. Trees crashed into the channel. The tug moved slower and slower and finally stuck fast. She could move neither ahead nor astern. Withes snared the *Carondelet* and held Porter in a vise. Equipped with saws, knives, cutlasses, and chisels, sailors dropped over the side to clear out the boughs. After four hours of toil, the *Carondelet* had moved less than a foot.

The Confederates raked the ironclad with shots from seven field pieces. Below the level of the banks, Porter's 11-inch guns were powerless. No word came from Sherman. Porter sent off hasty messages, one written on toilet paper. The Yankees unlimbered their smaller guns and, for a time, silenced the Johnnies' cross fire. But Porter stayed stranded in the willows. The possibility of Confederates' damming up the channel at both ends and draining off the water crossed the admiral's mind. This would put him in the ridiculous position of being high and dry, and it would take months for Grant's Army to haul him out. Where was Sherman?

Porter readied his command to blow up all the ironclads if the Confederates attempted to board. Seamen dragged out turpentine, oil, and camphene; spread the decks with powder; dropped below to shut up the ironclads and await the outcome.

Three thousand Rebels commenced firing briskly, but the hesitant General Featherston refused to assault.

From out of the willows, a Negro ran toward Porter, yelling, "Your folks is coming, your folks is coming." Beating off the Rebels, the 6th and 8th Missouri arrived at the beleaguered ironclads. Fatigue parties started to free the *Carondelet* and *Thistle*. The Rebels brawled with the 8th Missouri, but slowly fell back and retreated.

Sherman came riding out of the woods on a donkey. "Halloo, Porter," he called, "what did you get into such an ugly scrape for? So much for you Navy fellows, getting out of your element; better send for the soldiers always. This is the most infernal expedition I was ever on; who in thunder proposed such a mad scheme? Your gunboats look sick."[30]

When the fleet reached Black Bayou again, Negroes in high glee swarmed to the banks, parading on horses and mules, hurrahing "going to freedom sure."[31] As Porter headed into Steele's Bayou, retracing his steps, Admiral Farragut's private secretary boarded the *Carondelet* and startled him by announcing that Farragut and the *Hartford* were anchored just below Vicksburg.[32]

13

"It Is Great, Mr. Welles, It Is Great"

Hurrying to the *Hartford*, Porter met with Farragut, who sat on the propeller block drawing idle diagrams with his fingers.[1] Dwarfed by the bluffs at Port Hudson, blocked and hurled back by the Confederate cannon, his fleet lay crippled in the river below. Only the *Hartford* and the gunboat *Albatross* had survived the engagement at Port Hudson and labored on to Vicksburg.

Farragut knew how desperately the Navy Department, indeed the nation, wanted to clear the Mississippi River. He had been optimistic that his fleet, cooperating with ground forces under General Nathaniel P. Banks, could move safely through the gauntlet at Port Hudson and control the waters to Vicksburg.

General Banks had superseded Benjamin Butler in command of the Department of the Gulf in December 1862.[2] Overwhelmed by civil administrative duties, the assessment of taxes and fines, the regulation of trade, the confiscation of Confederate property, the routine affairs of his military department, Banks had stayed in New Orleans, drilling 10,000 troops and attending operas and concerts.[3] January and February had glided by. Rumors spread southward that the *Queen of the West* and *Indianola* were in Rebel hands. Washington was concerned

over the failure to make concerted efforts against Port
Hudson. Finally, Banks and Farragut had decided upon
a combined assault.[4]

After quick farewells in Baton Rouge on a crisp March
afternoon, sailors, high in the rigging, had flung hats in
the air and given "one tremendous tiger" as Farragut's
ocean-going ships stood up-river for Port Hudson. From
the deck of the *Mississippi,* Captain Melancton Smith had
glimpsed his wife on the ruined, terraced steps of the
state capitol building, waving a handkerchief.[5] As the
cheers faded, there were several in the squadron that
were gloomy over the prospect that lay ahead.[6] Atop the
precipitous bluffs at a right-angle bend, the batteries of
Port Hudson scowled down at the river, their guns so
high that it was impossible for the Yankee gunners to
elevate sufficiently their broadsides.

Surrounded by his staff, a spyglass thrust under his
arm, Farragut moved about the poop deck of the *Hartford,* watching his steamers astern, looking ahead, alert
to the enemy. Jovial and talkative, Admiral Farragut—
still "Cap'n Davy" to his men—was a conservative seaman,
prone to distrust new and untried weapons of war, not
doubting the efficiency of the rifled guns and armored
ships, but fearful that their impact upon the Navy might
be detrimental to the spirit of the service. "A ship of
wood and a heart of iron are as good as an ironclad,"
Farragut frequently told his officers.

On the deck below, Captain John L. Broome and his
marines—who manned the quarter-deck guns—prepared
to repel Confederate boarders. Engineer Speights, who
occupied the most exposed position on the sloop, was
stationed at the bell that communicated with the engine
room. In the bowels of the *Hartford,* Chief Engineer

James B. Kimball and his black gang stood at their posts. In the rigging, lookouts scanned the river for mines.[7]

At Profit Island, the squadron stopped engines, anchored, and communicated with the ironclad *Essex* and the mortar boats moored to the banks. Farragut and his commanders conferred on the flagship and sketched out tactics for the night attack. The *Essex* and the mortars were to fire, enfilading the Rebel batteries, as Farragut's squadron charged past the bluffs. To protect the slow-paced sloops-of-war if they became disabled in the strong current, seamen lashed the gunboat *Albatross* to the *Hartford's* port quarter, the *Genesee* to the *Richmond*, the *Kineo* to the *Monongahela*. No gunboat was assigned to the *Mississippi*, a side-wheeler.

That night, March 14-15, the ships prepared for the onslaught. On the *Richmond*, at 9:30 p.m., the Officer-of-the-Deck's orderly knocked on a cabin door.

"What is it?" asked Captain James Alden.

"A signal from the admiral—two red lights under the stern of the flagship."

The captain, who was conversing with his executive officer and divisional commanders, promptly rose and said sternly, "Gentlemen, you hear the message; each one will go to his place of duty and the ship will be got under way as soon as possible."

The crew peered out toward the banks and the bluffs, but saw nothing except darkness and shadows. Behind the cannon, deck hands placed square wooden boxes filled with sawdust, "like the spittoons one used to see in the country barrooms." Old salts informed the recruits that these held an "absorbent" to be thrown upon the blood-splattered decks.[8]

At Port Hudson taps sounded. Near 11:00 p.m., the

discharge of a distant cannon roused the Confederates from their bunks. The enemy was coming up-river. The drum roll sounded and officers, scrambling toward the guns, shouted, "Fall in, fall in." The soldiers jumped into their clothes and out into the darkness. The 20-pounder Parrott, served by the 1st Tennessee and the 1st Alabama, let go.[9]

The mortars and the *Essex's* 9-inchers howled. For some reason, the admiral's order to get under way was not instantly obeyed, and it was not until 10:45 that the squadron was moving.

The river was red with the glare of exploding shells. Slowly delivering her broadsides, the *Hartford* groped forward. From the poop deck, Farragut cried to his men, "That's your sort, boys, now's your time!" Broadside responded. Yelling into his speaking trumpet, Farragut unconsciously stepped on the tarpaulin covering the hatchway. It gave way and the admiral fell, thinking he was shot. A seaman grabbed him and helped him to his feet.

The *Hartford* quivered at each discharge of her Dahlgrens. Smoke from the admiral's cannon rolled back into the oncoming ships, blinding their pilots.

At the right-angle bend, the current spun the *Hartford* and swept her toward the bluffs and the Rebel batteries. The bowsprit of the *Richmond* loomed up over the *Hartford's* quarter. For a split second, the flagship grounded. To the *Albatross*, Farragut barked, "Back! Back!" The *Albatross* backed full, trembled, and swung the *Hartford* into deep water.

The pilot in the mizzen top reported a steamer bearing down. Farragut seized his sword lying on the signal locker and shouted, "Let them come!" It was a false alarm. The *Hartford* and *Albatross,* grappling in the current, gradually passed the blazing guns and reached safety above. Farragut searched in vain for his ships.[10]

The *Richmond* and *Genesee* were swallowed up in the smoke. Confederate shells chewed them up mercilessly. Splinters from the masts, ravelings from the sails and lines showered the decks of the *Richmond.* Lieutenant Commander A. Boyd Cummings, her executive officer, yelled to his gunners, "You will fire the whole starboard battery, one gun at a time, from bow gun aft. Don't fire too fast. Aim carefully at the flashes of the enemy's guns. Fire!"[11] The *Richmond* shuddered and shuddered again.

Cummings stood on the bridge. A shell plunged over the starboard gangway and exploded. Cummings crumpled to the deck, his left leg shattered.[12] The *Richmond* faltered and sheered toward the bank beneath the Rebel guns. A shell tore into her side, knocked out a gun crew, and set her afire. Sailors hurried forward with hoses and buckets to extinguish the flames. Partially damaged, the *Richmond* was exposed to a cross fire, which raked her from stem to stern. A mine exploded on the starboard quarter. A shot hit the steam chest and jammed open the safety valve. As she turned her prow toward the Confederate cannon, a shell crashed through the forecastle and a double charge of grape swept the decks. "Don't shoot any more!" screamed a bluejacket. "We are sinking!!"[13] Leaking profusely, losing headway despite the *Genesee's* help, the *Richmond* turned and headed southward.

Lashed to the *Kineo,* the *Monongahela* was barely making two and a half knots against the current. Opposite the principal Confederate battery, where *Richmond* met disaster, the *Monongahela* was hit hard. On the port quarter, the *Kineo* shot ahead awkwardly and parted her lines, carrying off part of the *Monongahela's* rigging, hammock nets, and anchor chain. An overheated crank pin stopped the *Monongahela's* forward engines. Unmanageable, she drifted helplessly after the *Richmond*.

The *Mississippi* steamed into the tempest. Orders were quietly given and executed. Leisurely smoking a cigar, Melancton Smith saw dimly through the smoke the disabled *Richmond* and *Monongahela* pass by. Abreast of the upper batteries and nearly out of danger, Smith congratulated his crew and ordered the engines ahead full. Gaining speed, the *Mississippi* veered and ran hard aground on a sand bar, keeling over on her port side, throwing a dark shadow across the river. She stuck fast. For thirty minutes, the side-wheeler tried to back off. Her engines throbbed. The Rebels scorched her with a cross fire. To remain, reasoned Smith, was to murder his men. Calmly lighting another cheroot, he inhaled deeply and ordered the crew to abandon ship. Sailors jumped overboard into the river and clung to bits of wood in the swift current. Others lowered the lifeboats and clambered in.

Captain Smith and his executive officer, Lieutenant Commander George Dewey, made a last check, sprinkled turpentine in the wardroom, applied the match, hurried into a lifeboat, and pulled away for the *Essex*. Relieved of the weight of 300 men, the *Mississippi* slowly righted herself and slid into the channel. The side-wheeler, wrapped in flames and with water pouring into the shot holes, was caught in the current and drifted downstream.[14]

A lookout on the *Richmond*, now anchored below the

batteries, hailed the Officer-of-the-Deck: "Halloo! A large fire ahead!"

"Where away?"

"Just above the bend."

"What is it like?" called the officer.

"Like a fire raft."

Captain Alden sang out, "Keep a good look out. Man the bow guns, and stand by to slip the cable."

Flames shot skyward. The *Mississippi* neared the *Richmond*. Just as she cleared, her starboard guns, heated from the blaze, began to explode. Suddenly, she blew up. The historic *Mississippi*, the side-wheeler that had carried Perry's pennant beneath the sunny skies of Japan and battle flags through the smoke of the Mexican War, disappeared in the surging waters of the Mississippi River.[15]

The river fell silent now. Inland, General Banks's Army was still seeking its initial position. Without starting a diversionary attack, it withdrew to Baton Rouge.[16]

Up-stream, above Port Hudson, Farragut waited anxiously. He had heard the cannon and, for an instant, had seen the masts and spars of the *Richmond*. He asked Captain Wainwright, "My God! What has stopped them?" A depressed Farragut went below to rest, blaming General Banks's inaction for the repulse.[17] The battle was an almost complete failure but, although he had pushed through only two vessels, they alone were enough to dominate the Mississippi and snuff out the Red River traffic.

The *Hartford* and the *Albatross* were now imprisoned between Port Hudson and Vicksburg, cut off in both directions from communications and supplies. The flagship and her consort steamed up-river past Natchez, fired salvos into Grand Gulf, discovered the wreck of the *Indianola,* and destroyed sugar and corn along the banks.

Returned from the willow trees of Steele's Bayou, Porter arrived at the *Hartford* below Vicksburg. Farragut poured out a stream of complaint about his losses and Banks's retreat, still idly tracing designs on the propeller block, and begged Porter to send down his ironclads from Helena. Porter informed him that the Western Flotilla could spare none.[18]

Upon Farragut's urgent request, General Alfred Ellet, bypassing Porter's authority, ordered the rams *Switzerland* and *Lancaster* down-river past Vicksburg. Commanded by the youthful Charles Ellet, the rams started out in broad daylight at full speed. The first fifteen Rebel shells were badly aimed, but, as the rams closed the range to Vicksburg, the Confederate fire became accurate and rapid. Afront the enemy's heaviest guns, the *Switzerland* caught nineteen shells. A 10-inch shell detonated her center boiler. The explosion was "God-awful." Her engines stopped, disabled. With steam hissing through her pilot house, the *Switzerland* floated with the current. From her deck, her crew saw the *Lancaster* suddenly blow up and sink rapidly bow first, her stern gun firing until the last.[19]

At Helena, Porter blazed in a show of temper. By what authority, he stormed, did General Ellet send those rams? He turned on Charles Ellet for running the batteries in broad daylight.[20]

With the *Hartford,* the repaired *Switzerland,* and the *Albatross* towing the coal and provisions barges sent down by Porter, Farragut moved southward and commenced the blockade of the Red River.

General Banks, he learned, was marching overland from Opelousas, Louisiana, to Alexandria, on the Red River, to hunt down the enemy and seize a hundred thousand bales of cotton. Along the way, Banks destroyed the *Queen of the West, Diana,* and *Hart,* and twelve transport steamers; captured 2,000 Rebels and twenty heavy guns; demolished the Confederate foundries at Franklin and New Iberia.[21]

From Washington, Halleck berated Banks for "eccentric movements" and for his failure to occupy Port Hudson and cooperate with Grant at Vicksburg.[22] The Cabinet held a lengthy session to discuss western affairs. Gustavus Vasa Fox speculated that the Confederate ram *Tennessee* might sneak out of Mobile Bay and sink the wooden blockading fleet in the Gulf. On April 6, 1863, the nation momentarily turned its attention away from Vicksburg toward Charleston, South Carolina, where the ocean-going Ericsson monitors were poised for an all-out attack on Fort Sumter. "The people," said Fox, "will have nothing but success, and they are right. The old cry is commencing against Mr. Welles for not giving it to them."[23] Within days, the news arrived that the monitors had failed.

At Milliken's Bend, General Grant was too busy to worry about Charleston. He continued to hold sway at his headquarters in the ladies' cabin on the *Magnolia.* The sentry at the gangway stopped no one from going on board. The general was accessible to all and welcomed Northern merchants, congressmen, plantation owners, and the ordinary. "I hain't got no business with you, General," mumbled one civilian, "but I just wanted to have

a little talk with you, because the folks will ask me if
I did."[24]

One evening in April military commanders dined with
Grant on board the *Magnolia*. There were many suggestions, many doubtful schemes, but the objective remained
the same: capture Vicksburg. The operations on the
Yazoo had failed. The canal projects had failed. The conference was about to break up without a solution when
General John A. Rawlins, Grant's chief of staff, after
whispering to Colonel James H. Wilson, announced that
"Wilson and I have a plan for taking Vicksburg none of
you have referred to yet."

"What is it, Rawlins, what is it?" General Sherman
asked nervously.

"Oh, you will condemn it as too dangerous."

"Never mind that," snapped Sherman, "let us have it."

Rawlins explained his plan to run the Vicksburg batteries with gunboats and empty troop transports, march
the Army down the Louisiana banks to the first feasible
crossing, and ferry it to Mississippi.

"It can't be done," Sherman exclaimed. "It is impracticable. The transports will be destroyed. The enemy's
guns will sink them or set them afire."[25]

Brushing aside Sherman's warnings, Grant sent 20,000
soldiers through from Milliken's Bend to New Carthage,
Louisiana, below Vicksburg, to straighten out the wagon
road, widen the intermediate bayous to transport ordnance and supplies, and hold the route.[26]

At twilight on April 16, Porter lined up his gunboats
fifty yards apart: the *Benton* secured to the tug *Ivy*; the
Lafayette, to the *General Price*; and then, singly, the
Louisville, *Mound City*, *Pittsburg*, and *Carondelet*, three
transports, and *Tuscumbia*.[27]

On the *Henry Von Phul,* moored at Milliken's Bend, Grant and his staff, like front-row spectators at a fireworks display, settled back to watch the action. One of Grant's children frolicked on his knee, while Mrs. Grant sat by his side and amused the other youngsters.[28]

The *Benton*—with Porter on board—got under way, slid past the *Henry Von Phul,* and was lost in the gloom, followed by the *Lafayette,* the *Louisville,* and the others. The Rebels lighted bonfires on the beach, silhouetting the gunboats in bold relief. The Confederate battery on Force Hill opened up. Rounding the point, the ironclads' bow and port quarter cannon fired percussion shells; the broadsides, shrapnel and grape. Enveloped in smoke, the gunboats stood in the swift current with its dangerous eddies.

The *Benton* hurled eighty shells into the town, fragments striking the Washington Hotel and buildings in Walnut Street. Never before under fire in an ironclad, Porter felt cooped up in that "iron pot" of a pilot house. He walked out on the spar deck, where he could see the whole show. One 32-pounder rattled into the *Benton's* after casemate, grazed the combings of the pitman hole, struck the cylinder timber, and lodged in a stateroom. A rifle shot hit the port casemate just above No. 8 gun, splattering wood, knocking off the planks, and wounding five sailors.[29]

On the *Lafayette,* Commander Walke heard the enemy shot grow more rapid, louder, nearer. He shouted to his gunners, "Run out and fire." The *Lafayette* trembled. Struck nine times, two hits thudding off the pilot house, one scattering fragments in all directions, she veered sharply, almost grounded, backed full, and nosed down-river.[30]

Confused by the glare and the noise, spinning in an eddy, the *Louisville* fired only six shots. As the *Mound City* passed the *Lafayette* and *Louisville*, a 10-inch Columbiad ball plowed through both her casemates.

Broadside after broadside roared into the Rebel batteries. With near misses splashing about them in the river, the *Pittsburg* and *Carondelet* glided by unscathed.

Confederate fire concentrated upon the oncoming transports and *Tuscumbia*. The *Silver Wave* romped by the guns. The captain of the *Tuscumbia* saw the *Henry Clay* and *Forest Queen* point their prows up-stream as if to retreat. Aware that Federal success hinged upon the transports running past Vicksburg, he nudged his gunboat closer and swung them back into line. Under heavy bombardment, the *Henry Clay* caught fire. The *Tuscumbia* grounded in a Louisiana bank, but backed off quickly. To avoid collision with the swerving *Forest Queen*, the *Henry Clay* stopped dead in the water, and her captain and crew abandoned ship. The *Henry Clay*, the flames still raging, sank out of sight. The *Tuscumbia* towed the crippled *Forest Queen* to safety below.[31]

When the smoke cleared, Porter discovered no material damage to the gunboats, now anchored below Vicksburg, and listed only fourteen sailors wounded.[32] The officers of the 69th Indiana serenaded the admiral who, smiling at the gangway, invited them to come on board for champagne. While they rejoiced, General Pemberton, in Jackson, wired: "I regard the navigation of the Mississippi River as shut out from us now. No more supplies can be gotten from the trans-Mississippi department."[33]

Sunday dawned clear. The officers and crew of the ironclads dressed early and, after the usual 8:00 a.m. inspection at quarters, signalmen hoisted the church flags

above the ensigns. All hands mustered around the capstans, where the captains read the services of the
Protestant Episcopal Church. On the *Lafayette*, a Mrs.
Holt, of the Sanitary Commission, passed out prayer book-
lets. After the collects, the voices of the *Lafayette's* crew
rose across the calm waters of the Mississippi:

> God bless our native land,
> Firm may she ever stand,
>   Through storm and light;
> When the wild tempests rave,
> Ruler of wind and wave,
> Do Thou our country save,
>   By Thy great might.[34]

Division officers called the roll, each man answering with
his name and rate. The services ended.

The Army's task of reaching the rear of Vicksburg was
by no means over. A week later six more transports—
*Tigress, Empire City, Moderator, J. W. Cheeseman, Anglo
Saxon,* and *Horizon*—steamed past Vicksburg and arrived
at New Carthage.

Ahead lay hard work. The defenses of Grand Gulf were
between the squadron and the point where Grant intended to cross the river. The Union military determined
to strike Grand Gulf with both gunboats and ground
forces, while an expedition under Sherman feinted up the
Yazoo River against Haynes Bluff.

Sherman started up the Yazoo with ironclads, tinclads,
and 10,000 for the diversionary assault. The expedition
ground to a halt below Haynes Bluff. At 9:30 a.m., April
30, the Federal ironclads *DeKalb* and *Choctaw* opened
fire. Sherman's troops landed, marched along the levee
toward the bluff into a blistering fire, retreated, and re-

embarked. At dawn the next day, Sherman rerouted his regiments toward the batteries, but again the Johnnies drove them back. The *DeKalb* and *Choctaw* ceased firing and convoyed the regiments back to the Mississippi River. That same night, Sherman marched his men southward to New Carthage to rejoin Grant.[35]

Perched eighty feet above the river on the bluffs of Grand Gulf were four forts defended by 100-pounders, 64-pounders, 7-inchers, and Parrott rifles. Porter's squadron loitered momentarily, waiting for the Army to arrive in transports. The admiral handed out battle plans. Going into action, the *Benton*, *Lafayette*, and *Tuscumbia* were to knock out the first fort. The *Louisville*, *Carondelet*, *Mound City*, and *Pittsburg* were to advance slowly and pass the first battery, firing grape, canister, and shrapnel cut at one-half second. The *Louisville* was to peel off from the battle line, come up-stream, and engage the second fort. The *Carondelet* was to assail the third; the *Mound City*, the fourth. The *Pittsburg*, doubling back up-stream, was to hit the fourth, the the third.[36] At New Carthage, Osterhaus's and Carr's divisions, 7,000 strong, boarded the transports.

During the morning watch on April 29, the ironclads, maneuvering in single file, moved down-stream—the *Benton*, *Lafayette*, and *Tuscumbia* and a string of Pook turtles. The tall, bearded admiral stood in the pilot house of the *Benton* at the head of the column. The battle line descended slowly, the river curving tightly against the rough bluffs. Minute merged into minute. The river grew slightly wider; the pace of the ironclads, a trifle faster.

Suddenly, abreast of Grand Gulf, they opened fire. The *Benton*, *Lafayette*, and *Tuscumbia* punished the upper fort at Bald Head. A rifle shot exploded on board the *Benton*, knocking Porter out. Gaining consciousness, he staggered about. Just as he passed through the hatch, a shot screamed into the pilot house, struck where the admiral had stood minutes before, cut off the pilot's leg, and shattered the wheel. The *Benton* veered out of action until the mechanics repaired her steering mechanism.

The battle raged on. With deficient engine capacity, the Pook turtles and *Tuscumbia* wavered and twisted in the current, exposed to Confederate fire on all sides.

The *Louisville, Carondelet, Mound City,* and *Pittsburg* hammered away at the batteries and by 11:00 a.m. had silenced the lowest gun emplacements. The *Pittsburg,* firing 429 times, principally her bow guns and starboard broadside, was hit by two shots that sailed through the pilot house, carried away the wheel, damaged the woodwork, dented the plates, and started a small leak.

The *Tuscumbia, Lafayette,* and *Benton* dueled with the upper battery. The *Benton* rounded to and fought bow-on. A shell penetrated the thin iron on the starboard quarter and exploded in a staterom. Seconds later, a shell from her No. 5 gun tore down the Rebel's flagstaff. Steaming into an eddy, the *Benton* swung around, dropped downstream 1,500 yards, ran into a bank, and backed off.

The upper battery pumped eighty-two shells into the clumsy *Tuscumbia*. With a sputtering port engine, buckled plates, and jammed gun ports, she drifted southward.

After five hours of incessant firing, all but one Rebel gun in the upper battery was out of commission. But this solitary, camouflaged cannon kept firing.

The *Benton* moved up to communicate with Grant, on a tugboat 1,200 yards away. The fleet had already suffered eighty casualties. Grant came alongside and stepped

on board, trailed by Governor Richard Yates, of Illinois,
Congressman Elihu B. Washburne, and a horde of reporters.[37] The general dared not risk his Army on a bloody
assault straight up the bluff.[38] He ordered his troops to
begin their march down the Louisiana shore.

At sunset, Porter stepped up the bombardment. The
empty transports, clinging to the Louisiana banks, passed
safely down-stream shadowed by the gunboats.[39]

Inside Grand Gulf, the Rebels realized that the Yankees
had gained their objective. They pulled out and fell back.

The Pook turtles came through with slight damage.
"But," remarked a Northern newsman, "the ironclads are
certainly losing their prestige, when seven of them, with
nine and eleven pieces, could not silence nine guns in a
fight of nearly five hours duration."[40] Porter blamed the
fuses. The Parrott shells had missed exploding three times
out of four.[41] The *Tuscumbia* was a shambles, and Commander James W. Shirk, her skipper, cursed her engines
and her rickety plates, green timber, weak hull, and unprotected magazines; he upbraided the shipbuilder,
Brown, for faulty construction. "Altogether," raged Shirk,
"the *Tuscumbia* is a disgrace."[42]

On the morning of April 30, Grant transported his Army
across the river to Bruinsburg, Mississippi, a village ten
miles south of Grand Gulf. He was in high spirits. After
four dreary months of disheartening trial and error, he
was on dry land on the Vicksburg side of the Mississippi.
By the end of the first week of May, he struck inland
from Grand Gulf to penetrate deep into enemy territory
and to face forces numbering double his own.

The Navy moved into abandoned Grand Gulf. The
heights were littered with cannon shot, shell fragments,
burst and dismounted guns, remnants of blown-up maga-

zines. Monuments in the cemetery were shattered and three graves dug out by solid shot.[43] Near a 10-inch Columbiad pointing toward the river, a lieutenant found a discarded letter: "They are firing very fast. I am uneasy, but not scared very bad. I have very little hope of ever returning to Arkn. except it be after this unholy war is closed and I should be fortunate enough to live."[44]

Porter left Grand Gulf astern and prowled southward to the mouth of the Red River, searching for the ram *Webb*. He wended his way up the Red River with the *Benton, Lafayette, Pittsburg, Switzerland,* and *Ivy* and captured deserted Fort DeRussy, a powerful casemated work of seven guns; ripped through a raft that obstructed the river; and steamed triumphantly into Alexandria, Louisiana, taking formal possession. Soon General Nathaniel Banks and his Army marched in and occupied the town.

There were three courses open to the general: pursue the enemy to Shreveport, join Grant at Vicksburg, or invest Port Hudson. Banks chose the last. His command marched out of Alexandria and crossed the Atchafalaya at Simmesport, toiling down the right bank of the Mississippi to Bayou Sara. Ferried over the river, the Army moved directly to the rear of Port Hudson.

Porter, hesitating to ascend the low water of the Red River to Shreveport, dropped down with his flotilla and, detailing the *Pittsburg* and *Lafayette* to blockade the mouth of the Red, headed northward past Grand Gulf to his station above Vicksburg.[45]

On May 18, the roar of the guns in the rear of Vicksburg announced the approach of Grant's Army, and the admiral saw the welcome sight of a portion of the Federal artillery, advancing to a position between Haynes Bluff and the city. The stronghold was besieged. The expectation of great events began to grow.

The *DeKalb, Choctaw, Linden, Romeo, Petrel,* and *Forest Rose* hastened up the Yazoo River to open communications with Grant's Army and pushed on to the now evacuated batteries at Haynes Bluff. Demolishing the forts there, the expedition swerved and continued up-river to Yazoo City. As it approached, the Confederates hurled torches into their unfinished ironclads. The Yankees gutted the navy yard, sawmills, and machine and blacksmith shops and all public buildings. Further on, they burned to the water line the steamers *John Walsh, R. J. Lockland, Golden Age, Scotland, Dew Drop, Emma Bett,* and *Cotton Plant.*[46]

From the Mississippi River, Porter's ironclads and mortars bombarded Vicksburg at close range day by day, night by night, the fleet firing into the upper gun emplacements, the squadron below, into the water and lower batteries. From the rear, Grant's artillery chastised the city.

Above Vicksburg, the *Cincinnati* steamed down-river to enfilade the rifle pits on the left flank of the defenses. Up on the hill, General Sherman, protecting Grant's extreme right, was ready to take advantage of the ironclad's shellfire. Suddenly, the *Cincinnati* rounded to and charged up-river at full speed. Rebel guns poured shot and shell into her. Two shots hit her shell room, one ricocheting up the recess of the paddle wheel, the other striking the side. A third ball entered her magazine and flooded it instantly as her starboard tiller was carried away. Plunging shot went through the deck and damaged the broadside guns.

The *Cincinnati* was sinking fast. Her skipper, Commander George Bache, ran her close to a bank, put out a plank, and removed the wounded. But before the *Cin-*

cinnati could belay a hawser to the trees, she sank in three fathoms of water, within range of enemy cannon. Immediately, the Navy started salvage operations.[47]

Despite the temporary loss of the *Cincinnati*, it was manifest that the ironclads had revolutionized the art of naval warfare. The length and savageness of the fights with the Vicksburg batteries demonstrated the superiority of armored gunboats. No wooden ship could have survived half an hour under such barrages as the ironclads sustained. The wooden-hulled squadron of Farragut had passed the New Orleans forts at night, but, off Vicksburg, the iron craft battled heavier guns in daylight and at closer range.

June continued hot and muggy. The Federal cannon that caged Vicksburg in the rear numbered 220. Shots, shells, and mortar bombs, fired from the right and left and from the river, plunged into Vicksburg, lighting the fires of a new era. It was perfect hell. There were starvation and desolation, vileness and gallantry, a sense of suffocation, and death. "What is to become of all the living things in this place, God only knows," reflected Miss Buford.[48] Shells ripped into schools and hospitals. The churches were shut tight except the Roman Catholic Church, its cross outlined against the red skies. Its priest was seen administering to the sick and suffering, while in the streets it was gossiped that Mr. Rutherford, the Presbyterian pastor, had taken his flock into the caves. In the river batteries, a Confederate soldier grumbled, "No place of safety, if you stand still there is danger from pieces of shell that fill the air, and if you move the danger becomes greater."

The stench of dead cattle, horses, and mules was awful. Everywhere mosquitoes swarmed. "Fricasseed kittens" proved popular fare. One man was horrified to see a rat caught, skinned, and cooked. Citizens herded together in caves, where all semblance of privacy vanished.[49]

The eyes of the Confederacy focused on embattled Vicksburg. "We must fight, whatever the odds," clamored the Richmond *Sentinel*. President Davis wired General Beauregard, in Charleston, and General Braxton Bragg, in Shelbyville, Tennessee, that control of the Mississippi was lost unless General Joseph E. Johnston was reinforced.[50] The Richmond *Enquirer* proclaimed that "Vicksburg cannot fall." In Jackson, the *Appeal* exclaimed, "Better far would it be to sacrifice Richmond, Charleston, Savannah, or Mobile than to yield the river."[51] In the trenches outside Vicksburg, soldiers signed a petition: "This army is now ripe for mutiny, unless it can be fed."[52]

Grant and Porter kept up the bombardment. On June 11 the mortar boats fired 193 shells at intervals of five minutes. "And why do they hold out?" asked the Cincinnati *Daily Commercial*.[53] "If we do not get Vicksburg now, we never will," Porter warned.[54]

Southward on the river Farragut and Banks were besieging Port Hudson. The *Hartford, Estrella, Albatross, Arizona,* and *Sachem* above and the *Richmond, Genesee, Essex, Monongahela,* and six mortars below shelled Confederate batteries daily. Inland, Banks's Army invested Port Hudson, its right resting on Thompson's Creek, its left, at Springfield's Landing.

Simultaneously, on May 27, Farragut's sloops opened fire, and Banks's troops moved through the woods and ravines. Confederates sprang from behind every tree and bush. The ravine was full of them. The fight was murderous, hand to hand. The Yankees, using clubbed muskets and bayonets, pressed forward and drove the Rebels into and then out of a six-gun battery. Banks's artillery shifted and tossed shot and shell into the enemy positions. The 6th Michigan and the 128th New York reached the enemy's interior lines, but, pinned down under a hot fire, they crawled back to safety as the Johnnies massed. With his casualties mounting almost to 2,000, Banks called off the attack. The siege of Port Hudson dragged on.

Banks badgered the Navy for heavier bombardments. Throughout June the mortars and the *Essex* alone silenced the lower batteries three times, the ironclads discharging 738 shells, the mortars, an aggregate of 2,800. Farragut ordered more ammunition from New York. Banks struck again, but failed.

As Farragut watched the progress of the siege, losing patience with Banks, the monotony was interrupted when Texans on the west bank of the Mississippi threatened Donaldsonville and New Orleans itself. Farragut hustled down-river to thwart the enemy. The *Winona* had already steamed to the rescue and shelled out the Rebels from Donaldsonville, but only after they had nearly sunk the *New London* with a direct hit in her boilers.[55]

Up-river, the third of July came hot and sultry to Vicksburg. But a cool breeze was soon blowing, and thunder in the distance indicated rain. Under a flag of truce, General Pemberton arrived on the hill where the Union's advance works lay. Grant approached. Colonel Montgomery, of the Confederate staff, said stiffly, "General Grant, General Pemberton." They shook hands and recalled the days when they had been lieutenants in the same outfit in Mexico. Sitting on the grass in a grove of fruit trees, the two generals talked in anxious, confidential tones, Pemberton pulling the leaves of grass, Grant puffing a cigar.[56] The surrender was arranged.

At 10:00 a.m., July 4, General Frederick Steele's division led the way into Vicksburg with colors flying, drums rolling. At noon, Lieutenant Colonel Strong hoisted the Stars and Stripes over the courthouse. Soldiers chanted:

> Vicksburg is ours,
> Hurrah!
> Treachery cowers
> Hurrah!
> Down reels the rebel rag!
> Up shoots the starry flag![57]

The Rebels marched out of their trenches, by regiments, onto the grassy field, where they stacked their arms, folded their colors, piled their knapsacks. The Confederates had lost the river, 27,000 soldiers as prisoners, 4,000 noncombatants, 102 field pieces, thirty siege guns, arms, ammunition, locomotives, railroad cars, everything. Twelve months had lapsed since Farragut's fleet had first steamed past the city, six months since the first abortive attempt up the Yazoo, two months since Grant arrived below Grand Gulf.

News flashed that General George G. Meade's Army of the Potomac had bloodily halted Lee at Gettysburg on July 3. At a stone house on the outskirts of Vicksburg —a Southern mansion with wide verandahs, almost hidden from view in the trees—notables of both armies gathered. In a damask-cushioned rocking chair sat General Pemberton. The stoop-shouldered, sandy-bearded Grant stood conversing with the Confederate officers. There was no vacant chair near, but neither Pemberton nor any of his generals offered Grant a seat. For five minutes Grant talked, then he turned and left the house.[58]

The principal underlying condition of Federal success in the West was the cooperation between the Army and the Navy. From the beginning of his Civil War career, Grant had utilized the Navy to its fullest extent—at Belmont, Forts Henry and Donelson, Shiloh, Vicksburg. Porter and Grant worked in close harmony. The general remarked that without the gunboats on the river and its tributaries, any military attempt to wrest the Mississippi Valley from the Confederacy would have been futile.[59] When Grant eventually went east to battle Lee, an essential feature of ultimate victory was his use of the Navy in Virginia waters.

After a Cabinet meeting, Gideon Welles returned to the Navy Department. He found a delegation from Maine waiting for him, criticizing the inadequate coastal defenses. An orderly stepped in and handed the Secretary a dispatch. Excusing himself, Welles literally ran to the White House with the news of Vicksburg. The President was discussing Grant's move with Secretary Chase and others when Welles handed him the telegram. Lincoln beamed with joy, pumped Old Gid's hand, and asked: "What can we do for the Secretary of the Navy for this glorious intelligence—he is always giving us good news. It is great, Mr. Welles, it is great."[60]

Together, in the twilight, they walked across the White House lawn toward the War Department. When the citizens of Washington learned the news, they ignited firecrackers, shot off rockets and Roman candles by the armful, and heaped barrels and boxes into huge bonfires.

Cannon roared in all parts of the city. A crowd cheered
Lincoln on the White House steps and snake-danced
through the streets shouting, "What of Vicksburg? What
of Vicksburg?" Speaking in the torchlight afront his house,
Secretary Seward cried out: "Vicksburg? Why, Vicksburg
fell on the Fourth of July." The parade marched off to
Stanton's, to Halleck's, where the bands blared "Hail
Columbia."[61]

It was quiet at the Welles's residence. The Secretary
was hurt that the crowd failed to serenade him, perturbed
when most newspapers did not allude to the Navy's part—
to the fleets of Farragut and Porter, which, passing the
batteries of Port Hudson and Grand Gulf, had sounded
the death knell for Vicksburg by severing the Red River
supply line.

That same week, Welles called on the President and
advised him that Porter should be made a permanent
rear admiral. Cheerfully Lincoln assented, but Stanton
claimed that the credit for the Mississippi River belonged
to the Army. Chase, Seward, and Blair sided with Welles,
and, at Vicksburg, Porter received the news of his promotion.[62]

On July 6 news reached General Banks and Admiral
Farragut that Vicksburg had fallen. The Confederates
inside Port Hudson realized that their position was now
untenable. Three days later, at dawn, Union bands played
"The Star-Spangled Banner" and "Yankee Doodle" and
two picked Federal regiments from each division marched
into Port Hudson. The Stars and Stripes were unfurled
to the breeze atop the highest bluff. Out in the river, the
guns of the *Richmond* thundered.[63]

The sudden appearance of the first-class steamboat
Imperial stirred New Orleans to a fever pitch. Freighted

with 600 head of cattle, the *Imperial* had arrived from St. Louis, her captain reporting a pleasant and unmolested trip all the way. It was not her size or her fine equipment or her cargo that impressed the eager crowds thronging the levee. The *Imperial* was the first freight boat to venture down the Mississippi since the fall of Vicksburg and Port Hudson, and all who gazed saw in her the embodiment of Union victory.[64] The Mississippi River was open.

Epilogue
The Mop-up

The Union Navy's objective in the West had been won, but skirmishes were fought for another year and a half. Admiral Porter flushed out pockets of resistance in the Cumberland, Tennessee, Arkansas, White, and Yazoo rivers; impounded cotton, amassing a fortune in prize money; and, with the nation, recoiled from the sight of the dead garrison at Fort Pillow, massacred by units of Confederate raiders operating in Tennessee. With General Banks, he thrashed up and down the Red River in an infamous campaign—a campaign that collapsed from Banks's ineptitude and from low water and the inter-service scramble for Confederate cotton.

On April 16, 1865, Lieutenant Commander Charles Read, C. S. N., under orders from Richmond to escape into the Gulf and scourge Federal merchantmen, boarded the ram *Webb* at Shreveport, Louisiana. The Rebel gunboat—converted into an ocean-going cruiser—eluded the blockade at the mouth of the Red River, swung her bow toward New Orleans, and steamed southward at full speed, leaving the Yankee ironclad *Lafayette* far astern.

The Union Navy at New Orleans, its ensigns at half-mast for Lincoln's death, scanned the river for the fast-charging, heavily armed ram. Disguised as an innocent

Army transport loaded with soldiers and cotton, flying the Stars and Stripes, the *Webb* was recognized by the pilot of the *Lackawanna* as she neared Algiers. The *Lackawanna* fired twice and missed. Instantly, the Confederates hauled down the American flag and twoblocked the Stars and Bars. The *Webb* lurched forward, past the *Portsmouth, Quaker City, Florida,* and *Ossipee,* whose batteries failed to fire, fearful of killing innocent bystanders thronging the streets and levee. Excitement was intense. Rumors spread that John Wilkes Booth commanded the *Webb* and President Jefferson Davis was a passenger.

Dipping her colors to a French man-of-war, the *Webb* veered past New Orleans and moved toward Forts Jackson and St. Philip. The masts of the *Richmond* loomed up in the distance. Commander Read, realizing that it was futile to battle the broadsides of a Federal sloop, ran the *Webb* into the mud, hurled torches on the deck, abandoned ship, and struck out into the swamps. Flames swallowed the ram.[1] Beginning with nothing, cursed with makeshift, ramshackle gunboats, the Confederate States Navy on the Mississippi ended with nothing.

Notes

The following abbreviations are used throughout:

L. C.   Library of Congress, Manuscript Division.
LPMR.   Loose Papers, Mississippi River, Record Group 45, National Archives.
LUS.   Military Order of the Loyal Legion of the United States.
NA.   National Archives.
OAR.   *The War of the Rebellion: A Compilation of the Official Records of the Union and Confederate Armies.*
ONR.   *Official Records of the Union and Confederate Navies in the War of the Rebellion.*
RG   Record Group, National Archives.
WTF   Water Transportation File, Record Group 92, National Archives.

CHAPTER 1

1. Cincinnati *Daily Commercial*, 18, 24, 25, 27, 31 May 1861.
2. Welles to Rodgers, *ONR*, XXII, 280.
3. Frank Moore, *The Rebellion Record*, 1: 27, 71, 117.
4. See Welles to his son, 4 March 1861, Gideon Welles Papers, L. C.; Charles A. Dana, *Recollections of the Civil War*, p. 170; William H. Russell, *My Diary North and South*, pp. 42, 43.
5. Smith to Hale, 16 January 1862, John Hale Papers, New Hampshire Historical Society.
6. David D. Porter, "Journal of Occurrences during the War of the

Rebellion," pp. 163–168, 401, David Dixon Porter Papers, L. C.; Virginia Woodbury Fox Diary, April–June 1861, Blair Family Papers, L. C.

7. Porter to Fox, n.d., & 24 May 1862, Gustavus Vasa Fox Papers, New-York Historical Society.

8. "Report of the Secretary of the Navy, 4 July 1861," *Senate Exec. Doc., No. 1*, 37 Cong., 1 sess.

9. Charles B. Boynton, *The History of the Navy during the Rebellion*, 1: 7, 72–74, 89, 125–127; Russell, *Diary*, pp. 502–503; W. V. McKean, "What the Navy has Done during the Civil War," *The United Service*, 1 (1864): 337–338.

10. News clipping, Welles Papers.

11. Lincoln to Welles, 14 May 1861, Abraham Lincoln Papers, Illinois State Historical Library.

12. James Gilmore, *Personal Recollections of Abraham Lincoln and the Civil War*, p. 27.

13. Russell, *Diary*, p. 490.

14. Welles to his wife, 21 April 1861, Welles Papers.

15. Blair to Cameron, 17 May 1861, Simon Cameron Papers, L. C.

16. Bates's memo, 15 April 1861, in Howard K. Beale, ed., *The Diary of Edward Bates, 1859–1866*, p. 182.

17. Bates to Eads, 17 April 1861, James B. Eads Papers, Missouri Historical Society.

18. Boynton, *Navy*, 1: 498–500.

19. Eads to Welles, 8 May 1861, Welles Papers.

20. Eads to Welles, 29 April 1861, *ONR*, XXII, 278.

21. Scott to McClellan, 3, 21 May 1861, George B. McClellan Papers, L. C.

22. For example, *Daily Missouri Democrat*, 10 May 1861.

23. McClellan to Scott, 26 April 1861, & McClellan to Townsend, 9 May 1861, McClellan Papers.

24. "Remarks of Gen. Scott on letter from Gen. Geo. B. McClellan dated April 27, 1861," *ibid.*

25. Meigs to McClellan, 17 June 1861, WTF, RG 92, NA.

26. Lenthall's memo, 1 June 1861, & Meigs to Welles, 28 September 1862, *ibid.*; Welles to John Foote, 4 June 1862, LPMR, RG 45.

27. Boynton, *Navy*, 1: 500.

CHAPTER 2

1. McClellan to Rodgers, 19 May 1861, WTF.

2. Rodgers to Welles, 7 September 1861, *ONR*, XXII, 318.

3. Rodgers to Welles, 8 June 1861, John Rodgers Papers, L. C.

4. See Phelps to Rodgers, 13 July 1861, *ibid.;* St. Louis *Republican,* 22 May 1861; Henry Walke, *Naval Scenes and Reminiscences,* p. 21.

5. Rodgers to Phelps, 23 July 1861, S. Ledyard Phelps's Letterbook, Missouri Historical Society.

6. Loose bills, Rodgers Papers.

7. Welles to Rodgers, 12 June 1861, *ONR,* XXII, 284.

8. Rodgers to Welles, 12 June 1861, *ibid.,* 286.

9. Cincinnati *Daily Commercial,* 1 July 1861.

10. Bishop to Rodgers, 14 August 1861, Rodgers Papers.

11. George Brown, "Service in the Mississippi Squadron," LUS, New York, *Personal Recollections,* p. 303.

12. Phelps to Welles, 10 October 1861, Welles Papers.

13. Rodgers to Collier, 29 June 1861, Rodgers Papers.

14. Phelps to Rodgers, 2, 12 July 1861, *ibid.*

15. Louisville *Daily Courier,* 27 June 1861.

16. Rodgers to Fremont, 10 August 1861, Rodgers Papers.

17. Cincinnati *Daily Commercial,* 12 June, 17 July 1861, 1 January 1862.

18. Rodgers to Welles, 22 August 1861, *ONR,* XXII, 302.

19. Cincinnati *Daily Commercial,* 11 July 1861.

20. Meigs to Cameron, 25 June 1861, Reports of the Quartermaster General, RG 92.

21. Pook to McClellan, 2 July 1861, WTF.

22. "Specification for building a gun-boat," *ibid.;* Isherwood to Welles, 20 July 1861, Subject File AD, RG 45. Also see H. Allen Gosnell, *Guns on the Western Waters, passim.*

23. Bates to Meigs, 31 July 1861, 3 August 1861, WTF.

24. Blair to Meigs, 31 July 1861, *ibid.*

25. Eads-Meigs contract, United States Navy Miscellaneous File, L. C. See also Rodgers to Merritt, 10 August 1861, Rodgers Papers.

26. See Temple to Lane, 14 August 1861, WTF; Scott to Meigs, 29 August, 1861, *ibid.;* Louisville *Daily Courier,* 9 August 1861; *Daily Missouri Democrat,* 12, 14 August, 18 September 1861.

27. Pook to Meigs, 20 August 1861, Rodgers Papers.

28. Rodgers to Eads, 10 August 1861, *ibid.*

29. Merritt to Meigs, 26 September 1861, WTF.

30. Cincinnati *Daily Commercial,* 1 January 1862.

31. Rodgers to Welles, 7 September 1861, *ONR,* XXII, 318.

32. Eads to Sibley, 14 September 1861, WTF.

33. Rodgers to Harwood, 8 July 1861, Letters from Naval Officers, RG 74.

34. Ripley to Rodgers, 6 August 1861, Rodgers Papers. See also Harwood to Rodgers, 20 August 1861, Letters Sent, RG 74.
35. Drayton to Rodgers, n.d., Rodgers Papers.
36. *OAR,* III, 390.
37. *Harper's Weekly,* 21 September 1861.
38. Fremont to Lincoln, 30 July 1861, *OAR,* III, 416.
39. Cincinnati *Daily Commercial,* 9 July, 3 August 1861.
40. Rodgers to Welles, 22 August 1861, *ONR,* XXII, 303.
41. Rodgers to Fremont, 3 September 1861, WTF.
42. Rodgers to Welles, 4 September 1861, *ONR,* XXII, 309.
43. Fremont to Blair, n.d., Fox Papers. Also see Robert E. Johnson, *Rear Admiral John Rodgers,* pp. 165–166.
44. Mercer to Paulding, 14 May 1861, Captains' Letters, RG 45.
45. Foote to Welles, 5 June 1861, Welles Papers.
46. Welles to Foote, 30 August 1861, *ONR,* XXII, 307.
47. Foote to Dahlgren, 5, 8 September 1861, John Dahlgren Papers, L. C.
48. Foote to Welles, 13 November 1862, LPMR.
49. Meigs to Rodgers, 31 August 1861, Rodgers Papers.
50. Welles to Rodgers, 30 August, 23 September 1861, *ibid.*
51. Foote to his wife, 17 December 1861, LPMR.
52. John Brinton, *Personal Memoirs,* p. 67.
53. Foote to Fox, 13 September 1861, *ONR,* XXII, 320.
54. Phelps to Foote, 10 September 1861, *ibid.,* 324.
55. Walke to Foote, 7 October 1861, *ibid.,* 362. See also Phelps to Foote, 5 October 1861, LPMR.

CHAPTER 3

1. Grant to Williams, 17 November 1861, *ONR,* XXII, 404.
2. Chicago *Post,* 9 November 1861.
3. Polk to Mackall, 10 November 1861, *ONR,* XXII, 407.
4. Walke, *Naval Scenes,* p. 37.
5. Trask to Polk, 14 February 1862, *ONR,* XXII, 425.
6. Pillow to Blake, 10 November 1861, *ibid.,* 412.
7. Walke to Foote, 9 November 1861, *ibid.,* 400; *Daily Missouri Democrat,* 10 November 1861.
8. Johnson to his son, 8 November 1861, Charles James Johnson Papers, Louisiana State University.
9. Polk to Davis, 8 November 1861, *ONR,* XXII, 406.
10. Johnson to his son, 8 November 1861, Johnson Papers.
11. Pillow to Blake, 10 November 1861, *ONR,* XXII, 412.

12. New Orleans *Daily True Delta,* 12, 26 November 1861; Memphis *Appeal,* 22 November 1861.

13. Harris to governors of Alabama, Mississippi, Louisiana, 20 November 1861, Governors' Correspondence, Tennessee Department of Archives.

14. Kroener to Trumbull, 7 February 1862, Lyman Trumbull Papers, L. C.

15. Foote to Welles, 9 November 1861, *ONR,* XXII, 399; Adams to Blair, 15 November 1861, Blair Family Papers.

16. Eads to Meigs, 29 October 1861, Eads Papers; Meigs to Eads, 13 November 1861, Letters Sent, RG 92.

17. See Henry W. Smith's testimony, War Claims Commission, Records of 3rd Auditor, RG 217; Meigs to Eads, 13 November 1861, Letters Sent, RG 92; Eads to Bates, 10 November 1861, Eads Papers.

18. Louis V. Bogy's testimony, War Claims Commission.

19. Fox to Foote, 5 March 1862, LPMR.

20. Adams to Fremont, 24 August 1861, WTF.

21. "War Claims at St. Louis," *House Exec. Doc., No. 94,* 37 Cong., 2 sess. See also Foote to Meigs, 7 November 1861, WTF.

22. Meigs to Adams, 29 October 1861, Letters Sent, RG 92.

23. Testimony of Barton Able, Ambrose Reeder, William Kountz, War Claims Commission.

24. J. G. Randall, *The Civil War and Reconstruction,* p. 423.

25. Cameron to Davis, 25 October 1861, Letters Sent, Secretary of War, RG 107.

26. Allen to Meigs, 20 December 1861, WTF.

27. Trumbull to Lincoln, 1 October 1861, Trumbull Papers.

28. *Daily Missouri Democrat,* 11 December 1861.

29. Foote to Dahlgren, 23 October 1861, Phelps's Letterbook.

30. Foote to Welles, 13 November 1862, LPMR.

31. Foote to Fox, 2 November 1861, *ONR,* XXII, 391.

32. Welles to Foote, 13 November 1861, *ibid.,* 429.

33. Dahlgren to Harwood, 20 January 1862, *ibid.,* 510.

34. Harwood to Foote, 30 August 1861, Letters Sent to Officers, RG 74.

35. Lavallette to Fox, 14 September 1861, Letters Received, RG 74.

36. Foote to Dahlgren, 8, 10 September 1861, Dahlgren Papers.

37. Foote to Sanford, 20 September 1861, *ONR,* XXII, 343.

38. Foote to Harwood, 18 September 1861, Letters Received, RG 74.

39. Foote to Meigs, 30 September 1861, *ONR,* XXII, 355.

40. Foote to Paulding, 17 September 1861, *ibid.,* 337.

41. Fox to Dahlgren, 9 September 1861, Letters Sent, RG 45.

42. Phelps to Foote, 1 November 1861, LPMR.

43. Welles to Carter, 12 October 1861, Letters Sent, RG 45.
44. Foote to Welles, 4 November 1861, *ONR*, XXII, 392.
45. Carter to Welles, 1 November 1861, Commanders' Letters, RG 45.
46. Dove to Foote, 24 November 1861, *ONR*, XXII, 442.
47. *Daily Missouri Democrat*, 30 October 1861.
48. Foote to Meigs, 7 November 1861, WTF; Eads's statement in *Daily Missouri Democrat*, n.d., WTF.
49. *Harper's Weekly*, 16, 30 November 1861.
50. Virginia Woodbury Fox's Diary, 14 November 1861.
51. McClellan to Stanton, 31 January 1862, McClellan Papers. See also Cincinnati *Daily Commercial*, 23 November 1861.
52. Gideon Welles, "Admiral Farragut and New Orleans," *The Galaxy*, 12 (1871): 673, 820; Montgomery Blair, "Opening the Mississippi," *The United Service*, 4 (1881): 34; statement in Miscellaneous File, Welles Papers.
53. Cincinnati *Daily Commercial*, 29 January 1862.
54. *Ibid.*, 26 February 1862.
55. See Foote to Meigs, 20 November 1861, WTF; Foote to Fox, 11 January 1862, *ONR*, XXII, 491; Fox to Foote, 26 December 1861, *ibid.*, 471.
56. *Daily Missouri Democrat*, 8 January 1862.
57. Chandler to Wade, 8 October 1861, Zachariah Chandler Papers, L. C.
58. For example, Proctor to Chase, 16 November 1861, Salmon P. Chase Papers, L. C.

Chapter 4

1. New Orleans *Daily True Delta*, 15 October 1861.
2. MacClure to Secretary of War, 18 January 1862, Letters Received, War Office; Davis to House & Senate, 12 January 1863, *Journal of the Open Sessions of the Senate*, RG 109.
3. For example, Richmond *Examiner*, 7 March 1863.
4. [Maury] to Richmond *Enquirer*, n.d., Matthew F. Maury Papers, L. C.
5. Mallory to his wife, 31 August 1862, Stephen R. Mallory Papers, University of North Carolina.
6. Mallory to Conrad, – May 1861, Subject File VN, RG 45.
7. Mallory to Davis, 26 April, 18 July 1861, *ibid.*
8. "Special Report of the Committee on Naval Affairs to the House of Representatives," *Documents of the First Session of the Sixth Legislature of the State of Louisiana* (1861).
9. New Orleans *Daily True Delta*, 28 April 1861.

10. For example, Hunton to Benjamin, 8 May 1861, Letters Received, War Office, RG 109.

11. Harris to Davis, 13 June 1861, *ibid.*

12. Walker to Twiggs, 17 July 1861, Letters Sent, *ibid.*

13. New Orleans *Daily True Delta*, 14 July 1861; New Orleans *Daily Picayune*, 1 September 1861.

14. New Orleans *Daily True Delta*, 14 August 1861.

15. Marcy to Mallory, 8 February 1862, Citizens File, RG 109.

16. Act No. 261, *Laws for the Army and Navy of the Confederate States* (1861), RG 109.

17. New Orleans *Daily Picayune*, 9 June, 18 September, 8 October 1861; New Orleans *Daily True Delta*, 6, 12, 14 July 1861; Thomas W. Knox, *Camp-Fire and Cotton-Field*, pp. 391–392; *Harper's Weekly*, 10 May 1862.

18. J. Thomas Scharf, *History of the Confederate States Navy*, p. 264.

19. Bill of sale, Subject File AY.

20. Warley to Mahan, 18 March 1883, LPMR.

21. Edward Tidball's testimony, *Report of Evidence Taken before a Joint Special Committee of Both Houses of the Confederate Congress, to Investigate the Affairs of the Navy Department* (1862), RG 109.

22. Mallory to Hollins, 31 July 1861, LPMR.

23. Contracts, Subject File AY; *Mobile's* contract, LPMR.

24. For actual construction see bills & receipts, Subject File AC. Also see Gosnell, *Western Waters*, pp. 18–19.

25. New Orleans *Daily True Delta*, 13, 15 October 1861.

26. Phelps to Pettus, 30 June 1861, Governor's Correspondence, Mississippi Department of Archives.

27. New Orleans *Daily True Delta*, 23 May, 19, 28 June, 6, 7 July, 4, 11 December 1861.

28. Mallory to Hollins, 22 November 1861, *Report of Evidence*, pp. 89–90.

29. Walker to Twiggs, 24 August 1861, Letters Sent, War Office.

30. Mitchell's notebook, 1862, John K. Mitchell Papers, Virginia Historical Society.

31. Hughes to Rousseau, 28 June 1861; Mallory to Baker, 18 February 1862, Subject File AD; Soper to his father, 4 April 1862, Ethan Allen Hitchcock Papers, L. C.

32. See Murray to Tucker, 29 December 1861, "Special Report," *Documents.*

33. Cincinnati *Daily Commercial*, 26 April 1862.

34. James Tomb's Memoirs, Subject File HA.

35. John K. Mitchell's testimony, *Report of Evidence*, p. 37.

Notes 291

36. Testimony of Asa & Nelson Tift, John Ray, John Tanner, Felix Senac, *ibid.*, 108, 392, 414. Also see New Orleans *Daily True Delta*, 13 November 1861.
37. Mallory to Memminger, 11 April 1862, Confederate Treasury Records, RG 56.
38. Sumner to Benjamin, 17 December 1861, Letters Received, War Office.
39. Hughes to Benjamin, 6 March 1862, War Office.
40. Anderson to Iven, 5, 9, 13, 25 September 1861, Letterbook, Tredegar Iron Works Records, Virginia State Library.
41. Anderson to Pointer, – September 1861, *ibid.*
42. Vouchers, John Armstrong, Bennett & Lurges, Leeds & Co., Citizens File.
43. Receipts, Subject File, AC; Montgomery to Davis, 22 February 1862, Letters Received, War Office.
44. Beverly Kennon's testimony, *Report of Evidence,* p. 136.
45. Vouchers, Subject File NR.
46. Mallory to Benjamin, 27 January 1862, Letters Received, War Office; Mallory to Davis, 16 August 1862, Subject File VN.
47. Barnard's memo, 28 January 1862, *OAR*, XV, 413.
48. For example, Stillwater to Davis, 18 September 1861, Letters Received, War Office.
49. Moore to Davis, 31 May 1861, *ibid.*
50. Lovell to Cooper, 22 May 1862, *OAR*, VI, 512; Davis to Moore, 26 September 1861, in Dunbar Rowland, ed., *Jefferson Davis, Constitutionalist,* 5: 137.
51. Lovell's testimony, Court of Inquiry, *OAR*, VI, 560, 562.
52. Benjamin to Mallory, – January 1862, Letters Sent, War Office.
53. Davis to Lovell, 17 October 1861, LPMR.
54. Kennon to Mahan, 12 March 1883, *ibid.*; Gosnell, *Western Waters,* pp. 19–20; Scharf, *Confederate States Navy,* pp. 249–251.
55. Taylor to Seddon, 20 June 1863, Citizens File.
56. Lovell's testimony, Court of Inquiry, *OAR*, VI, 562.
57. "Special Report," *Documents,* pp. 3–4.
58. Lovell to Benjamin, 1 January 1862, *OAR*, VI, 792.
59. Kennon to Mahan, 12 March 1883, LPMR.
60. Mitchell's testimony, *Report of Evidence,* pp. 37–40.
61. George Hollins's testimony, *ibid.*, 45–54.
62. Mallory to his wife, 31 August 1862, Mallory Papers.
63. William Whittle's testimony, *Report of Evidence,* pp. 8–9, 14.
64. James Martin's testimony, *ibid.*, 75–82.
65. Walker to Harris, 19 April 1861, Letters Sent, War Office.
66. Pillow to War Department, 15 May 1861, Letters Received, *ibid.*

67. Saunders to Polk, 5 December 1861, *ONR*, XXII, 807.
68. AGO, Special Orders No. 149, *OAR*, IV, 405.
69. Johnston to Cooper, 4 October 1861, *ibid.*, 436.
70. Harris to War Department, 25, 26 May, 15 October 1861, Governors' Correspondence, Tennessee Department of Archives.
71. Lovell to Johnston, 23 November 1861, 12 February 1862, *OAR*, VII, 693, 878.
72. Johnston to Cooper, 17 October 1861; Johnston to Benjamin, 8, 19 November 1861, *ibid.*, IV, 454, 528, 564.
73. Polk to his wife, 6 January 1862, Leonidas Polk Papers, University of North Carolina (microfilm copies).
74. Memphis *Avalanche*, 26 November 1861.
75. Mallory to Brown, 25 December 1861, *ONR*, XXII, 812.
76. Mallory to Davis, 16 August 1862, Subject File VN.

CHAPTER 5

1. Philadelphia *Inquirer*, 6 February 1862.
2. Albert D. Richardson, *The Secret Service*, p. 217.
3. William T. Sherman, *Memoirs of Gen. W. T. Sherman*, 1: 247.
4. Foote to Halleck, 28 January 1862, *ONR*, XXII, 524.
5. Grant to Halleck, 29 January 1862, *OAR*, VII, 121.
6. Halleck to Grant, 30 January 1862, *ibid.*, 121.
7. Foote to Pennock, 3 February 1862, LPMR.
8. *Daily Missouri Democrat*, 8 February 1862.
9. Foote to Welles, 3 February 1862, *ONR*, XXII, 534.
10. Moore, *Record*, 4: 72.
11. Tilghman's report, 9 August 1862, *OAR*, VII, 144.
12. Heiman to Mackall, 8 February 1862, *ONR*, XXII, 565.
13. Mary A. Newcomb, *Four Years of Personal Experiences of the War*, p. 23.
14. Eliot Callender, "What a Boy Saw on the Mississippi," LUS, Illinois, *Military Essays*, 1 (1891): 54.
15. James Laning's report, in David D. Porter, *The Naval History of the Civil War*, p. 145.
16. Charles Coffin, *Four Years of Fighting*, p. 78.
17. Tilghman to Cooper, 12 February 1862, *ONR*, XXII, 553.
18. Foote to Welles, 7 February 1862, *ibid.*, 537.
19. Moore, *Record*, 4: 77.
20. Heiman to Mackall, 8 February 1862, *ONR*, XXII, 567.
21. Natchez *Daily Courier*, 19 April 1862.
22. Cincinnati *Daily Commercial*, 12, 14 February 1862.
23. *Harper's Weekly*, 24 February 1862.

24. Leffingwell to Bacon, 10 November 1862, LPMR.
25. Foote to Welles, 6 February 1862, *ONR*, XXII, 537.
26. Foote to his wife, 6 February 1862, LPMR.
27. Laning's report, p. 146.
28. Scott to his wife, 7 February 1862, Anna E. Carroll Papers, Maryland Historical Society.
29. Richardson, *Secret Service*, p. 216.
30. *Harper's Weekly*, 1 March 1862.
31. Phelps to Foote, *ONR*, XXII, 571.
32. *Harper's Weekly*, 11 July 1863.
33. Moore, *Record*, 4: 69.
34. Louisville *Daily Journal*, 19 February 1862.
35. Wise to Foote, 10 February 1862, *ONR*, XXII, 549.
36. For example, *Harper's Weekly*, 22 February 1862.
37. Harris to Benjamin, 7 February 1862, Governors' Correspondence, Tennessee Department of Archives.
38. Louisville *Daily Journal*, 10 February 1862.
39. Johnston to Benjamin, 8 February 1862, *OAR*, VII, 130.
40. New Orleans *Daily True Delta*, 6, 7 February 1862.
41. Beauregard to Pryor, 14 February 1862, P. G. T. Beauregard Papers, L. C.
42. Beauregard to Cooper, 21 February 1862, *ONR*, XXII, 825; Beauregard to Johnston, *ibid.*, 822.
43. Grant to Halleck, 6 February 1862, *OAR*, VII, 125.
44. Halleck to Scott, 12 February 1862, Edwin M. Stanton Papers, L. C. See also Scott to Stanton, 6 February 1862, *ibid.*
45. Halleck to Foote, 11 February 1862, *ONR*, XXII, 582.
46. Walke to Foote, 10 February 1862, *ibid.*, 583.
47. Moore, *Record*, 4: 171.
48. Pillow to Derrick, 18 February 1862, *OAR*, VII, 278.
49. Floyd to Otey, 20 March 1862, *ibid.*, 270.
50. Walke to Foote, 15 February 1862, *ONR*, XXII, 587.
51. Foote to Welles, 15 February 1862, *ibid.*, 585. See also James Hoppin, *Life of Andrew Hull Foote*, p. 229.
52. Walke, *Scenes*, p. 82.
53. Haynes to Cooper, 24 March 1862, *OAR*, VII, 389.
54. *Daily Missouri Democrat*, 18 February 1862.
55. Walke to Foote, 15 February 1862, *ONR*, XXII, 590.
56. Foote to Welles, 13 February 1862, Andrew Hull Foote Papers, L. C.
57. Cincinnati *Daily Commercial*, 20 February 1862.
58. Floyd to Johnston, 27 February 1862, *OAR*, VII, 267.
59. Cincinnati *Daily Commercial*, 22, 27 February 1862.

60. Cairo *Gazette,* 17 February 1862.
61. Brinton, *Personal Memoirs,* p. 121.
62. Grant to Cullum, 16 February 1862, and other reports, *OAR,* VII, 159.
63. Moore, *Record,* 8: 37; reports, *OAR,* VII, 283–335.
64. Brinton, *Personal Memoirs,* p. 129.
65. Grant to Buckner, 16 February 1862, *OAR,* VII, 161.
66. Coffin, *Four Years of Fighting,* p. 83.
67. Walke, *Scenes,* p. 81.
68. Cincinnati *Daily Commercial,* 20, 22 February 1862.
69. Adam R. Johnson, *The Partisan Rangers of the Confederate States Army,* p. 71. See also Moore, *Record,* 4: 211; 5: 23.
70. Nashville *Times,* 1 March 1862.
71. Foote to his wife, 16, 17 February 1862, LPMR.
72. Foote to Welles, 20 February 1862, *ONR,* XXII, 615.
73. Cullum to Phelps, 20 February 1862, *ibid.,* 621.
74. Halleck to Cullum, 20 February 1862, *ibid.,* 622.
75. McClellan to Cullum, 21 February 1862, *ibid.,* 622.
76. Halleck to Grant, 18 February 1862, *ibid.,* 616.
77. Foote to his wife, 23 February 1862, LPMR.
78. Richmond *Whig,* 21 February 1862.
79. "Journal of the Secret Sessions of the House of Representatives," 25 February, 4 March 1862, RG 109.
80. Moore, *Record,* 4: 81.
81. Louisville *Daily Journal,* 22 February 1862.
82. Johnson to his wife, 22 February 1862, Charles James Johnson Papers.
83. For example, Bacon to Davis, 25 February 1862, Jefferson Davis Papers, Duke University.
84. Welles to his son, 16 February 1862, Welles Papers.
85. Quoted in Cincinnati *Daily Commercial,* 21 February 1862.
86. Foote to his wife, 23, 25 February, 9 March 1862, LPMR.
87. Stanton to McClellan, 18 February 1862, Letters Sent, War Office, RG 107; Fox to Foote, 1 March 1862, *ONR,* XXII, 648.
88. Meigs to Lincoln, 28 February 1862, Reports of the Quartermaster General; Adams to Meigs, 21 February 1862, WTF.

CHAPTER 6

1. Moore, *Record,* 4: 224.
2. Polk to Davis, 11 March 1862, *ONR,* XXII, 654.
3. Beauregard to Miles, 11 March 1862, Beauregard Papers.

4. Withers to certain members of Congress, 28 February 1862, *ONR*, XXII, 829.
5. Beauregard to Polk, 26 February 1862, Beauregard Papers.
6. Cincinnati *Daily Commercial*, 12 March 1862.
7. Pope to Halleck, 2 May 1862, *OAR*, VIII, 85.
8. Gray's notes, 24, 29 March 1862, *ONR*, XXII, 744, 748.
9. Beauregard to Lovell, 10, 14 March 1862, Beauregard Papers.
10. Hollins to Beauregard, 15 March 1862, *ONR*, XXII, 738.
11. Hollins to Mallory, 21 March 1862, *ibid.*, 756.
12. Johnson to his wife, 5 February, 10, 14 March 1862, Johnson Papers.
13. Polk to his daughter, 9 March 1862, Polk Papers.
14. Lindell to Brown, 31 March 1862, Letters Received, War Office, RG 109.
15. Scott to Stanton, 6 March 1862, Stanton Papers.
16. Cincinnati *Daily Commercial*, 17 March 1862.
17. Foote to Welles, 1 March 1862, *ONR*, XXII, 650.
18. Junius Browne, *Four Years in Secessia*, p. 87.
19. Cincinnati *Daily Commercial*, 5 March 1862.
20. Foote to Welles, 4 March 1862, *ONR*, XXII, 651.
21. Halleck to Foote, 4 March 1862, *ibid.*, 656.
22. Pope to Cullum, 14 March 1862, *OAR*, VIII, 81.
23. Hollins to McGown, 9 March 1862, *ONR*, XXII, 835.
24. Meigs to Foote, 15 March 1862, Letters Sent, RG 92.
25. Halleck to Cullum, 10 March 1862, *ONR*, XXII, 663.
26. Foote to Fox, 13 March 1862; Foote to Welles, 13 March 1862, *ibid.*, 686–687.
27. Cincinnati *Daily Commercial*, 25 March 1862.
28. Foote to ...., 9 March 1862, LPMR.
29. Foote to his wife, 12 March 1862, *ibid.*
30. Foote to Dahlgren, 31 March 1862, Dahlgren Papers.
31. "Message from the President of the United States, recommending A vote of thanks to Captain A. H. Foote," *House Exec. Doc., No. 141*, 37 Cong., 2 sess.
32. Foote to Halleck, 12 March 1862; Halleck to Strong, 13 March 1862, *ONR*, XXII, 685–686.
33. *Daily Missouri Democrat*, 19 March 1862.
34. *Ibid.*, 21 March 1862.
35. Richardson, *Secret Service*, p. 227.
36. Foote to Welles, 17, 19 March 1862, *ONR*, XXII, 693, 696.
37. Foote to Pennock, 17 March 1862, *ibid.*, 695.
38. Cincinnati *Daily Commercial*, 21 March 1862.

39. Foote to Welles, 20 March 1862, *ONR*, XXII, 697.
40. Pope to Halleck, 21 March 1862, *OAR*, VIII, 630.
41. *Daily Missouri Democrat*, 26 March 1862.
42. Richardson, *Secret Service*, p. 230.
43. Cincinnati *Daily Commercial*, 25, 28 March 1862.
44. *Daily Missouri Democrat*, 31 March 1862.
45. Quoted in Richmond *Dispatch*, 8 April 1862.
46. Davis to ...., 9 May 1862, in Charles H. Davis, *Life of Charles Henry Davis*, p. 222.
47. W. D. Porter to Hale, 6 February 1864, Hale Papers.
48. Scott to Stanton, 30 March 1862, Stanton Papers.
49. Cincinnati *Daily Commercial*, 1 April 1862.
50. Pope to Halleck, 23, 27 March 1862, *OAR*, VIII, 643.
51. Moore, *Record*, 5: 39; New Orleans *Daily True Delta*, 17 May 1862.
52. Mackall to Jordan, 31 March, 3 April 1862, *ONR*, XXII, 751; *OAR*, VIII, 809.
53. Hollins to Mallory, 9 April 1862, *ONR*, XXII, 839.
54. Pope to Halleck, 2 April 1862, *ibid.*, 708.
55. Bissell to Wade, 14 May 1862, *ibid.*, 734.
56. Cincinnati *Daily Commercial*, 10 April 1862; Walke, *Scenes*, pp. 124, 126.
57. *ONR*, XXII, 713–715.
58. Cincinnati *Daily Commercial*, 11 April 1862.
59. Walke to Foote, 8 April 1862, *ONR*, XXII, 726.
60. Pope to Halleck, 9 April 1862, *ibid.*, 724.
61. Foote to Halleck, 8 April 1862, *OAR*, VIII, 674.
62. *Daily Missouri Democrat*, 9 April 1862.
63. Randall, *Civil War and Reconstruction*, p. 281.
64. Gwin to Foote, 8 April 1862, *ONR*, XXII, 762.
65. Cincinnati *Daily Commercial*, 11 April 1862.
66. Beauregard to Cooper, 11 April 1862; Beauregard to Savannah *Republican*, 17 July 1862, Beauregard Papers.
67. Cincinnati *Daily Commercial*, 18 April 1862.
68. W. H. C. Michael, "The Mississippi Flotilla," LUS, Nebraska, *Civil War Sketches*, 1 (1902): 27; Grant to McClean, 9 April 1862, *ONR*, XXII, 765.
69. Richmond *Dispatch*, 10, 25 April 1862.
70. Foote to Welles, 14 April 1862, *ONR*, XXIII, 4.
71. Phelps to Davis, 5 June 1862, *ibid.*, 51.
72. Scott to Stanton, 16 April 1862, Stanton Papers.
73. Foote to Meigs, 23 April 1862, WTF; Foote to Welles, 14, 19 April 1862, *ONR*, XXIII, 5.

74. Halleck to Foote, 15 April 1862, *ibid.*, 5; and also see Foote to Welles, 15, 23, 30 April 1862, *ibid.*, 10, 12, 62.
75. Scott to Stanton, 19 April 1862, Stanton Papers.
76. Foote to Welles, 17 April 1862, *ONR*, XXIII, 8.
77. Welles to Foote, *ibid.*, 70.
78. *Daily Missouri Democrat*, 4 June 1862.
79. Mallory to Hollins, 10, 11 April 1862, *ONR*, XXII, 840.
80. Mallory to Davis, 16 August 1862, Subject File VN, RG 45.
81. Memphis *Argus*, 6 May 1862.
82. Natchez *Daily Courier*, 19 April 1862.
83. Beauregard to Cooper, 25 April 1862, Beauregard Papers.
84. Beauregard to Harris, 21 April 1862, *ONR*, XXIII, 696.
85. New Orleans *Daily True Delta*, 18 April 1862.

CHAPTER 7

1. Farragut to Welles, 1 May 1861, Captains' Letters, RG 45.
2. Welles Diary, 23 August, 2 September 1864, Welles Papers.
3. Porter, "Journal of Occurrences," p. 178.
4. William T. Meredith, "Farragut's Capture of New Orleans," in *Battles and Leaders of the Civil War*, 2: 70.
5. Bartholomew Diggins, "Recollections," MS, New York Public Library.
6. Fox to Farragut, 7 March 1862, Fox Papers.
7. David D. Porter, *Incidents and Anecdotes of the Civil War*, p. 95.
8. Porter, "Journal of Occurrences," p. 168.
9. Barnard to McClellan, 7, 15 February 1862, *OAR*, VI, 685, 691. Also see Barnard to Fox, 28 January 1862, *OAR*, XV, 413.
10. Andrew to Thomas, 27 November 1861; George to Butler, 3 April 1862, Benjamin F. Butler Papers, L. C.
11. Butler to Thomas, 18 November, 27 December 1861, *ibid.*
12. Stanton's memo, 19 January 1862, Stanton Papers.
13. Welles Diary, "Narrative of Events."
14. Gideon Welles, "Admiral Farragut and New Orleans," *The Galaxy*, 12 (1871): 820.
15. James Parton, *General Butler in New Orleans*, p. 191.
16. McClellan to Butler, 23 February 1862, Butler Papers.
17. Tyler Dennett, ed., *Lincoln and the Civil War in the Diaries and Letters of John Hay*, p. 240; Smith to his wife, 19 November 1864, Franklin E. Smith Papers, Duke University.
18. Virginia Woodbury Fox Diary, 5 December 1862.
19. Welles Diary, 14 April, 13 July 1863.

20. "List of Vessels of the Mortar Flotilla," Commanders' Letters, RG 45.
21. New York *Post*, 7 February 1862.
22. Mullaney to Harwood, 9 December 1861, Letters Received from Foundries, RG 74.
23. Welles to Porter, 21 December 1861, Letters Sent, RG 45.
24. *Harper's Weekly*, 1 February 1862.
25. Washington *Globe*, 15 February 1862.
26. Gregory to Welles, 14 January 1862, Admirals' Letters, RG 45.
27. Harwood to Mullaney, 31 January 1862, Letters to Inspectors, RG 74.
28. Virginia Woodbury Fox Diary, 18 February 1862.
29. Grimes to Fox, 3 February 1862, Fox Papers.
30. Farragut to Fox, n.d., *ibid.*
31. Butler to Fox, 2 March 1862, *ibid.*
32. Benjamin to Lovell, 8 February 1862, *OAR*, VI, 823.
33. Garner to Jones, 28 March 1862, *ibid.*, 867.
34. Benjamin to Lovell, 8 February 1862, *ibid.*, 823; Lovell to Benjamin, 12 February 1862, *ibid.*, 825.
35. Benjamin to Bragg, 18 February 1862, *ibid.*, 828.
36. Lovell to Cooper, 22 May 1862, *ibid.*, 513.
37. Benjamin to Lovell, 8 February 1862, *ibid.*, 823.
38. Shorter to Benjamin, 13 January 1862, *ibid.*, 803.
39. Moore to Davis, 1 April 1862, *ibid.*, 869.
40. Randolph to Moore, 2 April 1862, Telegrams Sent, War Office, RG 109.
41. D. W. Brickell's testimony, Court of Inquiry, *OAR*, VI, 577.
42. Davis to Moore, 17 April 1862, in Rowland, *Davis*, 5: 233.
43. Soper to his father, 4 April 1862, Hitchcock Papers.
44. Lovell's testimony, Court of Inquiry, *OAR*, VI, 560.
45. Hollin's testimony, *Report of Evidence*, p. 45.
46. Testimony of Kennon and Mitchell, *ibid.*, 40, 101.
47. Testimony of Whittle and Hollins, *ibid.*, 8, 45.
48. Parton, *Butler*, pp. 195, 208.
49. Mrs. Butler to Mrs. Heard, 30 March 1862, in Jessie Marshall, ed., *Private and Official Correspondence of Gen. Benjamin F. Butler*, 1: 387.
50. "Memorandum of Cargo," Butler Papers.
51. Parton, *Butler*, p. 203.
52. Richard S. West, *The Second Admiral: A Life of David Dixon Porter*, p. 123.
53. Albert S. Barker, *Everyday Life in the Navy*, p. 13.
54. Porter to Harris, 21 April 1862, Porter Papers.

55. Porter to Fox, 28 March, 8 April 1862, Fox Papers.
56. Diggins, "Recollections."
57. Duncan to Pickett, 30 April 1862, *OAR*, VI, 521.
58. Asher Taylor, *Notes of Conversations with a Volunteer Officer*, p. 8.
59. George Brown, "The Mortar Flotilla," LUS, New York, *Personal Recollections*, p. 178.
60. Higgins to Bridges, 27 April 1862, *OAR*, VI, 547.
61. "Letter from an officer at Fort Jackson, 23 April 1862," in Richmond *Dispatch*, 5 May 1862.
62. Porter to Welles, 25 April 1862, *ONR*, XVIII, 356.
63. Cooke to his wife, 22 April 1862, LPMR.
64. Porter to Welles, 30 April 1862, *ONR*, XVIII, 361.
65. Farragut's orders, 20 April 1862, *ibid.*, 162.
66. Testimony of John Wilkinson, George Shyrock, Wilson Youngblood, Court of Inquiry in the Case of John K. Mitchell, John K. Mitchell Papers, Virginia Historical Society; testimony of Lovell, Mitchell, Kennon, & Whittle, *Report of Evidence*, pp. 8, 37, 101, 217.
67. Diggins, "Recollections."
68. William B. Robertson, "The Water-Battery at Fort Jackson," *Battles and Leaders of the Civil War*, 2: 100.
69. Edward Higgins testimony, Court of Inquiry, *OAR*, VI, 590.
70. Willis J. Abbot, *Bluejackets of '61*, p. 235.
71. Harrison to Headley, 24 August 1866, LPMR.
72. Beverly Kennon, "Fighting Farragut Below New Orleans," *Battles and Leaders of the Civil War*, 2: 80.
73. Lovell to Cooper, 26 April 1862, *OAR*, VI, 510.
74. Diggins, "Recollections."
75. James Tomb's Memoirs, Subject File HA, RG 45.
76. John Russell Bartlett, "The 'Brooklyn' Below New Orleans," *Battles and Leaders of the Civil War*, 2: 66.
77. Diggins, "Recollections."
78. Taylor, *Notes*, p. 12.
79. Reports, *ONR*, XVIII, 131.
80. Porter, *Incidents*, p. 48.
81. Farragut to Porter, 24 April 1862, Porter Papers.
82. Butler to his wife, 26 April 1862, in Marshall, *Butler*, 1: 422.
83. Duncan to Pickett, 30 April 1862, *OAR*, VI, 531.
84. "Notes by Mitchell," Mitchell Papers.
85. David D. Porter, "The Opening of the Lower Mississippi," *Battles and Leaders of the Civil War*, 2: 51.
86. Whittle's testimony, *Report of Evidence*, p. 8.
87. Arthur Sinclair's testimony, *ibid.*, 61.

88. Lovell's testimony, *OAR*, VI, 565.
89. Diggins, "Recollections"; Howard Palmer, "New Orleans under General Butler," *The Louisiana Historical Quarterly*, 24 (1941): 454; New Orleans *Daily True Delta*, 25, 26 April 1862; Parton, *Butler*, p. 264.
90. Natchez *Daily Courier*, 6 May 1862.
91. Sarah Jane Johnston Diary.
92. *Journal of the Senate, November 1863 Session*, p. 182.
93. Ellis to his parents, 29 April 1862, E. John Ellis Papers, Louisiana State University.
94. Beauregard to Lovell, 13 May 1862, Beauregard Papers.
95. *Norfolk Day Book*, 29 May 1862; Atlanta *Intelligencer*, 27 April 1862; Alexandria, La., *Democrat*, 26 December 1862; Richmond *Dispatch*, 28, 29 April 1862.
96. Mallory to his wife, 11 May, 21 August 1862, Mallory Papers.
97. Philip Melvin, "Stephen Russell Mallory, Southern Naval Statesman," *Journal of Southern History*, 10 (1944): 158.
98. Quoted in *Frank Leslie's Illustrated Newspaper*, 14 June 1862.
99. Alfred Thayer Mahan, *Admiral Farragut*, p. 173.
100. Adams to Adams, 16 May 1862, in Worthington C. Ford, ed., *A Cycle of Adams Letters*, 1: 145.
101. Moore to Legislature, 15 December 1862, *Journal of the Extra Session, Sixth Legislature*, p. 13.
102. Parton, *Butler*, p. 281.
103. Mrs. Butler to Mrs. Heard, 2 May 1862, in Marshall, *Butler*, 1: 436.
104. Butler to Blair, 8 May 1862, Blair Family Papers.
105. Fox to Farragut, 12 May 1862, Fox Papers.
106. Farragut to Porter, 29 April, 1 May 1862, Porter Papers.
107. Porter to Fox, 24 May, 7 June 1862, Fox Papers.
108. Porter to Harris, 28 May 1862, Porter Papers.

CHAPTER 8

1. See letters to Naval Examining Board, 1862, RG 45.
2. Ellet to his mother, 11 March 1862, Ellet Family Papers, University of Michigan, Transportation Library.
3. Ellet to Stanton, 12, 13, 15 March 1862; Ellet to his brother, 30 March 1862, *ibid.*
4. Nimick to Stanton, 27 May 1862, Consolidated Correspondence File, RG 92.
5. Ellet to Stanton, 29 March 1862, Ellet Papers.
6. Ellet to Nimick, 6 April 1862, *ibid.*
7. Litherbury to Meigs, 1 May 1862, WTF.

8. Pennock to Davis, 16 May 1862, LPMR.
9. Ellet to Stanton, 19 April 1862, *ONR*, XXIII, 65.
10. William Porter's Memorial, Senate Records, RG 46; Porter to Welles, 6 May 1862, Commanders' Letters, RG 45; Porter to Harwood, 4, 20, 31 May 1862, Letters from Officers, RG 74; Wise to Meigs, 11 March 1862, WTF.
11. Cincinnati *Daily Commercial,* 11 December 1862.
12. Meigs to Foote, 15 March 1862, Letters Sent, RG 92.
13. Porter to Meigs, 9 March 1862, WTF.
14. *Daily Missouri Democrat,* 30 June 1862.
15. Phelps to Foote, 18 February 1862, *ONR*, XXII, 615.
16. Foote to Meigs, 10 April 1862, WTF.
17. Fox to Foote, 7 March 1862, LPMR. Also see Cincinnati *Daily Commercial,* 15, 18 August 1862.
18. Meigs to Welles, 27 March 1862, Reports of the Quartermaster General, RG 92; Porter to Welles, 5 March 1862, Commanders' Letters, RG 45.
19. Smith to Welles, 9 April 1862, Bureau Letters, RG 45; Contracts for Vessels, RG 19.
20. *Daily Missouri Democrat,* 2, 26 August 1862.
21. Eads to Hull, 10 October 1862, LPMR; Hull to Welles, 4 August, 19 September 1862, Admirals' Letters, RG 45.
22. See Welles to Stanton, 28 February 1863, Subject File OX, RG 45; Febiger to Welles, 9 June 1863, Squadron Letters, RG 45; Pennock to Porter, 18 June 1863, *ibid.*
23. "Specifications for an Ironclad Iron Propeller Gun-Boat for Western Waters," Monitor Correspondence, RG 19.
24. Porter to Welles, 5 June 1864, Squadron Letters, RG 45.
25. Porter to Welles, 7 February 1863, *ONR*, XXIV, 322.
26. Sanford to Hull, 11 September 1862, Letters from Officers, RG 19; Sanford to Foote, 8 September 1862, LPMR.
27. Brown to Lenthall, 24 September 1862, Miscellaneous Letters Received, RG 19.
28. Walker to Porter, 25 October, 1862, *ONR*, XXIII, 448.
29. Porter to Welles, 12 October 1862, Squadron Letters, RG 45.
30. Brown to Hull, 10 November 1862, LPMR.
31. Whittaker to Porter, 28 November 1862, Squadron Letters, RG 45.
32. Hartt to Hull, 9 February 1863, Subject File BG, RG 45.
33. King to Hull, 24 February 1864, Subject File AC, RG 45.
34. Hull to Lenthall, 16 August, 3, 4 September 1862, Letters from Officers, RG 19.
35. See Theodore Parker, "The Federal Gunboat Flotilla on the Western Rivers during its Administration by the War Department to

October 1, 1862" (Ph.D. dissertation), University of Pittsburgh, (1939).

36. Murphy to Foote, 19 February 1863, Letters from Officers, RG 24; Harty to Foote, 21 May 1863, *ibid.*

37. Welles to Davis, 30 April 1862, *ONR*, XXIII, 80.

38. Porter to Welles, 25 July 1863, Squadron Letters, RG 45.

39. Porter to Welles, 12 April 1863, *ibid.*

40. Porter to Foote, 16 May 1863, LPMR.

41. Scott to Porter, 25 October 1862, Squadron Letters, RG 45.

42. Sanford to Foote, 21 June 1862, LPMR.

43. Cincinnati *Daily Commercial,* 20, 24 June 1862.

44. Porter to Welles, 11 November 1862, Squadron Letters, RG 45.

45. Pennock to Welles, 30 October 1864, *ibid.*

46. Case No. 3337, Courts-Martial, Office of Judge Advocate, RG 45.

47. Farragut to Welles, 14 September 1862, Squadron Letters, RG 45.

48. William Bentley, *History of the 77th Illinois Volunteer Infantry,* p. 104.

49. "Notes on Torpedoes," Maury Papers.

50. Mallory to Carter, 3 October 1862, LPMR.

51. *Acts Passed by the Sixth Legislature at Its Extra Session, Held in the City of Shreveport, on the 4th of March 1863,* p. 25.

52. Brent to Magruder, 24 October 1863, Records of Navy Department, RG 109.

53. John Shirley's testimony, *Report of Evidence,* p. 405.

54. Brown to Mahan, 26 March 1883, LPMR.

55. George Gift, "The Story of the *Arkansas,*" *Southern Historical Society Papers,* 12 (1884): 48.

CHAPTER 9

1. Davis to ...., 9 May 1862, in Davis, *Davis,* pp. 222, 224.

2. Cincinnati *Daily Commercial,* 12 May 1862.

3. Thompson to Beauregard, 10 May 1862, *ONR*, XXIII, 54.

4. *Hinds County Gazette,* 15 January 1862.

5. Eliot Callender, "What a Boy Saw on the Mississippi," LUS, Illinois, *Military Essays,* 1 (1891): 62.

6. Davis to Welles, 11 May 1862, *ONR*, XXIII, 14.

7. Davis to Welles, 12 May 1862, *ibid.,* 17.

8. Ellet to Stanton, 26, 30 May, 4 June 1862, *ibid.,* 29, 36, 43.

9. Beauregard to Lovell, 10 June 1862, Individual Commands, RG 109.

10. Phelps to Davis, 5 June 1862, *ONR*, XXIII, 51.

11. Cincinnati *Daily Commercial,* 7, 11 June 1862.

12. Knox, *Camp-Fire and Cotton-Field,* p. 179.

13. Coffin, *Four Years of Fighting*, p. 103.

14. *Daily Missouri Democrat*, 18 June 1862.

15. Cabell to Mahan, 14 April 1883, LPMR.

16. Ellet to Stanton, 11 June 1862, *ibid.*

17. *Daily Missouri Democrat*, 18 June 1862.

18. Reports, *ONR*, XXIII, 119.

19. Cincinnati *Daily Commercial*, 11 June 1862.

20. Moore, *Record*, 5: 181.

21. Coffin, *Four Years of Fighting*, p. 108.

22. Foote to Welles, 13 June 1862, *ONR*, XXIII, 155.

23. Foote to Sanford, 11 June 1862, Gratz Collection, Pennsylvania Historical Society.

24. Cincinnati *Daily Commercial*, 20, 21 June 1862.

25. Halleck to Davis, 8 June 1862, *ONR*, XXIII, 160.

26. Cincinnati *Daily Commercial*, 24, 25, 30 June 1862; *Daily Missouri Democrat*, 26, 28 June 1862.

27. Browne to Gunn, 9 August 1862, Symmes Browne Papers, Ohio Historical Society.

28. Reports, *ONR*, XXIII, 165.

CHAPTER 10

1. McDonald to Mahan, 1 May 1883, LPMR.

2. Farragut to Welles, 30 May 1862, *ONR*, XVIII, 519.

3. Cincinnati *Daily Commercial*, 26 June 1862.

4. Charles W. Hassler, "Reminiscences of 1861–3," LUS, New York, *Personal Recollections*, p. 62.

5. *The Press*, 10 July 1862, in LPMR.

6. Harrison Soule, "From the Gulf to Vicksburg," LUS, Michigan, *War Papers*, 2 (1898): 69.

7. *The Press*, 10 July 1862.

8. Fox to Farragut, 17 May 1862, *ONR*, XVIII, 498.

9. Farragut to Welles, 30 May 1862, *ibid.*, 519.

10. Butler to Stanton, 1, 10 June 1862, Butler Papers.

11. Farragut to Porter, 31 May 1862, Porter Papers.

12. Butler to Williams, 1, 6 June 1862, Butler Papers.

13. Farragut to Bailey, 11 June 1862, *ONR*, XVIII, 551.

14. Isaac DeGraff's MS Journal, RG 45.

15. Farragut's order, 25 June 1862, Porter Papers.

16. Cincinnati *Daily Commercial*, 18 July 1862.

17. Rowland Chambers Diary, Louisiana State University.

18. Farragut to Welles, 2 July 1862, *ONR*, XVIII, 608.

19. Craven to Farragut, 28, 30 June 1862, *ibid.*, 597, 599.

20. Reports, *ibid.*, 614.
21. Farragut to Craven, 30 June 1862, *ibid.*, 602.
22. Farragut to ...., n.d., in Loyall Farragut, *The Life of David Glasgow Farragut*, p. 269.
23. Farragut to his wife, n.d., *ibid.*, 271.
24. Phelps to Foote, 6 July 1862, LPMR.
25. Russell to McPherson, 4 July 1862, Edward McPherson Papers, L.C.
26. *The Press*, 10 July 1862.
27. Farragut to Butler, 5 July 1862, Butler Papers.
28. Cincinnati *Daily Commercial*, 12 July 1862.
29. Hassler, "Reminiscences," p. 62.
30. Davis to his wife, 16 August 1862, in Davis, *Davis*, p. 274.
31. Halleck to Stanton, 15 July 1862, *ONR*, XXIII, 240.
32. Van Dorn to Davis, 14 July 1862, *ibid.*, XVIII, 652.
33. Porter's Memorial, Senate Records, RG 46.
34. Brown to Mahan, – – 1883, LPMR.
35. Grimball to his father, 2, 3, 25 July 1862, John Grimball Papers, Duke University.
36. Cincinnati *Daily Commercial*, 24 July 1862.
37. Phelps to Foote, 7 September 1862, LPMR.
38. Scharf, *Confederate States Navy*, p. 318.
39. Wharton to Mahan, 7 February 1883, LPMR.
40. Diggins, "Recollections."
41. Scharf, *Confederate States Navy*, p. 323.
42. Cincinnati *Daily Commercial*, 29 July 1862.
43. Davis to Welles, 16 July 1862, Squadron Letters, RG 45.
44. Diggins, "Recollections."
45. Porter to Hale, 19 December 1863, Hale Papers.
46. Porter to Davis, 22 July 1862, Squadron Letters, RG 45.
47. Davis's Diary, *ONR*, XXIII, 270.
48. Phelps to Foote, 29 July 1862, LPMR.
49. Diggins, "Recollections."
50. Farragut to Davis, 23 July 1862, *ONR*, XXIII, 239.
51. Cincinnati *Daily Commercial*, 31 December 1862.
52. Van Dorn to Cooper, *OAR*, XV, 15.
53. John Wilson's Diary, *ONR*, XIX, 131, 135.
54. Farragut, *Farragut*, p. 288.
55. Breckinridge to Kimmel, 30 September, *OAR*, XV, 76.
56. Porter to Welles, 6 August 1862, *ONR*, XIX, 117.
57. Porter to Hale, 26 January 1864, Hale Papers.
58. New Orleans *Daily True Delta*, 14 August 1862.
59. Davis's Diary, *ONR*, XXIII, 270.

60. Walke to Davis, 30 July 1862, *ibid.*, 272.
61. Porter to Fox, 26 July 1862, Fox Papers.
62. Cincinnati *Daily Commercial,* 7, 12, 21, 23 July, 7, 15 September 1862.
63. David Donald, ed., *Inside Lincoln's Cabinet: The Civil War Diaries of Salmon P. Chase,* p. 107.
64. Welles to Davis, 24 July 1862, *ONR*, XXIII, 269; Davis to Welles, 1 August 1862, *ibid.*, 278.
65. Porter to his mother, 7 October 1862, Porter Papers.

CHAPTER 11

1. Cincinnati *Daily Commercial,* 4 November 1862.
2. Porter, "Journal of Occurrences," p. 393.
3. Fox to Porter, 24 October 1862, *ONR*, XXIII, 443.
4. Fox to Welles, 11 November 1862, Welles Papers.
5. Ellet to his sister, 13 December 1862, Ellet Papers.
6. Winslow to Porter, 25 October 1862, *ONR*, XXIII, 447.
7. Porter to Welles, 27 October 1862, *ibid.*, 451.
8. See Russell, *Diary,* p. 37.
9. McClernand to Stanton, 10 October 1862, Stanton Papers.
10. Stanton to McClernand, 21, 29 October 1862, *OAR*, XVII, 282, 302.
11. McClernand to Stanton, 10 November 1862, Stanton Papers.
12. "Copies of Confidential Papers. Remarks," William T. Sherman Papers, L. C.
13. Porter to Sherman, 12 November 1862, *ONR*, XXIII, 479.
14. Porter, "Journal of Occurrences," p. 414.
15. *Ibid.*, 467.
16. Quoted in Porter to Foote, n.d., LPMR.
17. McClernand to Lincoln, 12 December 1862, Stanton Papers.
18. McClernand to Browning, 16 December 1862, John A. McClernand Papers, Illinois State Historical Library.
19. Earl Schenck Miers, *The Web of Victory,* p. 52.
20. Telegrams, *ONR*, XXIII, 709.
21. "Report of Heavy Batteries, Vicksburg," *OAR*, XV, 848, 852.
22. "Davidson's Notes of Torpedo Operations," Porter Papers.
23. Reports, *ONR*, XXIII, 544.
24. Selfridge's "Notes on the Civil War," Thomas O. Selfridge Papers, L. C.
25. Moore, *Record,* 6: 310.
26. Cincinnati *Daily Commercial,* 27 February 1863.
27. Moore, *Record,* 6: 297; Russell, *Diary,* p. 299.
28. Miers, *Web of Victory,* pp. 62, 67.

306 Battle Flags South

29. Porter to Welles, 27 December 1862, *ONR*, XXIII, 572.
30. Little to his mother, 27 December 1862, Sidney Little Papers, Louisiana State University.
31. Sherman, *Memoirs*, 1: 319.
32. Reports, *OAR*, XVII, 601.
33. Porter, "Journal of Occurrences," p. 467.
34. Porter to Welles, 3 January 1863, *ONR*, XXIII, 604.
35. Grimes to Fox, 9 March 1863, Fox Papers.
36. Welles Diary, 9 January 1863.
37. Cincinnati *Daily Commercial*, 15 January 1863.
38. "Copies of Confidential Papers. Remarks," Sherman Papers.
39. Porter to Sherman, 1 January 1863, *ONR*, XXIII, 597.
40. Sherman to Porter, 3 January 1863, *ibid.*, 605.
41. Moore, *Record*, 6: 370.
42. Porter's order, *ONR*, XXIV, 100.
43. E. Paul Reichhelm Journal, L. C.
44. Moore, *Record*, 6: 370.
45. Justin Meacham, "Military and Naval Operations on the Mississippi," LUS, Wisconsin, *War Papers*, 4: 391.
46. Perry to his wife, 14 January 1863, Presley Persons Papers, Duke University.
47. Reports, *ONR*, XXIV, 98.
48. Porter, "Journal of Occurrences," pp. 466, 482.
49. Porter to Grimes, 24 January 1863, *ONR*, XXIV, 194.
50. Porter to Bache, 17 January 1863, *ibid.*, 174.
51. Sherman, *Memoirs*, 1: 329.
52. Sherman to Sherman, 26 January 1863, Sherman Papers.
53. Grant to Halleck, 11 January 1863, *ONR*, XXIV, 106.

Chapter 12

1. Ramsey to Trumbull, 4 February 1863, Trumbull Papers.
2. *Harper's Weekly*, 4 April 1863.
3. Porter to Welles, 7 February 1863, *ONR*, XXIV, 321.
4. Reports, *ONR*, XXIV, 243; *OAR*, XXIV, 371.
5. Welles Diary, 17 March 1863; Porter, "Journal of Occurrences," p. 532.
6. Ellet to Porter, 2 February 1863, *ONR*, XXIV, 219.
7. Cincinnati *Daily Commercial*, 10 February 1863.
8. Ellet to Porter, 5 February 1863, *ONR*, XXIV, 223.
9. Cincinnati *Daily Commercial*, 4 March 1863.
10. Garvey to Porter, 28 August 1863, Squadron Letters, RG 45.
11. Cincinnati *Daily Commercial*, 4 March 1863.

12. Ellet to his sister, 22 February 1863, Ellet Papers.
13. Porter to Welles, 22 February 1863, *ONR,* XXIV, 382.
14. Ellet to Ellet, 26 February 1863, Ellet Papers.
15. *ONR,* XXIV, 379, 392, 402; New Orleans *Daily True Delta,* 5 April 1862; Gosnell, *Guns on Western Waters,* p. 192.
16. Ellet to Ellet, 28 February 1863, Ellet Papers.
17. Virginia Woodbury Diary, – – February 1863.
18. Welles to Porter, 2 March 1863, *ONR,* XXIV, 388.
19. Porter to Welles, 12 March 1863, LPMR.
20. Pemberton to Stevenson, 27 February 1863, *ONR,* XXIV, 409.
21. Adams to Reeve, 1 March 1863, *ibid.*
22. Porter to Pennock, 11 February, 4 March 1863, *ONR,* XXIV, 350, 456.
23. Phelps to Porter, 5 February 1863, *ibid.,* 312.
24. Smith to Porter, 10 February 1863, *ibid.,* 337.
25. Case No. 3322, Courts-Martial, RG 45.
26. Porter to Welles, 7 March, 12 April 1863, *ONR,* XXIV, 462, 543.
27. Porter to Welles, 16 April 1862, Squadron Letters, RG 45.
28. Porter to Grant, 14 February 1863, *ONR,* XXIV, 342.
29. Grant to Porter, 15 February 1863, *ibid.*
30. Porter, *Incidents,* p. 168.
31. Moore, *Record,* 6: 461; Reports, *OAR,* XXIV, 431; *ONR,* XXIV, 474.
32. Porter to Farragut, 22 March 1863, Squadron Letters, RG 45.

CHAPTER 13

1. Diggins, "Recollections."
2. Halleck to Banks, 8 November 1862, Nathaniel Banks Papers, University of Texas (microfilm copies).
3. Banks to his wife, 15 January, 24 February 1863, *ibid.*
4. Jenkins to Mahan, 3 May 1883, Subject File OO, RG 45.
5. James W. Kessler, "Loss of the U.S.S. *Mississippi," The United Service,* 12: 650.
6. Jackson to his wife, 12 March 1863, Samuel Jackson Papers, Pennsylvania Historical Society.
7. Farragut, *Farragut,* p. 316.
8. Thomas Bacon, "The Fight at Port Hudson: Recollections of an Eye Witness," *The Independent,* 13: 591.
9. Edward Y. McMorries, *History of the First Alabama Volunteer Infantry, C.S.A.,* p. 53.
10. Loyall Farragut, "Passing the Port Hudson Batteries," LUS, New York, *Personal Recollections,* p. 318.

11. Bacon, "Fight at Port Hudson," p. 594.
12. New Orleans *Era,* 18 March 1863.
13. Moore, *Record,* 6: 457.
14. New Orleans *Daily Picayune,* 23 March 1863.
15. Moore, *Record,* 6: 455.
16. Reports, *ONR,* XIX, 665; *OAR,* XV, 251.
17. Diggins, "Recollections."
18. Porter, "Journal of Occurrences," p. 551.
19. Ellet to his sister, 26 March 1863, Dreer Collection, Pennsylvania Historical Society.
20. Porter to Welles, 25 March 1863, Ellet Papers.
21. Banks to Farragut, 23 April 1863, *OAR,* XV, 707.
22. Halleck to Banks, 3 April 1863, *ibid.,* 1116.
23. Fox to Porter, 6 April 1863, *ONR,* XXIV, 553.
24. *Harper's Weekly,* 6 June 1863.
25. James H. Wilson, *Under the Old Flag,* 1: 158.
26. Grant to Porter, 2 April 1863, *ONR,* XXIV, 521.
27. Porter to commanders, 10 April 1863, Squadron Letters, RG 45.
28. Wilson, *Old Flag,* p. 163.
29. Porter, "Journal of Occurrences," p. 569.
30. Walke, *Scenes,* p. 354.
31. Cincinnati *Daily Commercial,* 27 April, 2 May 1863.
32. Reports, *ONR,* XXIV, 552.
33. Pemberton to Chalmers, 18 April 1863, *ibid.,* 717.
34. Walke, *Scenes,* p. 363.
35. Breese to Porter, 2 May 1863, *ONR,* XXIV, 589.
36. Porter to Welles, 27 April 1863, *ibid.,* 607.
37. Porter, "Journal of Occurrences," p. 591.
38. Porter to Harris, 2 June 1863, Porter Papers.
39. Reports, *ONR,* XXIV, 610.
40. Cincinnati *Daily Commercial,* 18 May 1863.
41. Porter to Dahlgren, 8 May, 27 June 1863, Letters from Officers, RG 74.
42. Shirk to Porter, 2 May 1863, *ONR,* XXIV, 659.
43. Clint Parkhurst, "Our First View of Vicksburg," *The Palimpsest,* 3: 78.
44. Jamison to "loved ones," 29 April 1863, Elihu B. Washburne Papers, L. C.
45. Porter to Welles, 7, 13 May 1863, *ONR,* XXIV, 645, 646.
46. Porter to Welles, 20, 24 May, 1 June 1863, *ibid.,* XXV, 5, 7, 133.
47. Bache to Porter, 29 May 1863, *ibid.,* 42.
48. Balfour Diary, Mississippi Department of Archives.
49. William A. Drennan Diary, *ibid.;* Rowland Chambers Diary,

Louisiana State University; Vicksburg *Daily Citizen,* 2 July 1863.

50. Davis to Beauregard, Bragg, 25 June 1863, in Rowland, *Davis,* 5: 531, 532.
51. Quoted in Cincinnati *Daily Commercial,* 25 May 1863.
52. "Many Soldiers" to Pemberton, 28 June 1863, *ONR,* XXV, 118.
53. Cincinnati *Daily Commercial,* 18 June 1863.
54. Porter to Welles, 9 June 1863, *ONR,* XXV, 65.
55. Reports, *ONR,* XX, 206; *OAR,* XXVI, 43.
56. *Harper's Weekly,* 25 July 1863.
57. Moore, *Record,* 7: 53.
58. *Ibid.,* 51.
59. W. H. C. Michael, "The Mississippi Flotilla," LUS, Nebraska, *Civil War Sketches,* 1 (1902): 21.
60. Welles Diary, 8 July 1863.
61. Cincinnati *Daily Commercial,* 10, 13 July 1863.
62. Welles Diary, 8, 13 July 1863.
63. Cincinnati *Daily Commercial,* 25 July 1863.
64. *Harper's Weekly,* 8 August 1863.

EPILOGUE

1. Scharf, *Confederate States Navy,* p. 364.

Bibliography

ABBREVIATIONS

L. C.   Library of Congress, Manuscript Division
LPMR.   Loose Papers, Mississippi River, Record Group 45, National Archives.
LUS.   Military Order of the Loyal Legion of the United States.
NA.   National Archives.
OAR.   *The War of the Rebellion: A Compilation of the Official Records of the Union and Confederate Armies.*
ONR.   *Official Records of the Union and Confederate Navies in the War of the Rebellion.*
RG.   Record Group, National Archives.
USNIP. *United States Naval Institute Proceedings.*
WTF.   Water Transportation File, Record Group 92, National Archives.

MANUSCRIPTS

Library of Congress, Manuscript Division. Papers of P. G. T. Beauregard, Asa Beetham, Blair Family, Benjamin F. Butler, Simon Cameron, Zachariah Chandler, Salmon P. Chase, John A. Dahlgren, Charles A. Dana, John Ericsson, Hamilton Fish, Andrew Hull Foote, William B. Franklin, Ethan Allen Hitchcock, Joseph

Holt, Samuel Philips Lee, John A. Logan, George B. McClellan, Edward McPherson, Ninian Pinkney, David Dixon Porter, George Haven Putnam, John Rodgers, Thomas O. Selfridge, John Sherman, William T. Sherman, Edwin M. Stanton, Lyman Trumball, United States Navy Miscellaneous, Benjamin F. Wade, Elihu B. Washburne, Gideon Welles, H. A. Wise. Diaries of Betty Herndon Maury, Stephen R. Mallory (typewritten), E. Paul Reichhelm.

National Archives. RG 19, Bureau of Ships: contracts for vessels; correspondence relating to wooden screw gunboats and double-turret wooden monitors; engineers' reports; letters from contractors and manufacturers; letters sent to contractors, officers, and the Secretary of the Navy; miscellaneous letters. RG 24, Bureau of Naval Personnel: bureau letters; letters from the Secretary of the Navy. RG 45, Naval War Records: admirals', commodores', commanders', captains', officers', bureaus', squadrons', and naval agents' letters; naval examining board; permanent commission letters. Office of the Secretary of the Navy: confidential letters sent; letters to Congress, Federal executive agents, flag officers; miscellaneous letters sent and received. Office of the Judge Advocate General: general courts-martial records. Area files: Mississippi River. Subject files: armor, battles, coal and wood for ships, designs and general characteristics, distribution of vessels, engines, guns and gunnery, joint military and naval operations, lines of supply, naval policy, operations of fleets and squadrons, purchases and sales, recruiting and enlistments. Journals of Edward Latch and Isaac DeGraff. RG 74, Bureau of Ordnance: letters sent to and received from Secretary of the Navy, foundries, inspectors, and officers. *RG 92*, Quartermaster General: consolidated correspondence file, letters sent and received, reports, water transportation file. *RG 94*, Adjutant Generals Office: letters received, Smith-Brady Commission records. *RG 107*, Secretary of War: letters sent and received. *RG 109*, Confederate Records: journals of the House and Senate; individual commands; departments of War, Navy, Treasury; records relating to Louisiana and Mississippi; Union Provost Marshal's citizens' file. *RG 56*, Confederate Treasury; Third Special Agency. *RG 217*, Third Auditor: western gunboat flotilla records. *RG 59*, Consular Correspondence: Mexico. *RG 46*, Senate Committee on Naval Affairs.

Delaware Historical Society. James Wilson journal.

Duke University. Papers of J. T. Billenstein, John Cabell Breckinridge, Frederick Clark, Nathan Dye, Jefferson Davis, Oren Farr, John Grimball, James Hill, George W. Thomas Jefferson, Duncan McLaurin, Presley Persons, John Routh, Daniel Ruggles, Franklin E. Smith, Eugene Southwick, Henry Spaulding.

Henry E. Huntington Library. Eldridge, Nicholson, and Brock collections. Papers of David G. Farragut, David D. Porter, Gideon Welles.

Illinois State Historical Library. Papers of Nathaniel Banks, John A. McClernand, Abraham Lincoln, Lewis B. Parsons.

Louisiana State University. Papers of P. L. Bonny, Louis A. Bringier, Butler family, Eggleston-Roach, Thomas C. W. Ellis, J. D. Garland, Charles James Johnson, Lemanda E. Lea, Sidney O. Little, Thomas O. Moore, William Nicholson, Prudhomme family, Jared Y. Sanders, Julia N. Skinner, Elias Wyckoff. Diaries of Rowland Chambers, Alexander R. Miller.

Maryland Historical Society. Papers of Anna E. Carroll.

Mississippi Department of Archives and History. W. R. Barry Papers. Governors' correspondence. Diaries of Joseph D. Alison, Miss Balfour, William A. Drennan.

Missouri Historical Society. Papers of James B. Eads, Bates family, Charles Parsons. Letterbook of S. L. Phelps.

New Hampshire Historical Society. John P. Hale Papers.

New-York Historical Society. Papers of Gustavus Vasa Fox, Henry A. Wise.

New York Public Library. David G. Farragut Papers. "Recollections" of Bartholomew Diggins.

Ohio Historical Society. Symmes Browne Papers.

Pennsylvania Historical Society. Dreer and Gratz collections. Samuel Jackson Papers. Diary of John C. Huntley.

Tennessee Historical Society. Governors' correspondence. John Trotwood Moore Confederate Collection.

Tulane University. Louisiana Historical Association Collection: Papers of William W. Hunter, Henry F. Wade.

University of Kentucky. Benjamin F. Buckner Papers.

University of Michigan. Transportation Library. Ellet family Papers (microfilm).

University of North Carolina. Southern Historical Collection: Papers of John Comstock, Gustavus A. Henry, H. C. Lockhart, George William Logan, Stephen R. Mallory, Leonidas Polk (microfilm copies). Diaries of William Steward, J. W. Wilson, "Reminiscences" of M. Jeff Thompson.

University of Texas. Nathaniel Banks Papers (microfilm).

University of Virginia. Cabell-Ellet Papers.
Virginia Historical Society. John K. Mitchell Papers.
Virginia State Library. Tredegar Iron Works Papers.

UNITED STATES GOVERNMENT DOCUMENTS

"Certain War Vessels Built in 1862-1865," *Senate Report No. 1942*, 57 Cong., 1 sess.; "Communications from the Secretary of War, on the Subject of the armed flotilla on western rivers," *House Exec. Doc., No. 5*, 37 Cong., 2 sess.; *Congressional Globe;* "Journal of the Congress of the Confederate States of America, 1861-1865," *Senate Doc., No. 234*, 58 Cong., 2 sess.; "Letter from the Secretary of the Navy, addressed To the Committee on Naval Affairs, in relation to iron-clad ships, ordnance, etc.," *House Misc. Doc., No. 82*, 37 Cong., 2 sess.; "Letter of the Secretary of the Navy, In answer to A resolution of the Senate of the 9th instant, relative to the employment of George D. Morgan, of New York, to purchase vessels for the government," *Senate Exec. Doc., No. 15*, 37 Cong., 2 sess.; "Letter from the Secretary of the Navy, transmitting Statement of all the contracts made by the different bureaus connected with the Navy Department," *House Exec. Doc., No. 150*, 37 Cong., 2 sess.; "Letter from the Secretary of the Navy, transmitting Report of Admiral Foote in relation to naval depot on western waters," *House Exec. Doc., No. 48*, 38 Cong., 1 sess.; "Letter of the Secretary of War, in answer to A resolution of the Senate of the 30th day of January, in relation to the vessels purchased or chartered for the use of the War Department since the 1st day of April last,' *Senate Exec. Doc., No. 37*, 37 Cong., 2 sess.; "Message from the President of the United States, Recommending A vote of thanks to

Captain A. H. Foote, of the United States Navy, for his eminent services in organizing the western flotilla and conducting operations in western waters," *House Exec. Doc., No. 141,* 37 Cong., 2 sess.; *Official Records of the Union and Confederate Navies in the War of the Rebellion,* 26 v.; *Regulations for the Government of the United States Navy. 1865;* "Report by the Quartermaster General Relative to Vessels Bought, Sold, and Chartered Since April 1861," *House Exec. Doc., No. 337,* 40 Cong., 2 sess.; "Report in regard to the chartering of transport vessels for the Banks expedition," *Senate Report, No. 84,* 37 Cong., 3 sess.; "Report of a select committee (investigating) . . . the circumstances attending the surrender of the navy yard at Pensacola, and the destruction of the property of the United States at the navy yard at Norfolk, and at the armory at Harper's Ferry . . . ," *Senate Report, No. 37,* 37 Cong., 2 sess.; "Report of the Joint Committee on the Conduct of the War," *Senate Report, No. 108,* 37 Cong., 3 sess.; "Report of the Joint Committee on the Conduct of the War," *Senate Report, No. 142,* 38 Cong., 2 sess.; "Report of the Secretary of the Navy, communicating . . . a copy of the record . . . to inquire into and determine how much the vessels-of-war and steam machinery contracted for by the department . . . cost the contractors over and above the contract price and allowances for extra work," *Senate Exec. Doc., No. 18,* 39 Cong., 1 sess.; *Reports* of the Secretary of the Navy, 4 July 1861-4 December 1865; "Report of the Secretary of the Navy in Relation to Armored Vessels," *House Exec. Doc., No. 69,* 38 Cong., 1 sess.; *Reports* of the Secretary of War, 1 July 1861-1 March 1865; "Report on Government Contracts," *House Report, No. 2,* 37

Cong., 2 sess.; "Report on Marine Engines," *House Report, No. 8,* 38 Cong., 2 sess.; "Report on Naval Supplies," *Senate Report, No. 99,* 38 Cong., 1 sess.; "Report on the manner of chartering and condition of vessels for the Banks expedition," *Senate Report, No. 75,* 37 Cong., 3 sess.; "Report on the Massacre at Fort Pillow," *Senate Report, No. 63,* 38 Cong., 1 sess.; *The War of the Rebellion: A Compilation of the Official Records of the Union and Confederate Armies,* 128 v.; "War Claims at St. Louis," *House Exec. Doc., No. 94,* 37 Cong., 2 sess.

STATE GOVERNMENT DOCUMENTS

Louisiana. *Acts Passed by the Twenty Seventh Legislature of the State of Louisiana in Extra Session at Opelousas, December, 1862, & January, 1863; Acts Passed by the Sixth Legislature . . . at Its Extra Session, Held in the City of Shreveport, on the 4th of March, 1863; Documents of the First Session of the Sixth Legislature of the State of Louisiana; Journal of the Senate of the Extra Session, Sixth Legislature.* Mississippi. *Journal of the Senate and House of Representatives, December Session of 1862 and November Session of 1863; Laws Passed at a Called and Regular Session of Mississippi Legislature, Dec. 1862 and Nov. 1863.*

NEWSPAPERS

Boston *Transcript*; Chicago *Post*; Cincinnati *Daily Commercial*; *Hinds County Gazette* (Raymond, Miss.); Louisville *Daily Courier, Daily Journal*; Memphis *Appeal, Avalanche, Bulletin*; Natchez *Daily Courier*; New Orleans *Daily Picayune, Daily True Delta*; New York *Times, Tribune*; Norfolk *Day Book*; Philadelphia *Pub-*

lic Ledger; Richmond *Daily Dispatch, Enquirer, Examiner*; Sacramento *Union*; St. Louis *Daily Missouri Democrat, Republican*; Washington *Globe, National Intelligencer.*

PERIODICALS
Frank Leslie's Illustrated Newspaper; *Harper's Weekly*; *The United States Army and Navy Journal*; *The United States Service.*

OTHER PRINTED MATERIALS
Abbot, Willis J., *Blue Jackets of '61* (New York, 1886); Abbott, John, "Heroic Deeds of Heroic Men," *Harper's New Monthly Magazine*, 32, 33 (1866); Alden, Carroll S. & Allan Westcott, *The United States Navy* (Garden City: Doubleday, Doran, 1943); Ambrose, Stephen E., *Halleck* (Baton Rouge: Louisiana State University Press, 1962); Ammen, Daniel, *The Atlantic Coast* (New York, 1883); Bacon, Thomas, "The Fight at Port Hudson," *The Independent*, 53 (1901); Barker, Albert S., *Everyday Life in the Navy* (Boston: Richard G. Badger, 1928); Barnes, James, *David G. Farragut* (Boston, 1899); Basler, Roy P., ed., *The Collected Works of Abraham Lincoln*, 9 vols. (New Brunswick, N. J.: Rutgers University Press, 1953); Baxter, James P., *The Introduction of the Ironclad Warship* (Cambridge: Harvard University Press, 1933); Beale, Howard K., ed., *The Diary of Edward Bates, 1859-1866* (Washington, D. C.: American Historical Association, 1930); Beale, Howard K., & Alan W. Brownsword, eds., *Diary of Gideon Welles*, 3 Vols. (New York: Norton, 1960); Bennett, Frank M., *The Monitor and the Navy under Steam* (Boston: Houghton, Mifflin, 1900); Bennett,

Frank M., *The Steam Navy of the United States* (Pittsburgh, 1896); Bentley, William, *History of the 77th Illinois Volunteer Infantry* (Peoria, 1883); Blakeman, A. Noel, "Some Personal Reminiscences of the Naval Service," LUS, New York, *Personal Recollections* (1897); Bland, T. A. *Life of Benjamin F. Butler* (Boston, 1879); Bowen, James L., *Massachusetts in the War* (Springfield, 1889); Boynton, Charles B., *The History of the Navy during the Rebellion*, 2 vols. (New York, 1867-68); Brand, W. F., "The Capture of the Indianola," *Maryland Historical Magazine*, 4 (1909); [Brent, J. L.], "Capture of the Indianola," *Southern Historical Society Papers*, 1 (1876); Brinton, John, *Personal Memoirs* (New York: Neale, 1914); Brodie, Bernard, *A Guide to Naval Strategy* (Princeton: Princeton University Press, 1944); Brodie, Bernard, *Sea Power in the Machine Age* (Princeton: Princeton University Press, 1941); Brown, George, "Service in the Mississippi Squadron," and "The Mortar Flotilla," LUS, New York, *Personal Recollections* (1891); Browne, Junius, *Four Years in Secessia* (New York, 1865); Butler, Benjamin F., *Autobiography* (Boston, 1892), commonly referred to as *Butler's Book*; Butler, Edward, "Personal Experiences in the Navy, 1862-1865," LUS, Maine, *War Papers*, 2 (1902); Callender, Eliot, "What a Boy Saw on the Mississippi," LUS, Illinois, *Military Essays*, 1 (1891); Carpenter, Cyrus, "James W. Grimes, Governor and Senator," *Annals of Iowa*, 1 (1894); Church, William, *The Life of John Ericsson*, 2 vols. (New York: Scribners, 1906); Clark, James S., *The Thirty-Fourth Iowa Regiment* (Des Moines, 1892); Coffin, Charles, *Drum-Beat of the Nation* (New York, 1888); Coffin, Charles, *Four Years of Fighting* (Boston, 1866); Coffin, Charles, *Marching to Victory* (New York, 1889); Coffin, Charles, *Redeeming the Republic* (New York, 1890); Commager, Henry S., ed., *The Blue and the Gray*, 2 vols. (Indianapolis: Bobbs-Merrill, 1950); Coleman, S. B., "A July Morning with the Rebel Ram 'Arkansas,'" LUS, Michigan, *War Papers*, 1 (1890); Crabtree, John, "From Helena to Vicksburg in August, 1862," LUS, Illinois, *Military Essays*, 4 (1907); Crooker, Lucien, "Episodes and Characters in an Illinois Regiment," *Ibid.*; Dahlgren, M. V., ed., *Memoir of John A. Dahlgren* (Boston, 1872); Dana, Charles A., *Recollections of the Civil War* (New York: Appleton, 1902); Davis, Charles H., *Life of Charles Henry Davis* (Boston, 1899); Davis, Charles W., "New Madrid and Island No. 10," LUS, Illinois, *Military Essays*, 1 (1891); Davis Jefferson, *The Rise and Fall of the Confederate Government*, 2 vols. (New York, 1881); Dennett, Tyler, ed., *Lincoln and the Civil War in the Diaries and Letters of John Hay* (New York: Dodd, Mead, 1939); Donald, David, ed., *Inside Lincoln's Cabinet: The Civil War Diaries of Salmon P. Chase* (New York: Longmans, Green, 1954); Durkin, Joseph T., *Stephen R. Mallory* (Chapel Hill: University of North Carolina Press, 1954); Fairbanks, Henry, "The Red River Expedition of 1864," LUS, Maine, *War Papers*, 1 (1898); Farragut, Loyall, "Passing the Port Hudson Batteries," LUS, New York, *Personal Recollections* (1891); Farragut, Loyall, *The Life of David Glasgow Farragut* (New York, 1879); Ford, Worthington C., ed., *A Cycle of Adams Letters*, 3 vols. (Boston: Houghton, Mifflin, 1920); Fowler, William, *Memorials of William Fowler* (New York, 1875); Franklin, Samuel R., *Memories of a Rear-Admiral* (New York, 1898); Freeman, Douglas S., *R. E. Lee*, 4 vols.

(New York: Scribners, 1935); Gerdes, F. H., "The Surrender of Forts Jackson and St. Philip, on the Lower Mississippi," *The Continental Monthly*, 3 (1863); Gift, George, "The Story of the *Arkansas*," *Southern Historical Society Papers*, 12 (1884); Gilmore, James, *Personal Recollections of Abraham Lincoln and the Civil War* (Boston, 1898); Goodloe, Albert, *Some Rebel Relics from the Seat of War* (Nashville, 1893); Gordon, George, *A War Diary of Events in the War* (Boston, 1882); Gosnell, H. Allen, *Guns on the Western Waters* (Baton Rouge: Louisiana State University Press, 1949); Grant, Ulysses S., *Personal Memoirs*, 2 vols. (New York, 1886); Hall, Charles B., "Notes on the Red River Campaign," LUS, Maine, *War Papers*, 4 (1915); Hanna, Kathryn A., "Incidents of the Confederate Blockade," *The Journal of Southern History*, 11 (1945); Hassler, Charles W., "Reminiscences of 1861-3," LUS, New York, *Personal Recollections* (1891); Hill, Jim Dan, *Sea Dogs of the Sixties* (Minneapolis: University of Minnesota Press, 1935); Hendrick, Burton J., *Lincoln's War Cabinet* (Boston: Little, Brown, 1946); Hendrick, Burton J., *Statesmen of the Lost Cause* (Boston: Little, Brown, 1939); Holley, Alexander L., *A Treatise on Ordnance and Armor* (New York, 1865); Hollins, George N., "Autobiography of Commodore George Nicholas Hollins, C.S.A.," *Maryland Historical Magazine*, 34 (1939); Holzman, Robert S., *Stormy Ben Butler* (New York: Macmillan, 1954); Hoppin, James, *Life of Andrew Hull Foote* (New York, 1874); How, Louis, *James B. Eads* (Boston: Houghton, Mifflin, 1900); Howard, Richard, *History of the 124th Regiment Illinois Infantry Volunteers* (Springfield, 1880); Hunt, George, "The Fort Donelson Campaign," LUS, Illinois,

Military Essays, 4 (1907); Hutchinson, William, "Life on the Texan Blockade," Rhode Island Soldiers and Sailors Historical Society, *Personal Narratives*, 3 (1883); Jenney, William, "With Sherman and Grant from Memphis to Chattanooga," LUS, Illinois, *Military Essays*, 4 (1907); [Johnston, Adam R.], *The Partisan Rangers of the Confederate States Army* (Louisville: Fetter, 1904); Johnson, Ludwell, *Red River Campaign* (Baltimore: Johns Hopkins Press, 1958); Johnson, Robert E., *Rear Admiral John Rodgers* (Annapolis: U. S. Naval Institute, 1967); Johnson, Robert U. & Clarence C. Buel, eds., *Battles and Leaders of the Civil War*, 4 vols. (1884-7); Jones, J. B., *A Rebel War Clerk's Diary*, 2 vols. (Philadelphia, 1866); Jones, Jenkin, *An Artilleryman's Diary* (Madison: Wisconsin Historical Commission, 1914); Jones, Virgil C., *Civil War at Sea*, 3 vols. (New York: Holt, Rinehart, Winston, 1960-2); Knox, Thomas W., *Camp-Fire and Cotton-Field* (New York, 1865); Leech, Margaret, *Reveille in Washington* (New York: Harpers, 1941); [Lewis, C. B.], *Field, Fort, and Fleet* (Detroit, 1885); Lewis, Charles L., *David Glasgow Farragut*, 2 vols. (Annapolis: U. S. Naval Institute, 1943); Lyon, Adelia, ed., *Reminiscences. Compiled from the War Correspondence of Colonel William P. Lyon* (San Jose, Calif.: William Lyon, 1907); McAuley, John, "Fort Donelson and Its Surrender," LUS, Illinois, *Military Essays*, 1 (1891); MacBride, Robert, *Civil War Ironclads* (Philadelphia: Chilton, 1962); McMorries, Edward Y., *History of the First Alabama Volunteer Infantry, C.S.A.* (Montgomery: Brown, 1904); MacCord, Charles W., "Ericsson and his 'Monitor,'" *North American Review*, 149 (1889); Mahan, Alfred T., *Admiral Farragut* (New York, 1892); Mahan, Alfred

T., *From Sail to Steam* (New York: Harpers, 1907); Mahan, Alfred T., *The Gulf and Inland Waters* (New York, 1883); Marshall, Jessie, ed., *Private and Official Correspondence of Gen. Benjamin F. Butler during the Period of the Civil War*, 5 vols. (Norwood, Mass.: Plimpton, 1917); Mason, F. H., *The Forty-Second Ohio Infantry* (Columbus, 1876); Martin, Isabella D. & Myrta Lockett, eds., *A Diary from Dixie* (New York: Peter Smith, 1929); Meacham, Justin, "Military and Naval Operations on the Mississippi," LUS, Wisconsin, *War Papers*, 4 (1914); Melvin, Philip, "Stephen Russell Mallory, Southern Naval Statesman," *The Journal of Southern History*, 10 (1944); Meredith, William, "Admiral Farragut's Passage of Port Hudson," LUS, New York, *Personal Recollections* (1897); Merrill, James M., "Confederate Shipbuilding at New Orleans," *The Journal of Southern History*, 28 (1962); Merrill, James M., *The Rebel Shore* (Boston: Little, Brown, 1957); Michael, W. H. C., "How the Mississippi Was Opened," and "The Mississippi Flotilla," LUS, Nebraska, *Civil War Sketches*, 1 (1902); Miers, Earl S., *The Web of Victory* (New York: Knopf, 1955); Milligan, John D., *Gunboats Down the Mississippi* (Annapolis: U. S. Naval Institute, 1965); Millis, Walter, "The Iron Sea Elephants," *The American Neptune*, 10 (1950); Moore, Frank, *The Rebellion Record*, 12 vols. (New York, 1866-73); Morison, Samuel Eliot, & Commager, Henry S., *The Growth of the American Republic*, 2 vols. (New York: Oxford, 1957); Morse, John, ed., *Diary of Gideon Welles*, 3 vols. (Boston: Houghton, Mifflin, 1911); Newcomb, Mary A., *Four Years of Personal Reminiscences of the War* (Chicago, 1893); Newsome, Edmund, *Experiences in the War of the*

Great Rebellion (Carbondale, Ill., 1880); Nicolay, John G. & John Hay, eds., *Complete Works of Abraham Lincoln,* 12 vols. (New York, F. D. Tandy, 1905); Osbon, B. S., ed., "Journal of the Cruise of the Flagship Hartford, 1862-63 . . . From the Private Journal of William C. Holton," *The Magazine of History with Notes and Queries,* 22 (1922); Osborn, P. R., "The American Monitors," *USNIP,* 62 (1937); Palmer, Howard, "New Orleans under General Butler," *The Louisiana Historical Quarterly,* 24 (1941); Parkhurst, Clint, "Our First View of Vicksburg," *The Palimpsest,* 3 (1922); Parton, James, *General Butler in New Orleans* (New York, 1864); Paullin, Charles O., "The Navy Department during the Civil War," *USNIP,* 38 (1912); Paullin, Charles O., "President Lincoln and the Navy," *The American Historical Review,* 14 (1909); Pemberton, John C., *Pemberton, Defender of Vicksburg* (Chapel Hill: University of North Carolina Press, 1942); Perkins, George H., *Letters of Capt. Hamilton Perkins* (Concord, N. H.: Rumford, 1901); Porter, David D., *Incidents and Anecdotes of the Civil War* (New York, 1885); Porter, David D., *The Naval History of the Civil War* (New York, 1886); Potter, E. B., *et al., The United States and World Sea Power* (Englewood Cliffs, N. J.: Prentice-Hall, 1955); Powers, George, *The Story of the Thirty-Eighth Regiment of Massachusetts Volunteers* (Boston, 1866); Quaife, M. M., ed., *Absalom Grimes, Confederate Mail Runner* (New Haven: Yale, 1926); Randall, James G., *The Civil War and Reconstruction* (Boston: D. C. Heath, 1937); Read, Charles, "Reminiscences of the Confederate States Navy," *Southern Historical Society Papers,* 1 (1876); Richardson, Albert, *The Secret Service* (Hartford, Conn., 1865); Rodgers,

W. L., "A Study of Attacks upon Fortified Harbors," *USNIP*, 30 (1904); Rogers, Henry, *Memories of Ninety Years* (Boston: Houghton, Mifflin, 1928); Rowland, Dunbar, ed., *Jefferson Davis*, 10 vols. (Jackson: Department of Archives and History, 1923); Russell, William H., *My Diary North and South*, (London, 1863); Salter, William, *The Life of James W. Grimes* (New York, 1876); Scharf, J. Thomas, *History of the Confederate States Navy* (New York, 1887); Schley, Winfield S., *Forty-Five Years Under the Flag* (New York: Appleton, 1904); Seaton, John, "The Battle of Belmont," LUS, Kansas, *War Talks* (1906); Sherman, William T., *Memoirs of Gen. W. T. Sherman*, 2 vols. (New York, 1892); Soley, James R., *Admiral Porter* (New York: Appleton, 1903); Soley, James R., *Sailor Boys of '61* (Boston, 1888); Soley, James R., *The Blockade and the Cruisers* (New York, 1887); Soley, James R., "Rear Admiral John Rodgers, President of the Naval Institute, 1879-82," *USNIP*, 8 (1882); Southwood, Marion, *'Beauty and Booty,' The Watchword of New Orleans* (New York, 1867); Soule, Harrison, "From the Gulf to Vicksburg," LUS, Michigan, *War Papers*, 2 (1898); Sprout, Harold & Margaret, *The Rise of American Naval Power, 1776-1918* (Princeton: Princeton University Press, 1939); Stevenson, Benjamin, *Letters from the Army* (Cincinnati, 1884); Stevenson, Thomas, *History of the 78th (Ohio) Regiment* (Zanesville, 1865); [Stevenson, William G.], *Thirteen Months in the Rebel Army* (New York, 1862); Stewart, Edwin, "Address on Admiral Farragut," LUS, New York, *Personal Recollections* (1912); Still, William N., Jr., "Confederate Naval Strategy: The Ironclad," *The Journal of Southern History*, 27 (1961); Still, William N., Jr., "Confederate

Naval Policy and the Ironclad," *Civil War History*, 9 (1963); Still, William N., Jr., "Facilities for the Construction of War Vessels in the Confederacy," *The Journal of Southern History*, 31 (1965); [Taylor, Asher], *Notes of Conversations with a Volunteer Officer of the United States Navy, on the Passage of the Forts below New Orleans* (New York, 1868); Thompson, Robert & Richard Wainwright, eds., *Confidential Correspondence of Gustavus Vasa Fox*, 2 vols. (New York: Naval History Society, 1918); Trexler, H. A., "The Confederate Navy Department and the Fall of New Orleans," *Southwest Review*, 19 (1933); Tunnard, William, *The History of the Third Regiment Louisiana Infantry* (Baton Rouge, 1866); Walke, Henry, *Naval Scenes and Reminiscences* (New York, 1877); Ware, Eugene, *The Lyon Campaign in Missouri, Being a History of the First Iowa Infantry* (Topeka: Crane, 1907); Weigley, Russell F., *Quartermaster General of the Union Army* (New York: Columbia University Press, 1959); Welles, Gideon, "Admiral Farragut and New Orleans," *The Galaxy*, 12 (1871); West, Richard S., *Gideon Welles* (Indianapolis: Bobbs-Merrill, 1943); West, Richard S., "Gunboats in the Swamps: The Yazoo Pass Expedition," *Civil War History*, 9 (1963); West, Richard S., *The Second Admiral: A Life of David Dixon Porter* (New York: Coward-McCann, 1937); Whitney, Henry C., *Life on the Circuit with Lincoln* (Boston, 1892); Williams, Ben Ames, ed., *A Diary from Dixie* (Boston: Houghton, Mifflin, 1949); Williams, E. Cort, "Recollections of the Red River Campaign," LUS, Ohio, *Sketches of War History*, 2 (1888); Williams, G. Mott, "The First Vicksburg Expedition, and the Battle of Baton Rouge, 1862," LUS, Wisconsin, *War Papers*,

2 (1896); Williams, T. Harry, *P.G.T. Beauregard* (Baton Rouge: Louisiana State University Press, 1955); Wills, Charles W., *Army Life of an Illinois Soldier* (Washington, D.C.: Globe, 1906); Wilson, H. W., *Ironclads in Action*, 2 vols. (London, 1896); Wilson, James G., "The Red River Dam," LUS, New York, *Personal Recollections* (1891); Wilson, James H., *Under the Old Flag*, 2 vols. (New York: Appleton, 1912).

DISSERTATION

Parker, Theodore. "The Federal Gunboat Flotilla on the Western Rivers during its Administration by the War Department to October 1, 1862." Ph.D. dissertation, University of Pittsburgh, 1939.

Index